THE WEST LANCASHIRE YACHT CLUB

1894–1994

A CENTENARY HISTORY

by
Roger Ryan

Carnegie Publishing Ltd., 1993

The West Lancashire Yacht Club 1894–1994: a centenary history
by Roger Ryan
Copyright © Roger Ryan, 1993

Published by Carnegie Publishing Ltd., 18 Maynard Street, Preston
Typeset by Carnegie Publishing Ltd
Printed in the UK by Cambridge University Press

British Library Cataloguing-in-Publication Data
A CIP catalogue record for this book is available from the British Library

ISBN 0-85936-010-6

Contents

Abbreviations

In the main text, the West Lancashire Yacht Club is usually called the WLYC, although the term 'West Lancs' has been widely used by members and non-members for at least fifty years. Other abbreviations are identified in each chapter. Among these, note that the Southport Corinthian Yacht Club members were widely referred to locally as the 'Corinthians', and I have kept to this where there is little chance of confusion with other clubs using this term in their title.

Apart from standard bibliographical abbreviations, the following appear regularly in the Reading Notes for sources and, where appropriate, I have used them in the text if this was the usual term adopted by that organisation, such as the YRA.

HYM	*Hunt's Yachting Magazine*
LRO	Lancashire Record Office
MMMRC	Merseyside Maritime Museum Record Centre
RMYC	Royal Mersey Yacht Club
RYA	Royal Yachting Association (since 1952)
SC	after a place name for any Sailing Club
SG	*Southport Guardian*
SV	*Southport Visiter*
WLYC	West Lancashire Yacht Club
YC	after a place name for any Yacht Club
YM	*The Yachtsman* magazine
YRA	Yacht Racing Association, 1875–1952
YW	*Yachting World*, another journal

Preface

THE INAUGURAL MEETING of the West Lancashire Yacht Club took place at the Scaris-brick Hotel in Southport on 16 June 1894. Above all else, this book has been written to celebrate the club's achievement of its centenary in 1994. Today's members owe a great deal to the club's founders who were innovators in the field of small yacht design, as well as helms of note, and gained an early recognition for the WYLC well beyond its local waters in the North West. Yachting, however, has never been easy at Southport. Access to the Ribble estuary was fairly difficult in 1894, due to continuous silting in the notorious 'Bog Hole' off Southport pier, and since then it has slowly become worse. The various attempts to come to terms with this problem, which have included an ultimately successful use of Southport's large Marine Lake, form a constant theme in the history of the club. From the gloomy perspective of the late 1930s, few members would have given the WLYC much chance of surviving for long and certainly not until 1994. The fact that it did so, and thrives today is a tribute to a new generation of members who appreciated the need for changes and successfully organised support within the club to achieve them. Meanwhile, external social and economic influences have always played a part in what hapened within the WLYC and I have discussed them wherever they have been relevant to the course of events at Southport.

This book has been produced as one of the many tasks facing the Centenary Committee of West Lancashire Yacht Club. John Hayward (the chairman), Michael Parker, Royce Blenkiron, Ray Goulden, Kirk Wilson, Jim Morgan and John Batten have all given me help and I thank them for their constant encouragement through some two years of monthly committee meetings. With the sad news of Royce Blenkiron's death in September 1993, the Committee has lost the support of a former WLYC President, Honorary Secretary and Sailing Secretary. It has been a privilege to have benefited from Royce's expertise and his advice on the script of this book.

I am also grateful for the support given by the commodores serving during this period, Tony Halliwell and then Michael Parker from 1993. They have both given their personal support and ensured that I have been given access to all of the documents and sources available within the club. Many other members have also taken the time and trouble to help with the project. They have included some past commodores who kindly drafted brief accounts of their experiences with the West Lancashire Yacht Club, while other members and friends of the club have arranged for me to meet past employees, answered questions and provided me with photographs, press cuttings and documents. Apart from those mentioned above, I am particularly grateful to the following people for their contribu-tions: Dick Atkinson, Joe Bond, Mrs Marjorie Davies, Ron Harper, Alan Houghton, Philip Lindsay, Adrian Moran, Tom Percival, Cyril Porter, Brian Randall, Andrew Read, Bill Sutton, John Sutton, Frank Thompson, John Thorougood, Jack Whiteley and Bob Willetts.

Beyond the club, I have received an immense amount of help from Southport College. As a member of staff at the college, I have received full support from the principal and governors who have allowed me free use of our facilities in preparing this book. In particular,

I have had the benefit of Steven Oakden's advice as the College Librarian, both in providing bibliographical information and putting me in touch with local historians who have a knowledge of maritime history. Beyond that, Betty Pavey, the Deputy Librarian, has given me a great deal of support by obtaining various texts and articles from other libraries which were essential as background reading. Photographic work has been equally important. I am very grateful to John Wardle, a senior technician at the college, for his care and expertise in reproducing the majority of the photographs in the book. Meanwhile, the clarity of the maps and figures is entirely due to work done by Gavin Allan-Wood, a lecturer, who used our computer facilities to prepare them. Finally, the photocopying of text, maps and notes has been carried out very efficiently by Sheila Jones' reprographics section; and Eric Baker, a lecturer in Building, advised me about inter-war residential property values in Southport.

The Royal Mersey Yacht Club has proved another source of valuable help. I am most grateful to the commodore and flag officers of the RMYC for permission to have access to their library and records. Thanks to the courtesy and help of Barbara Roberts, the Steward-ess of the club, I have been able to use RMYC documents in the clubhouse and borrow a large number of yachting journals. Without that help, much of my research would have been impossible in the limited time available.

The Southport newspapers and pier company records have also provided me with essential information. I am very grateful to Joan Tarbuck, the Local History Librarian, and other staff in the Southport Reference Library for their help. For the later years in the study, I also owe much to Jim Morgan's invaluable collection of local press cuttings from 1954 to 1969, while John Batten provided many details about yachting at Southport and across the Mersey at West Kirby. John Millar's history of the West Kirby Sailing Club has also proved immensely helpful. Further advice was given to me by Leonard Lloyd of the Maritime History Group of the Friends of the Botanic Gardens Museum in Southport. Leonard very kindly read my first chapter and helped me through the intricacies of the late nineteenth-century yacht rating rules. Jack Dakres, author of The Last Tide, helped me with the history of the Ribble estuary, while A. Burt Briggs produced information about the Lytham Yacht Club. Other local sources were researched with the help of staff at the Lancashire Record Office, Liverpool City Library, Blackburn Reference Library, and the Merseyside Maritime Museum Records Centre.

Beyond local sources, I have received considerable help through correspondence from Sally Skilling at the Ulster Folk and Transport History Museum, Belfast. Other questions were answered by the National Maritime Museum, Greenwich; the Royal Geographical Society; the British Newspaper Library; the Public Record Office of Northern Ireland; and Jim Perkins, the Honorary Secretary of the Yachting World Heron Class Association. Furthermore, I am very grateful to Robin Duchesne, Secretary General of the Royal Yachting Association and F. W. Roberts, Commodore of the Royal Temple Yacht Club, for answering specific questions about the early history of the West Lancashire Yacht Club. Bernard Pilbrow of the RYA also provided me with valuable information about the history of that association. More generally, Dr John Lowerson, Reader in History at the University of Sussex, gave advice on middle-class involvement in yachting before 1914. Similar help came from Oliver Westall of the University of Lancaster. Oliver has also read and commented on much of my text and I am very grateful for his advice and support throughout the past two years while I have been carrying out research and then writing this book.

More than anyone else, though, my wife Merylyn and our children Paul and Emma have very generously given their full support and help. I thank Merylyn for reading through various draft versions and for her invaluable comments, while I am equally grateful for Paul and Emma's practical help in printing out the text and putting everything together. It is entirely due to their willingness to tolerate my preoccupation with the 'Club History' that I have been able to finish this book on time!

Roger Ryan
Southport College
September 1993

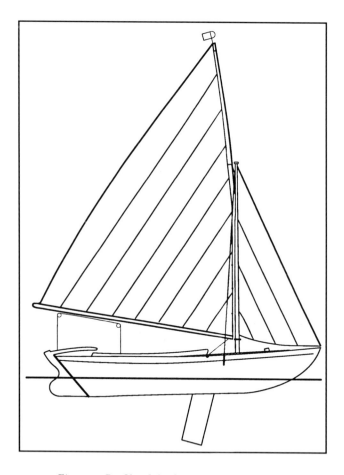

Figure 1. Profile of the Seabird class one-design.

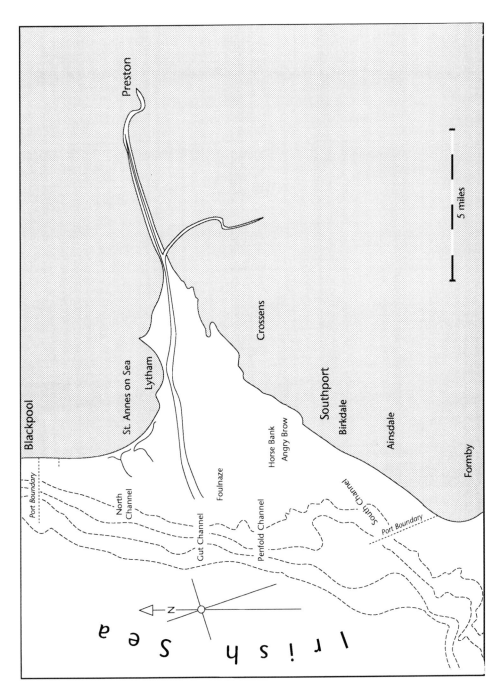

Map 1. Survey of the Ribble and Estuary, 1925.

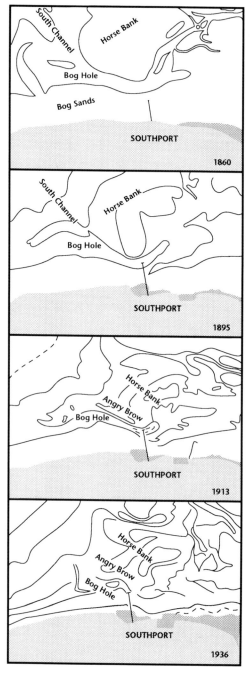

Map 2. Changes in the South Channel and 'Bog Hole', 1860 to 1936.
Source: J. Barron, A History of the Ribble Navigation, *pp. 40–1.*

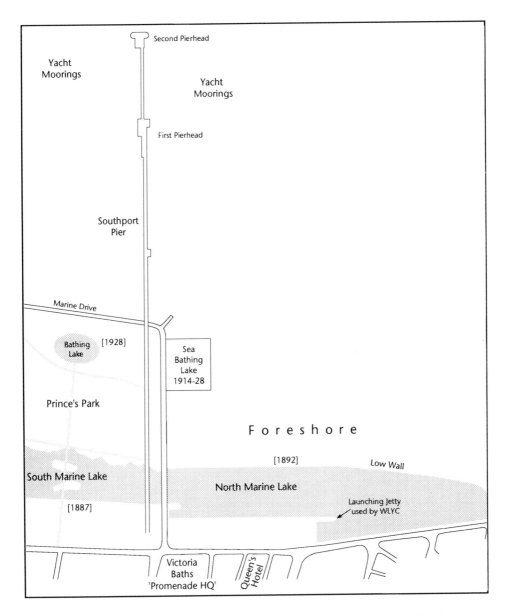

Map 3. *Southport Pier and the Marine Lakes, showing the pier as it existed between 1897 and 1933, and the Marine Lake area between 1892 and 1962. Source: Report on the pier to Southport Corporation, 28 July 1934, held in Southport Reference Library 'Pier Box'.*

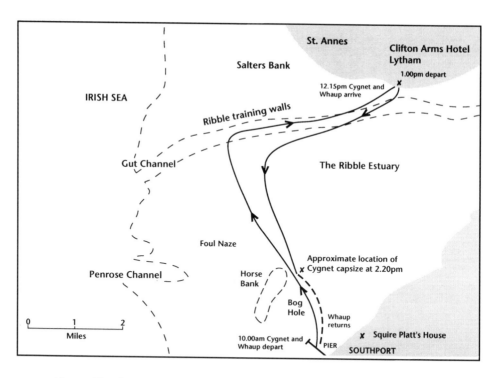

Map 4. Sketch map of events leading up to the capsize of Cygnet, *20 July 1913.*

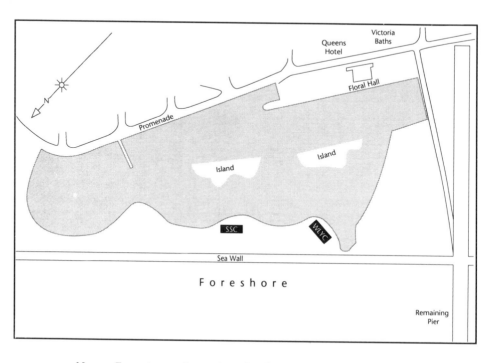

Map 5. Extensions to the northern Southport Marine Lake from 1962,
showing the sites of the new WLYC and SSC clubhouses.

Chapter 1

Southport Yachting—Origins and Background

1. Early Days at Southport

WHAT WAS IT about Southport which made the town an important yachting centre during the thirty years before the First World War? Known by some quirk of the Victorian imagination as the 'Montpellier of England',[1] Southport's clean and remarkably extensive sands fringed one of the most dangerous stretches of coastline in Britain. Since the late eighteenth century, well-to-do visitors had been drawn in growing numbers to the rugged beauty of the local beaches, but Southport's foreshore was also notorious among fishermen and other mariners for its treacherous currents, shifting sandbanks, and predominantly onshore wind from the south-west. Frequent storms, especially in autumn and winter, wrecked moored boats and often carried them for miles along the shore of the Ribble estuary towards Preston. As if that was not enough, Victorian Southport's outlet to the sea relied upon a rapidly silting access through the Ribble's wayward South Channel, known locally with a mixture of affection and despair, as the 'Bog Hole'.[2]

For all that, the Southport coastline had a well-established shrimping and fishing trade[3] which eventually enhanced its bracing attractiveness as a seaside resort within fairly easy reach of industrial Lancashire.[4] Of course, before the railway reached Southport in 1855, travel to the town by horse-drawn vehicle was expensive and time consuming. The journey was by no means difficult but it did provide a measure of isolation which helped to enhance Southport's reputation as an exclusive resort offering those visitors who could afford it—and a growing core of wealthy residents—the kind of social life and hotel comforts previously confined to such seaside resorts as Brighton in southern England or watering places like Bath.[5]

Early signs of an effort to use yachting as a means of enhancing this image were evident by 1835 when a handful of yachtsmen were drawn to Southport for the town's first regatta. One of the leading local landowners, Peter Fleetwood Hesketh—MP for Preston from 1832 to 1847 and created a baronet in 1838—provided the prize money for races in rowing and fishing boats as well as one for the yachts. In one respect, Hesketh was an appropriate patron because he owned the substantial cutter Lancaster Rose.[6] But he became preoccupied with a disastrously expensive effort to develop Fleetwood while also maintaining a fashionable 'in town' residence in Piccadilly. Even as a member of the élite Royal Yacht Squadron he was far more interested in events at Cowes than with sailing off the bleak coastline at Southport where, in any case, there were still very few yachts to be seen on a regular basis. Despite the intention of promoting the town's respectability, another problem was that by the early 1850s these early so-called 'regattas' had become notorious for their rowdiness and gambling, attracting an interest in the rowing and fishing boat races which seems to have gone well beyond the purely nautical!

By this stage Sir Peter Fleetwood Hesketh's fortune had been drained. He sold his Lancashire estates to his younger brother, the far more cautious and austere Reverend Charles Hesketh, who had founded the Southport Total Abstinence Society in 1836 and then played a leading part in the formation of the Lord's Day Society in 1855. Like Charles Scarisbrick—the other major landowner in Southport—he was more concerned, as a Lord of the Manor with a large financial stake in the town, with protecting local morality and public order than with encouraging such brash forms of public entertainment.[7] They simply banned the regatta in 1853[8] and it was not revived until 1883, when poor organisation rather than rowdiness brought further discredit.[9] Regardless of such obstacles to organised events, visiting yachts appeared during the summer months far more frequently once the opening of Southport's impressive pier in 1860 had greatly eased access to the shore.[10]

Like many other Victorian coastal towns, however, the development of yachting at Southport stemmed from the demands of the urban middle classes rather than from local initiatives. With a growing interest nationally in yachting as an organised sport for more than just the immensely wealthy, the pressure for access to sailing water and moorings increased. Because Liverpool, Manchester and the rest of industrial Lancashire were within easy reach of Southport by rail from 1855 there was good reason to hope that the town would become a regular port of call if not a home base for amateur yachtsmen.[11] Whereas there were only twenty-two yacht clubs in Britain in 1855, for instance, at least sixty-four existed by 1874 and growth on this scale reflected a new interest in yachting which went well beyond such bastions of élitism as Cowes and Torquay.[12]

2. The National Scene

Previously, clubs beyond southern England were confined to a handful of centres where the scale of mercantile or landed wealth could hardly be denied. At its 'marine station' in Birkenhead, for instance, the Royal Mersey Yacht Club had stood as witness to Liverpudlian prosperity since 1844.[13] Others included the Royal Yorkshire at Hull and Carnarvon's Royal Welsh, both dating from 1847, as well as Glasgow's prestigious Royal Northern at Rothesay from 1824, and the Royal Clyde at Hunter's Quay, founded in 1856. Ireland also had some eminent clubs, including the Queenstown based Royal Cork which began in 1720. Clubs of such wealth and prestige were clearly no threat to élitism; with most members owning large yachts capable of lengthy voyages, and what was at best a lukewarm attitude towards smaller vessels. In 1866, for instance, a meeting of Royal Mersey members decided that 'yachts with moveable keels or centreboards must sail in a class by themselves', while the club's prime interests continued to focus upon the racing of the generally far larger schooners and yawls.[14]

Despite such thinly veiled disapproval, smaller yachts—often with centreboards rather than deep fixed keels—were growing in popularity, as interest in the sport widened and the number of clubs trebled within twenty years. The arrival of so many new clubs prompted discussions among leading yachtsmen throughout Britain, but principally in the South, who then formed the Yacht Racing Association (YRA) in 1875. From the start, the YRA set out to co-ordinate racing activities, including the all important handicapping system used to allow yachts of different sizes and designs to compete with one another, as well as seeking to maintain a high standard of conduct within this competitive side of the sport as participation widened.[15] The urgent need for some kind of regulation is evident from the continued rise in the number of clubs, with just over 120 established by the end of the year of the West Lancashire Yacht Club's foundation in 1894 and some 200 ten years later.[16]

Recognition by the YRA became an essential factor in any yacht club's success. It was the only means by which a club could compete with others in racing events and offer members the level of sport which most boat owners increasingly expected. The YRA refused to give any clear ground rules for recognition, which was clearly only granted to those clubs able to demonstrate a combination of a substantial fleet of competently sailed yachts and social acceptability. One hint as to the YRA's outlook appeared in Dixon Kemp's authoritative *Manual of Yacht and Boat Sailing*—he was the Association's first Secretary from 1876 to 1898 and editor of the *Field*[17]—who wrote that

> any 'yacht club' is considered 'recognised' which is organised by yacht owners for the promotion of properly conducted yacht matches, and which do not enrol mechanics and labourers as members.[18]

The ban on working men reflected a widespread fear in middle-class sporting circles of their physical strength and skills which were regarded as a source of unfair advantage when competing with true 'corinthians' who were amateurs in every sense with no financial interest in the outcome of their sporting activity. Rugby, rowing, athletics, cricket, angling and golf were among other sports faced by this dilemma.[19] The possiblity of gambling, dependent upon individual performance, might provide some justification for this attitude.[20] Nevertheless, it was at root a straight forward desire to project the social barriers of Victorian society into the growing world of sport, while the public school and Oxford or Cambridge university influence gave such 'athleticism' a moral approval which served to enhance the image of these activities in the minds of 'status-hungry' middle-class merchants, stockbrokers and other professionals.[21] More specifically, amateur yachtsmen had every reason to fear the expertise of the men who sailed in the still numerous fishing fleets scattered around the coast. Trawler skippers who took to the sea throughout the year, knew local waters extremely well and they would have been formidable competitors. Many local fishermen, in fact, were hired as paid hands in larger yachts during the summer and played a key part in racing even though the YRA rules prevented them from taking the helm.[22]

Even so, the YRA realised that there was little need for rigid rules in the late nineteenth century. Entry to club membership was in itself sufficiently well controlled by the elaborate vetting procedures of existing yacht owners that most clubs with a serious interest in racing managed to gain recognition in the 1880s and 1890s, although it was sometimes necessary to make more than one attempt.[23] Indeed, the barriers to club entry also arose from the sheer costs of owning and maintaining any boat, as well as the time needed to travel to moorings and sail regularly.

Furthermore, each club had its own code of conduct centred upon rules about dress, behaviour and a system of flag officers—based upon naval principles—ensuring that standards of behaviour were set firmly in a middle-class pattern which required as much commitment socially as on the water. Male dominance was also taken for granted, despite the emergence of some obviously highly capable women yachtsmen by the late nineteenth century. Of course, there were contrasting shades of élitism, from the excesses of Cowes to the more down-to-earth activities of, say, the Humber Yawl Club which, from its inception in 1883, 'fostered carefully a stern image of Viking northerners with little time for the soft living of the south'.[24] A similar approach characterised the growing number of clubs in and around the Mersey. For all that, any late Victorian or Edwardian yachtsman who belonged to a YRA 'recognised' club would have fitted in well at any of the others; and the ability to do so was clearly one of the characteristics expected of membership in what remained a selective, albeit gradually less exclusive, world.

One sign of the yacht clubs' confidence in the strength of these social barriers was that their entry fees and annual subscription rates were surprisingly low. They were certainly comparable to, say, those of most suburban tennis or golf clubs.[25] The Cowes based Royal Yacht Squadron's £100 entrance fee and £11 annual subscription of the 1890s, for instance, was wholly exceptional. Only one other club—the Royal St George at Kingstown in Ireland—exceeded a £10 entrance fee and the vast majority of clubs charged 2 guineas or less with annual subscriptions at an equally modest level.[26] This allowed many yachtsmen to belong to more than one club; with a few of the leading personalities having a string of memberships covering a whole region or even beyond that, if they had the time and money, allowing them access to club facilities wherever they took their boat.

Walter Scott Hayward—Commodore of the WLYC 1895–1903

Clear evidence of multiple club membership can be found in the North West where many of the key figures in local clubs such as those at Southport or along the coast of North Wales, were also registered as members of the Royal Mersey Yacht Club.[27] Quite apart from the convenience of having access to the Royal Mersey's fine clubhouse and its moorings, membership of this, the 'senior' local club, entitled a yachtsmen to hold a prestigious admiralty warrant allowing the use of the blue ensign with the club's prominent liver bird crest beneath the Union Jack. West Lancashire Yacht Club members must have been particularly impressed by the irony of this practice in 1899 when one of the leading specialist journals, *The Yachting World*, produced a glowing 'yachting celebrities' report on their commodore, Walter Scott Hayward. Amidst an account of how he had formed the WLYC in 1894, and his contribution towards its rapid rise to success, is a full plate photograph of him proudly wearing his Royal Mersey cap complete with its liver bird badge![28]

On numbers alone, however, the WLYC could count itself successful in comparison with most other local clubs. With about 150 members in 1904, it was still slightly larger than the élitist Royal Windermere Yacht Club whose membership had risen steadily from some thirty members in 1877 to 120 by this date.[29] Nearer to Southport, both the West Kirby and Blackpool & Fleetwood Sailing Clubs had between 120 and 130 members in the immediate pre-war years.[30] Even the top ranking clubs remained relatively small due to their tight control over the selection of new members. Of course, the Royal Mersey Yacht Club remained well above 200 during the Edwardian period but the Royal Welsh Yacht Club at Carnarvon still had only 164 in 1913.[31] Another point is that these figures obviously 'double-counted' those yachtsmen who belonged to more than one club in an area like the North West where clubs were within easy travelling distance of one another. The pressure to gain YRA recognition was a complicating factor in that respect. It certainly helped to have over a hundred members in the first place. Once recognised, clubs fell into a pecking order which, although never specified, clearly depended upon a combination of seniority, total yacht tonnage and the number of members.[32] Clubs were therefore eager to keep as many 'members' on their books as they could, even though a proportion of them might have ceased to play an effective part in the club. With annual subscriptions remaining relatively low, there must have been a good many 'outport' members—that is living away and having no vote—who kept up their payments even though their contribution to club life was negligible.

For all that, a membership of from 100 to 200 was regarded as perfectly viable. Indeed some commentators in the 1900s implied that larger clubs were too impersonal. In particular, younger members who were keen to crew found it difficult to find a slot when the membership was, say, three or four hundred. As the *Yachting World*'s 'Corinthian Yachts-man' argued in 1909 this frequently happened because 'in a large club the majority of members are strangers to one another and the wants of an owner are not known beyond his immediate circle'.[33]

To that extent, the smaller club found it easier to sustain a level of enthusiasm and friendly cooperation which probably did as much for its survival as the higher member-ship fee income and prestige of their larger 'sister' clubs. Nevertheless, there were successful large clubs which would have disagreed with this. The Royal Clyde Yacht Club's 859 members surely knew in 1911 that they belonged to one of the world's most prestigious clubs, and the 613 members of an 'old established Thames Estuary club' doubtless felt equally secure in 1909.[34] Finally, we can pause to admire the spirit of the 510 members of the proud Horning Town Sailing Club, in Norfolk, who showed a healthy disregard for anyone else in 1910 and simply claimed to belong to the largest sailing club in the world![35]

Of course, the appearance of any new club anywhere worried the more conservative among the old guard. For example, A. H. Bridson JP, was commodore of the Dart Bay Sailing Club and the originator of the West of England Yacht and Boat Sailing Conference, established in 1890.[36] It was almost certainly, the same A. H. Bridson who wrote to the editor of *The Yachtsman* in 1893 to point out that the licensing law prevented anyone but 'permanent members (so called) ... paying for alcoholic liquors, cigars and billiards' in a yacht clubhouse. Few readers could have objected to that statement of the obvious, and this might be another reason why many took up multiple club membership. But Bridson continued his letter with an evident indignation which implied that, in his view, the barriers were coming down too fast.

> It is true that the hospitality of most English yacht clubs is seemingly conspicuous by
> its absence, but in these days when many sailing clubs, with a hut on the shore for a
> club house, call themselves yacht clubs, and when the status of members varies very
> greatly in different clubs, there are many reasons against indiscriminate hospitality
> altogether apart from the licensing difficulty.[37]

The absence of any response to Bridson's letter in the journal's weekly column where debate arose over most issues, indicates that few yachtsmen shared his fears about declining social standards. He was certainly well out of line with current thinking at the YRA which had the sense to realise that survival depended upon attracting a larger number of participants with the money and time to invest in a boat which they were prepared to race.

Only at one stage, from about 1907 to 1914, did the yachting 'establishment' grow unduly nervous about newcomers. Increasingly, by the 1890s and 1900s the type of person described by *Yachting Monthly* as the 'man of moderate means'—often employed in the middle ranks of companies in banking, insurance or similar activities—had Saturday afternoons free.[38] Wherever such people could reach sailing waters from their desk in town, the opportunities for regular racing changed from an occasional luxury to a regular event. The social constraints upon Sunday competition remained, but with improving commuter rail links and reasonable coastal lodging rates yachting boomed in popularity around the turn of the century as it began to tap new fields for potential members. In the industrial North, many new members were attracted from Manchester into clubs on the Lancashire coast and in the Mersey estuary.

But this was overshadowed by the pressure upon those waters which could easily be reached from London. As a letter about 'Trains for Yachtsmen' in the *Yachting World* pointed out in 1911, even the South coast had become accessible on a regular basis with, in this case, the prospect of needing to travel for less than two hours to reach Southampton on a Friday evening and returning to London for work on Monday morning.[39] More significantly, Southend and Burnham-on-Crouch were much closer to the City and they changed remarkably fast, with new clubs springing up against a background of growing waiting lists for moorings and reports of increasing pressure on club house facilities.[40]

At first, through its powerful influence upon the yachting columns of the *Field* magazine, the YRA became excessively defensive about the emergence of a large number of so-called 'minor' clubs, particularly around the East coast and in the Thames Estuary. Their presence among Britain's 200 clubs could not, however, be ignored for long, particularly as they could become members of either the Boat Racing Association or the smaller Sail Boat Association. Under considerable pressure from the leading yachting journals from 1907 onwards,[41] the YRA gradually conceded the point that recognition was less of a threat than official isolation. During the next few years the pace of recognition increased until the First World War forced such matters to one side. Then, after some rearguard quibbles about what was and what was not a 'yacht' among small sailing boats, any well organised club could gain recognition by the mid-1920s if it was willing and able to abide by the Association's rigorous rules of behaviour on the water. Unlike some other sports, including athletics, rugby, and rowing, this meant that yachting in Britain has not had to suffer a lengthy conflict between rival governing bodies.[42] By balancing the interests of the yachting establishment against the demands for recognition of newcomers, the YRA—which became the Royal Yachting Association in 1953—retained firm control of all sailing activities in Britain during the crucial decades of growth and change before the First World War.[43]

3. The Attractions of Southport

Despite the obvious hazards and inconveniences of local sailing waters at Southport, these powerful external social and economic influences brought organised yachting to the resort in the late nineteenth century. The Southport Corinthians were formed in 1884, followed by the West Lancashire Yacht Club (WLYC) ten years later. Just as elsewhere in late Victorian Britain, the railway played a key part in the development of Southport as a successful Victorian residential outpost as well as a seaside resort.[44] From 1855, with the opening of a link with Manchester, the railway brought Southport within a few hours of Lancashire's industrial and commercial wealth.

This immensely increased the town's appeal not only to the rich but also to those professional and business people of more limited means who could afford to sail at the weekends once the railway made their travel to the resort fairly staightforward. They were to be found among the growing number of middle-class people who preferred to live in Southport and commute to Liverpool or Manchester. Apart from that, those weekend visitors who had the money could easily find suitable rented housing, or rooms, in a leasehold property market controlled by the two dominant ground rent holders, the Scarisbrick Trustees and the Heskeths.[45] Their leases prohibited serried ranks of cheap terraces in favour of more 'respectable' and substantial detached or semi-detached properties which included a large number of well-to-do guest houses. They slotted easily into the wide tree-lined avenues which all led towards the sheltered gentility of Lord Street and a central area dominated socially and in architectural style by the numerous clusters of impressive 'villas' owned by a wealthy élite who held sway over local political and business life. From this vantage point, at least, the town's claim to have become a 'seaside garden city' was firmly based in reality by the late-nineteenth century.[46]

Southport's burgeoning middle class therefore included a fair proportion of weekend and daily commuters, together with numerous semi-retired men of means, all of whom could well afford to sail. At the same time, as explained earlier, the town possessed a reputation and social life of sufficient weight to attract many wealthier individuals. As Peter Aughton explains, 'Southport began life as a seaside variant of the Regency Spa Town', in which those with wealth enjoyed numerous 'galas and balls, whist and quadrille in the evenings'.[47] Such exclusive entertainments, as well as the emerging and equally select clubs for golf, tennis, rowing and, by the 1900s, motoring, were well able to survive the arrival of huge crowds of weekend 'trippers' from the industrial working class homes of East Lancashire. These transient masses, greater in fact than those going to Blackpool until the turn of the century and essential to the profitability of local businesses, were readily diverted to the the sands, or to the 'boating' lake and the pier with its entertainments and steamer trips to other coastal resorts on the Fylde Coast or across to Rhyl.[48]

From the pier, or the decks of crowded steamers, the trippers gazed at yachtsmen, doubtless with a mixture of admiration and envy, but only at a distance which merely enhanced the status of this form of leisure activity and emphasised its remoteness from the day-to-day lives of even those factory workers, shop-girls, dockers and the like who could afford a break.[49] Moreover, the local press, principally in the form of the *Southport Guardian* and the *Visiter*, regularly admired their town's 'yachting' activities. At one extreme, 'Belle's Tea Table Talk', presented a hopefully at least slightly tongue in cheek report in this vein for the *Visiter*'s readers about a WLYC race held on a cold and wet day in June 1903.

> The 'Vikings bold' who, in life-belt encased, trusted their lives to such merciless rhapsodies, and inconsequent capers on the restless tide, commanded my intense admiration. My poor badly balanced brain [added the mercifully anonymous journalist] would have been describing whirligigs and eccentrics for weeks after! It looked like rare good sport for those engaged in it—they seemed to enjoy the excitement of it. No doubt the elements of danger and daring appealed to those our 'gentlemen sailors'![50]

More realistically, it was normal to report the arrivals and departures of big yachts in rather glowing terms. In June 1894, for instance, the *Southport Guardian* noted that

Sir Geo. Pilkington and Lady Pilkington are about to leave Southport for a time. Their handsome yacht, the Jullanar, arrived in the Channel on Thursday, and has been lying at anchor there. She will sail, with Sir Geo. and Lady Pilkington, today, the destination of the party being the North of Scotland, where the yacht will cruise for a couple of months. We wish the voyageurs a long spell of fair weather and favourable winds.[51]

Sir George Pilkington–President of the WLYC 1894–1916

Sir George, to his credit, was at pains to admit—even to emphasise—his 'figure-head' status as a sailor while serving as the WLYC President from 1894 to 1910. In contrast to many in such a role, he was genuinely respected and liked by club members for this honesty, which was matched by his considerable moral support for those who took their racing seriously. That apart, the obvious local press approval of 'yachting' in its broadest sense, mirrored in the incredibly lengthy column space devoted to it nationally in *The Times* and the *Field* magazine, must have attracted some new club members who saw the sport primarily as a means of expressing their middle class status. Others, of course, were simply inspired to develop what they found to be an almost addictive pastime. For them, social approval merely sanctioned something which they would have done anyway once the means existed!

Against this background, the formation of the Southport Corinthian Yacht Club in 1883 had been viewed locally as a long over-due development rather than something novel. In particular, the organisation of the revived annual 'regatta' off the pierhead in July 1883 had lapsed into a farce. The public had been promised impressive fishing boat, rowing and yacht races, with entries 'hailing from Southport, Marshside, Liverpool, Tranmere, Lytham, Fleetwood and Morecambe.' Captain Gladstone, the Honorary Secretary of the Royal Mersey Yacht Club, agreed to start and judge the sailing events, while the then Dr George Pilkington acted as judge for the rowing races. Further weighty support came from Colonel Edward Fleetwood Hesketh JP who acted as President for the event from the local steamer Wellington which had been hired as a flagship. In the event, all of their plans went awry as the sailing vessels set off into the Channel, rather than the promised inshore course which, the *Visiter* claimed, would allow spectators to 'see the whole of the race'. The fiasco, in terms of stimulating more interest in yachting, led the disappointed *Visiter* correspondent to complain that 'the management was extremely bad, no arrangements whatever having been made for either pleasure seekers or', perhaps more significantly, 'the Press'![52]

4. The Southport Corinthians

Nevertheless, even the *Visiter* admitted that the event highlighted the potential advantages of Southport as a yachting venue during the summer months. The Pier Company Directors also felt that there were gains to be made. A thriving yacht fleet could only enhance the pier's reputation as an amenity for those who liked to 'promenade' over the sea. They agreed to support the cost of buoying the Bog Hole[53] and this essential task was completed by a Lieutenant Crawley of the Royal Naval Artillery Volunteers who had, by the 1884 season, ensured that 'the channel is now well buoyed from the southern bar to the pier, a distance of four miles'. This in itself, according to the *Visiter*, meant that the newly formed yacht club would 'in their races ... have a good course out into the open, and no difficulty will be experienced in working up to Southport at all states of the tide'.[54] Beyond that, the Pier Company had contributed five guineas towards the Regatta prizes and agreed to do the same for the new club, while the Directors also provided adequate changing and 'punt' launching facilities at the first pierhead for a modest rent of £30 a year.[55]

Initially known as the Southport Corinthian Sailing Club, the new venture took over the pierhead premises of the Southport Corinthian Rowing Club which had found life impossible among the shifting sandbanks and treacherous currents around the Bog Hole.[56] While the rowers retreated to an artificial lake at the Alexander Gardens on the Scarisbrick Road, several miles inland,[57] the Southport Corinthian yachtsmen enjoyed a well publicised club opening ceremony supported by the mayor and other local worthies. Within months of starting the new club had over forty members and its racing programme was ready by May 1884 for the start of the new season.[58]

More significantly, in yachting terms, the Southport Corinthians quickly gained YRA recognition and decided to adopt the title of 'yacht' club at a time when the term still carried a higher social cachet than the humble term 'sailing'. A further stamp of official acceptance came with the reporting of its events in *Hunt's Yachting Magazine*.[59] At the time, *Hunt's Magazine* was the only specialist journal for yachting. Its staid pages drearily listed race wins and prizes together with laborious reports of each club's annual general meeting; all in a manner designed, it seemed, to dispel any hint of commercialism in a world where the amateur status of the true 'corinthian' yachtsman was paramount.

However, there was clearly a disagreement—albeit a gentlemanly one—with regard to the Southport Corinthians' future. The vast majority of members appeared happy to 'cruise' in their yachts, of varying sizes, and showed little if any desire to take part in regular racing. Most of these owners had larger vessels capable of sea voyages for which the help of paid crewmen was at least worth considering and, in most cases, absolutely essential. By contrast, the declared aim of the Southport Corinthian had been from the start to 'encourage a class of small yachts not exceeding three tons'. Strict measurement rules were laid down, limiting costs and, in the true amateur spirit of it's 'Corinthian' title, 'give all members a chance in the races which it is proposed should be held every alternate Saturday during the season'.[60]

The thinking behind this approach came from Walter Scott Hayward, who as a junior member of the Temple Yacht Club some fifteen years earlier would have met a similar attitude at its Charlton clubhouse on the Thames where you were expected to take part in races and purely 'social' members were frowned upon.[61] Moreover, as explained later on, the idea of restricting a class to one-design was taken up with increasing enthusiasm in the late-nineteenth century as there was a general reaction against the escalating costs of racing between vessels of different design. The idea of having regular and fairly short races on a local course was also a prospect close to the hearts of the Southport Pier directors who obviously preferred the timed and visible event as an attraction for their crowds of ticket buying weekend promenaders.

Even so, the enthusiasm for racing among the majority of members seems to have been on the wane by the early 1890s. In May 1891, the SCYC reported its plans for a race programme of two open handicaps and six events for the '3-ton matches', while there were to be nine races for a 12-foot centreboard class of a type recognised increasingly in yachting as belonging to a so-called 'mosquito' fleet. Meanwhile, however, more emphasis was put upon what can only be described as the social life of the club. As *The Yachtsman* reported at the start of the 1891 season, the Southport Corinthian Yacht Club

> now numbers over a hundred members with every prospect of a large increase this year in consequence of having taken commodious shore premises, consisting of smoke and billiard rooms, library &c. Until now the Club had tended to attract only those prepared to walk or take the [pier] tramway out to the launching stages. [This] disadvantage of being so far from the water has long been apparent, and has militated seriously against the acquisition of numbers of would-be members who are not so seriously interested in the sport as those who are at present on the list.[62]

Certainly, the new Southport Corinthian shore-based clubrooms at the pier entrance on the promenade offered an appropriately 'commanding view of the Channel'.[63] But as an attempt to strengthen the Corinthian's long term position as a yacht club, it was to prove an unexpected disaster. While most Club members were preoccupied with cruising and social activities, the small boat men emerged as the only true amateur competitors. Above all, the mosquito fleet sailors presented a remarkable contrast to the others in the club. Sailing single handed, or in pairs, they made little if any use of the paid hands who played such a significant part on the larger yachts.[64] The mosquito fleet also provided an opportunity for those with less money to sail, while their use of centreboards and the small size of their boats enabled them to use the new Marine Lake, which was opened by Southport Corporation in 1893, to start a modest but keenly competitive winter sailing programme.[65]

Among these enthusiasts, there was an influential group of keen racing sailors led by Walter Scott Hayward, the vice-commodore, and J. J. Bailey, an Oldham engineer and amateur photographer who was also famed for his exploits as an Amazon and Arctic explorer.[66] Walter Scott Hayward's leading contribution to the foundation of the club ensured that he could at least continue to promote competitive sailing. Certainly, he was gaining recognition throughout the north-west for his skills as a yacht designer as well as for being a highly capable helmsman. Quite apart from initiating the 21-foot restricted class of 3-tonners, he designed the 12-foot centre-board dinghy used by the mosquito fleet and then produced plans for a modestly sized yacht known as a three-quarter-rater in 1893. His 0.75-rater class was so obviously aimed at cost controlled racing in the difficult waters of the Ribble Estuary that it could hardly be ignored.[67]

Scott Hayward's influence attracted a core of loyal support from those Southport Corinthian members who expected the 'social' element of yachting to serve the sporting aims of a club rather than becoming an end in itself. Evidently, they failed to convince a silent majority among the Southport Corinthians and the outcome was the agreement to disagree which led to the formation of the WLYC in June 1894.[68] From the start the WLYC's approach reflected a progressive line of thinking which was gradually making inroads in yachting generally by the early 1890s and this undoubtedly contributed to the new club's almost immediate success. The sport was undergoing cultural and technical changes at a time of rising costs and increasing social pressures for a wider participation. Go-ahead individuals who were willing to take a chance managed to take others with them whereas they would previously have been marginalised as eccentrics.

5. Changing Attitudes

A striking example of how yachting was changing nationally can be seen in the fate of the somewhat dry *Hunt's Magazine*. Established in 1851 and funded entirely by readers' subscriptions, the journal was driven out of business in 1887.[69] Instead of its cumbersome print and heavily serious articles illustrated with line drawings, yachtsmen evidently preferred the knowledgeable and stylish writing of Dixon Kemp in his role as editor and yachting correspondent of the *Field*. Dixon Kemp bridged the gap between the wealthy élite and a very rapidly growing band of small boat sailors with his reputation as 'the greatest authority upon the general theory and practice of all branches of yachting that the world has ever known'.[70] As secretary to the Yacht Racing Association from its inception in 1875 until he resigned in 1898, he had an immense influence upon all classes of yachtsmen, with his massive *Manual of Yacht and Boat Sailing* continuing to run as revised editions for some thirty years after his death in 1899.[71]

Meanwhile, another more commercial element appeared on the scene as the social base of yachting widened. The first editions of the journal *The Yachtsman*, from 1891, and its rival from 1894, the *Yachting World*, took the sport into the twentieth century. Glossy paper, 'gossipy' local reports, informative articles, high quality photography and, above all, advertising, left readers in little doubt as to the presence of a new emphasis in the sport. Both journals paid immediate attention to the WLYC when it was formed and their early support at a national level undoubtedly gave the club the stamp of approval so essential for credibility among older clubs.

At 3d. a week both *The Yachtsman* and the *Yachting World* were relatively cheap. But they were still obviously aimed at the middle class, with a commercially healthy touch of sycophancy towards the extremely rich, and to that extent they merely reflected wider social trends. On the one hand, their columns said virtually nothing about the vast majority of the population, the wage earners and small traders for whom yachting remained too remote a prospect to be worthy of a moment's serious thought. Even so, the continual growth of yachting represented the start of a gradual, but irreversible, widening of its appeal. Of course, the arrival of salaried professionals and modestly successful local businessmen into the ranks of many clubs, despite the existence of a long trade depression from the late 1870s to mid-1890s, raised some eyebrows and introduced yet further elements of snobbery and division. Some older clubs went to almost ridiculous lengths to emphasise their 'seniority' and much energy was devoted to the quest to gain the coveted right to the title of a 'Royal' club.[72]

Add to this the public perception of yachting as a sport for the exceedingly wealthy who raced in large boats; usually on the English South coast with royalty aboard. Clearly there were grounds for questioning the extent to which yachting was really opening its doors to a wider social circle by the turn of the century, despite all the signs of change at the club level. In the 1880s much racing, and certainly most of that reported in the national press such as *The Times* or *The Field*, still took place in large yachts whose ability to compete with others was determined on an elaborate handicap system.[73] To make matters worse, the development of British yachting was almost constantly being disrupted during the late Victorian period by a series of quarrels concerning the methods of rating which were most appropriate for determining a fair system of handicap when yachts of different sizes and design wished to race one another. At times, the intensity of these arguments was so great that the modern reader could be forgiven for overlooking that this was a sport and not the world of competitive business or of warfare! No club, particularly newcomers like the WLYC, could afford to ignore the rating issue which had a profound influence upon how yachting in boats of all sizes developed during the late nineteenth century and the Edwardian period.

Rating systems were originally based upon the displacement of sailing vessels as determined by an Act of 1719 intended to tax mercantile capacity according to tonnage carrying capacity. Keel length and beam, however, figured prominently in the calculation and this provided an acceptable guide to a yacht's speed because handicap penalties were very broadly in line with sail carrying ability and load water line length.[74] The so-called Builder's Measurement Rule of 1773 adopted these principles for time allowances which were aimed at giving yachts of similar size the chance to compete with each other on equal terms. These early rating sytems were established by mutual agreement between senior clubs, including the Royal Yacht Squadron, the Royal Thames and the Royal Mersey. Little progress was made in design, with yachts tending towards a solid form having a straight stern and bluff bows, recognisable as the distinctive 'cod's head and mackerel tail' shape of the traditional cutter until British complacency was shaken in 1851 by the arrival at Cowes of the sleek United States yacht America which won every race it entered before returning home.[75]

British designers learnt fast. By raking the bow and stern to maximise length on the water line for the same measured keel dimension, yacht speed could be increased without altering the handicap time-allowance. The conservative attitudes which had dominated designs for nearly a century were abandoned as clubs realised that this so-called 'tonnage cheating'— designing yachts to exploit loopholes in the rules—had become acceptable practice among the leading owners.[76] A succession of handicap rule changes, in 1855, 1866, 1879, 1881, 1886, 1896, 1901 and 1907 attempted to check design trends regarded as unsafe or impracticable.[77] On each occasion, different weightings were given to those variables which were believed to have most effect upon boat speed. Until 1886, the formulae adopted were based solely upon beam and length; first at the keel, then from stem to stern post and finally at load water line. Then sail area was introduced to the calculation in 1886. Little wonder that the costs of yacht building rose, despite a general fall in raw material prices from the mid-1870s to the 1890s, as designs changed almost continuously. Terms like 'plank on edge'—reducing beam to extremes of narrowness in the 1860s and 1870s —and 'skimming dish'—aimed at cutting down wetted surface area without reducing length or beam during the 1880s and early 1890s—give an idea of the changes in hull shape of the most radical yacht designs.[78]

In one respect, the rating rule alterations were a stimulus to innovation and development. Against that, however, costs became prohibitive. Of course, in 1875 the YRA was formed principally with that concern in mind and during the next six years the Association took over responsibility for rating as its authority in the sport widened.[79] Like their predecessors, the YRA rating committees consisted chiefly of experienced yacht owners who struggled to prevent extreme designs without ruining the chances of more conventional boats built within the bounds of a current rule. Nevertheless, because the top boats of all sizes were increasingly being built for speed at the cost of comfort by the 1880s, the customary career of a yacht—from racer to cruiser—was curtailed with serious effects upon resale values.[80]

A further change devised by Dixon Kemp in 1886 led to a 'length and sail area rule' which did not penalise beam. The calculation used a denominator of 6,000 simply to yield figures similar to the previous 'tonnage' rules for yachts which had not been taken to the 'plank-on-edge' extremes where the ratio of length to beam could be up to a 'ridiculous' 6.0 compared to the 4.0 preferred by most owners who liked to cruise as well as race. A 5-'tonner' with a reasonably conventional hull shape resulting from a ratio of 4.0 now became a 5-'rater'.[81] Had it not been for the decision to build some of the one-design yacht classes according to the same calculation, the term would have passed into obscurity after the next handicap rule change in 1896, because the word 'rater' then ceased to have any purely technical validity. As its creator Dixon-Kemp pointed out just after the new rule had been introduced in 1896, 'it can only be regarded as a slang term'.[82]

That curt remark reflected the preoccupation of the YRA which continued in its quest for a rating rule that would allow fair time handicaps for races between dissimilar yachts. In fact, the new rules in 1896, 1901 and 1907 gradually introduced a measure of sanity into racing yacht design. They owed much to Professor Froude's research twenty years earlier proving that speed varied inversely to wetted surface area as well as in direct relation to the other known variables—beam, load waterline length and sail area—used previously.[83] The new ratings therefore penalised those yachts designed for maximum length and sail area with a minumum of sumbmerged hull area—the so-called 'skimming dishes'—which were certainly uncomfortable as cruisers but were also viewed as potentially unstable.[84]

Even after 1896, yachts with minimal cabin space enjoyed a modest handicap advantage until this loophole was penalised in 1901. In the meantime, the pace of changes hit small yacht owners particularly hard. Wealthy fanatics could have a new small racer, designed to exploit every possible loophole in a rule, from drawing board to water within months—eight days if it happened to be for the Duke of York!—so what chance did the man of moderate means have?[85] And yet, as Linton Hope put it, from his vantage point as a key member of the 1896 YRA rating committee, 'the small class has been a most useful nursery and one of the best for the sport, as many could go in for an 18-footer who could not afford several hundred pounds for one of the larger classes'.[86] The obvious logic in this point explains, better than anything else, the origin of one-design racing. Any immediate loss of pace in technical progress was eventually offset by the growth in participation. British sailing remained open to new one-design classes so that the financial need for continuity has not inhibited the pace of change.

Moreover, the early founders of one-design classes in the 1880s and 1890s took a liking to the term 'rater' and it continued to be adopted even after the 1896 change in the official rating rules. Chapter 3, for example, will show how Walter Scott Hayward's three-quarter (0.75)-rater class designed for the Southport Corinthians in 1894 was immediately adopted by the WLYC. Indeed, it is more than likely that the indifference of most Corinthians towards Scott Hayward's enthusiasm for this small yacht played a key part in his decision to found the new club![87] Add to that his leading part in designing the WLYC Seabird half-raters in 1898 and it becomes clear that this 'slang' term remained of more than passing significance for yachtsmen in the north west as it did for those one-design class owners who sailed raters elsewhere in the country. Because these new classes had rigid design specifications, they obviously required no handicap system when they raced as a fleet. Furthermore, costs were usually strictly controlled by their class rules, often with the specific intention of encouraging participation by people who had previously found sailing too expensive. As a result, the one-design classes proved a major stimulus to the continued growth of yachting as a sport at a time when its upper echelons were facing a crisis of confidence.

It was against this background of changes in yachting at the national level that the WLYC was formed in May 1894 and, as explained earlier, Walter Scott Hayward played the leading role in bringing about this break with the Southport Corinthians. Meanwhile, John Bailey took on the unenviable task of secretary to the new club and it was largely due to his tact and energy that the venture went smoothly. In fact, nineteen of the Southport Corinthian members also joined the WLYC, including all of the flag officers, giving it an initial stamp of almost paternalistic approval.[88] Bailey also persuaded the Pier Company directors to let the new club fit out its own clubhouse and changing rooms on the pier in lieu of paying rent for the first two years and the WLYC was ready for its opening cruise by July 1894.[89]

As chapter 4 explains, the new club achieved some remarkable successes during its early years. In developing highly competitive one-design racing fleets, with boats which were relatively cheap and easy to handle when compared to those of only twenty years earlier, it attracted the attention of the yachting press. With twenty-one of the West Lancashire Seabird class of one-designs sailing by 1902, the *Yachting World* was prompted to remark the 'there is promise of the class becoming the largest one-model class in the British Isles. This speaks well for the admirable way in which the class has been managed by that young and energetic organisation, the West Lancashire Yacht Club'.[90] Few, if any, new clubs could have enjoyed such prominent recognition at such an early stage in their history and this achievement is, if anything, the more remarkable for a club based at Southport, where all yachtsmen had to contend with the hazards and frustrations of sailing in the Ribble Estuary.

Chapter 2

Sailing Waters 1894 to 1937

1. Introduction

FROM ITS FOUNDATION in 1894, the WLYC faced increasing difficulty in gaining access to suitable open water for regular racing. The basic problem was the silting of the South Channel of the Ribble Estuary which ran close to the foreshore. By the mid-nineteenth century this part of the estuary had acquired the perhaps regrettable, but certainly unforgettable, local name of the 'Bog Hole', describing the stretch of deep water which persisted long after the South Channel's access to the Ribble had been cut-off by sand and mud at most stages of the tide (map 1). It was not impossible for a yacht club to move elsewhere if faced with such diffculties or simply in a search for better sailing water. The Temple Yacht Club[1] and the Great Yarmouth Yacht Club provide two examples in the period before 1939.[2] Even so, most clubs chose to stay put. The rapid growth in numbers, with each club understandably keen to have its own stretch of water, made it increasingly difficult to find a new location that had not been claimed. Besides, local pride led many to show an almost stubborn determination to adapt to local conditions and one advantage of this was that British sailing clubs developed an immense range of yacht designs.

Of course, the Southport Corinthian Yacht Club never moved. Apart from the obvious ties implied by its name, the foundation of the WLYC took away the core of enthusiasts who were ever likely to initiate such a radical change. Despite a brief burst of more serious racing activity from 1910 to 1913, the club was gradually overtaken by events. In 1922 its committee half-heartedly discussed a merger with the WLYC members, but the idea came to nothing. After that, the Corinthians never stood a serious chance of survival at a time when yachting was generally facing hard times and the Bog Hole was continuing to silt up. Their membership dwindled to the point that the club had closed downby 1932.[3]

For all its reputation as a go-ahead club before 1914, the WLYC also had little choice but to remain at Southport. One obvious reason for staying was that it relied heavily on strong support from those members who actually lived in the town, known in the club rules as 'inport' members. They figured strongly in the one-design racing and provided the core of week-to-week attendance which ensured that the WLYC had a notably high rate of sailing participation with, for instance, a regular turnout of about fifty members on the water in the years just before the First World War. Meanwhile, many of the so-called 'outport' members also belonged to other clubs such as the Royal Mersey, the Lytham, and the Rhyl Yacht Clubs. The Lytham Yacht Club, for instance, began in 1889 under very similar circumstances to the creation of the Southport Corinthians. Indeed, among its founding members the club included Frank Coddington, the wealthy Blackburn cotton manufacturer who was also a leading Southport Corinthian member and then supported the creation of the WLYC.[4] Quite apart from the likely resentment among neighbouring clubs such as this, any attempt to move the WLYC from Southport either further north into Lancashire or southwards down the coast towards Hightown, home of the thriving new Blundellsands

Sailing Club from 1887, would have led to a heavy loss of subscriptions as members simply gave up sailing or switched interest to their other yacht clubs.[5]

2. The North Marine Lake

Only the North Marine Lake offered an alternative to sailing on the sea at Southport. Construction of a lake on the south side of the pier had started in 1887, as part of an amusement park, while a separate North Lake was opened for boating in 1892. Although the two were joined by a wide channel in 1895, the North Lake remained to all intents and purposes isolated from the growing range of rather brash amusements sited around the southern stretch of water, including a large water chute from 1903.[6] It was obviously worth trying to sail on the North Lake out of season when there were few, if any, holidaymakers rowing about. From 1893 onwards this became the venue for various attempts to race the smaller one-design sailing dinghies, with the Southport Corinthians launching a few of their 12-footers for Saturday afternoon races in the early Spring of that year.[7]

In some respects, the North lake must have seemed quite good for sailing in the quieter months. Its water was sheltered, fairly shallow and tide free, covering an area some 1300 yards long by 400 yards wide (map 3).[8] The ever keen *Yachting World* had no doubts concerning its advantages. In October 1894, the journal reported with great approval that the WLYC had gained the Corporation's 'permission to put their small craft on the Marine Lake'. And its correspondent regarded a plan to bring in a new small one-design class as highly appropriate for that particular stretch of water.

> This young club certainly intends to keep the 'ball rolling', for I hear they have formed a new class for next year—a 10-foot single-handed one—and if members can get them built in time, they are willing to give prizes to be sailed for during the winter months on the lake.[9]

As it happened, some of those involved with the Corinthians' efforts a year earlier—including Frank Coddington—were now supporting these early WLYC races. It is clear that the WLYC—but not the Southport Corinthians—attempted to run an out of season racing programme on the North Lake during just about every year before the First World War. The Star one-design class certainly became a part of these plans after its introduction in 1906 and it is even possible that there were at least a few attempts to sail the larger Seabird class boats on there in some years. In October 1905, for instance, the 'Sea Birds Skua and Sea Snipe are', said the *Yachting World*'s man, 'on the Marine Lake, Southport, presumably for winter sailing'.[10] Sail or not, there were no Seabird series on the lake. Furthermore, in these pre-wet suit days, the average Club member remained healthily unimpressed about the advantages of winter sailing. Except for some special invitation events and ladies races, only two or three boats raced with any regularity until things began to warm up towards the end of March. And who could blame them when, as in January 1907, a planned 'all-comers' race organised by the WLYC 'had to be postponed for the second time on Saturday. On this occasion the Marine Lake was frozen over.'[11]

Pride might well have added to the deterrent effects of chilly water. Early reports of racing on the Marine Lake clearly suggest that it was only viewed as a winter stop-gap. As the *Yachting World* put it in November 1894, the sheltered lake 'gives the new members a golden opportunity for practice for the more serious work in the channel'. And even experienced helms were sometimes liable to have their all too visible mistakes exposed to critical comment. A sense of humour was essential, as Herbert Baggs—co-designer of the Seabird with Walter Scott-Hayward—discovered in October 1904. He was racing in his 12-footer Flirt and although these events were treated in a fairly light hearted way he would, presumably, have preferred to forget about that particular Saturday. But the *Yachting World* clearly regarded accuracy as important for its readers.

> Flirt more than maintained her lead and on the rounding was well ahead. Unfortu-
> nately her skipper, in a preoccupied moment, evidently thought he was at the tiller of
> his 7-tonner, and forgetting the amount of care required in the handling of a boat of
> such different dimensions, much to the amusement of all concerned, took an invol-
> untary bath, and his interest in the race was, in the fullest sense of the word, damped.[12]

Of course, such a spectacle was far removed from the snobbery of the large yacht clubs on the south coast. The *Yachting World*'s lively style was popular with a growing number of readers, who did not seem to object if they were the target for amusement. And it does indicate how yachting was beginning to change at the turn of the century, with a sense of fun and participation becoming key elements for success in clubs whose roots now lay among a prosperous but not necessarily wealthy and isolated middle class. Even so, it is equally clear that other Lake users could make life difficult in spells of good spring weather. Early in March 1893, for instance, *The Yachtsman* had reported that the Southport Corinthians' dinghies 'were much bothered during the race by the rowing boats getting in the way',[13] and this undoubtedly put yet another restriction upon the use of the Marine Lake by either yacht club.

Understandably, then, most WLYC yachtsmen clearly preferred to get out on to the wider expanse of the Bog Hole Channel at the earliest opportunity. There could have been yet another reason for their desire to escape on to the sea. With the Marine Lake being so close to town, they were no more able to escape the rigours of Southport's strong Sabbatari-anism than any other pleasure seekers. Unlike Blackpool before the First World War, where the corporation gave in to a 'general awareness that Sunday observance was no longer a paying proposition',[14] Southport continued to ban the use of boats on the Marine Lake. It even turned off the Municipal fountains on Sundays and would not allow taxis and trams to run, so the sailors stood little chance of getting on the lake on the Sabbath at any time of the year, whereas it was fairly easy to escape attention on the sea in the summer even though there was no racing!

Finally, it is worth questioning the apparently trouble-free state of the Marine Lake as portrayed by successive holiday brochures at Southport or, for that matter, by any of the growing number of other corporations at Victorian and Edwardian seaside resorts who copied this well-intentioned effort to improve facilities.[15] Weeds, particularly a variety known as 'American weed', seem to have been a problem which could, as at Bournemouth in 1908, only be cured by the 'prohibitively expensive' method of dredging 4 inches from the lake bottom.[16] Dredging was, therefore, avoided in Bournemouth as well as at West Kirby where, by April 1908, it was reported in *Yachting World* that 'the District Council have allowed the Marine Lake to silt up so much as to be quite unsuitable for racing'.[17]

Yet even at West Kirby, as at Rhyl Marine Lake and in Southport itself, reference was very frequently made to the perceived value of these large stretches of shallow salt water as tourist attractions. Clearly, the costs of maintaining them were more than the local authori-ties could have bargained for when they built them—Southport actually being the earliest of note[18]—in the 1890s. One *Southport Visiter* correspondent, a W. B. Marsden, who objected to the development of the new North Lake, complained that:

The South Lake after only five or six years use became such an intolerable nuisance and gave off such pestilent odours that it cost over £1000 to empty, clean it out and refill it with purer sea water.[19]

Proof of Mr Marsden's point followed. The two lakes had been linked beneath what, perhaps to the surprise of modern conservationists who want to save it, he described as 'an unsightly and unnecessary iron bridge [which] will irretrievably ruin the foreshore'.[20] The results of these developments were vividly described by a businessmen, Mr Ellis Leaver who, in a vain attempt to get the pier moved further north towards Marshside, claimed in a letter to the pier directors in 1897 that

> I am credibly informed that the sickening stench from the stagnant and putrid waters of the Marine Lakes on each side of the present pier is the subject of daily complaint by residents and visitors.[21]

Few who used the lakes on a regular basis would have argued with these views. Nevertheless, until 1910 when Southport became one of the earliest seaside resorts to build a sewage farm—as a condition of its 'long-desired' amalgamation with Birkdale—the town did little to respond to the obvious burdens put on its essentially Victorian public health services by the massive influx of summer visitors.[22] To be fair Southport's particularly inadequate sewerage system was due to the very shallow local gradients and the sandy subsoil, both of which hindered the flow of waste into the sea. At times, this also caused overflows into the Marine Lakes.

Furthermore, sluicing the lakes could create a massive surge of water into the—at this stage—unusually deep Bog Hole just off the foreshore, causing extensive beach erosion in the area around the pier foundations. The Pier Company's directors took a successful legal action to gain £150 compensation from the Corporation when this mistake was made in December 1894 [23] and, more significantly, the Town Clerk's written 'assurance that the Corporation would not allow the water to escape from the Culverts in such a way as to do further damage to the pier'.[24] After that the Corporation became understandably reluctant to drain the lakes on a regular basis and the state of the water was regarded by local people with at least some caution. That was probably another reason why the WLYC Members were not overkeen on sailing on the North Lake, except in the Spring before the new season's flood of holidaymakers put paid to any natural improvements during the winter.

It is clear, then, that despite many difficulties, WLYC members far preferred to use the sea for racing as well as for those owners of larger boats who wished to use the Southport pierhead mooring area as a base for cruising. That is why the founding members put so much effort into setting up their own changing facilities and club room on the pier, while a 'shore' base only came as an afterthought. This consisted of rented rooms in the Scarisbrick Hotel, in 1894, followed in 1895 by the Queen's Hotel for over twenty years until, in an ironic twist which could not have been lost on older members, the WLYC gained its own club headquarters for the first time when it took over the rooms above the Victoria Baths vacated by the Southport Corinthians before their club was wound up.[25]

Meanwhile, the WLYC had also brought an end to its out-of-season use of the Marine Lake during the First World War. Despite several half-hearted negotiations with the Corporation during the 1920s and 1930s, lake sailing was not revived until 1949.

3. The Bog Hole

For the first forty or so years, then, the WLYC's history was inextricably linked to the Bog Hole, with the need to gain access to moorings on this stretch of water via Southport Pier serving as a constant reminder of the club's vulnerability. The name 'Bog Hole' probably originated from its proximity to the site of the 'Old Bugg' and 'New Bug' sandbanks shown on a 1736 chart at the seaward end of the South Channel of the Ribble Estuary.[26] The location of the Bog Hole within the Estuary can be seen from one of many maps in a very detailed 1938 report by James Barron entitled *A History of the Ribble Navigation* (see maps 1 and 2). Barron's study of the Ribble Estuary was based upon his experience as the civil engineer in charge of the building of training walls and dredging operations for the Port of Preston from 1901 to 1933. Barron had an obvious interest in the case for the development of an accessible channel into Preston for seagoing vessels. Nevertheless, he was a highly professional Member of the Institute of Civil Engineers and his book, which was thoroughly illustrated with many charts and diagrams, gave a balanced account of how the Estuary developed during this period.

Earlier studies representing different views as to how the Estuary should be developed were included as Barron built up a full and fair account of the differences which arose, particularly from the 1880s onwards, between various interest groups. These included the Mersey Docks and Harbour Board, which relied on the Formby Channel, as well as those interests within Southport who depended upon the sea for their livelihood or pleasure.[27] Meanwhile, to the north of the estuary Preston had to face the more immediate worries of Lytham, with its own docks and small shipbuilding industry, and the resort of St Annes which, like Southport, had no wish to see its pier become a white elephant isolated from the sea by sand and mud.[28]

Barron's 1925 chart of the Ribble Estuary has been used for Map 1. It marks out the full extent of the various channels and sandbanks—some 57 square miles in all—as well as showing the Preston Port Boundaries to the north and south. These boundaries were established by legislation in 1896, consolidating a series of measures taken since the start of the nineteenth century to gradually extend Preston's jurisdiction as a Port and Customs Authority.[29] Southport's position within the Ribble Estuary can also be seen on the map with its pier clearly marked, although by 1925 the Bog Hole had been virtually closed as an anchorage for sea-going vessels of any size. The gradual but obvious onset of such conditions from the mid-1890s had considerable significance to Southport as a whole and there was an upsurge in local political activity intent upon improving access to the sea. Understandably, in this context the possible fate of the town's two yacht clubs aroused far less public interest and concern than the threat to the tourist trade and local fishing grounds. The question of sailing waters was therefore highly specific to the members of the WLYC and the Southport Corinthians, with the decline of the Bog Hole threatening the existence of their clubs. Rather than simply waiting and hoping for the best, members in both clubs realised that they needed to seek an alliance of interests with others, such as the fishermen and the Pier Company, who were better able to attract publicity and could hope to arouse wider opposition to Preston's plans for the Ribble Estuary.

Of course, the WLYC had in Sir George Pilkington a president who counted for much locally having served as the town's mayor and Liberal MP from 1885–6 and 1899–1900. For a brief spell, also, Sir Naylor Leyland, Bart, the Liberal MP from 1898 until his death the following year, was a WLYC vice-president, while the Conservative MP Sir Godfrey Dalrymple White, 1910–23 and 1924–31, accepted the same position.[30] Furthermore, Dudley Coddington, commodore from 1906 to 1910 had served during this period as a Conservative councillor for the town's wealthy Marine ward. And yet despite having such connections and being for the most part relatively well-off, local yachtsmen never gained any effective local political influence. In part, this arose because neither club owned property and the employment which they offered to the local boatyards did not amount to much when compared to the activities of the town's business interests. To make matters worse, the two yacht clubs' dealings with the pier directors also became less friendly as the Company's profits were squeezed by rising maintenance costs and falling receipts. Life was certainly not made easy for anyone connected with the sea at Southport. At root, all of these problems stemmed from the deteriorating state of the Ribble's South Channel which threatened many local interests in Southport and at Crossens, several miles to the north, which housed much of the fishing fleet and the two local boatyards of Wrights & Co. and Latham & Co.

Reports from a number of surveys from 1761 onwards leave no doubt as to the frequency with which the direction and depth of the Ribble channels could change. From the mid-eighteenth to the early nineteenth century, the South Channel was the main outlet for the Ribble. But the Central, or 'Gut', Channel gradually took over in the 1820s and 1830s, until an 1850 survey by William and Webb found the southern waterway much restricted 'having lost its connection at low water with the Ribble'.[31] Later investigations put the blame for this firmly upon land reclamation in the upper reaches of the estuary which diverted the Ribble's flow towards the north.[32]

In the meantime, however, those mid-Victorian yachtsmen who visited Southport found an anchorage which remained a haven of certainty amid the shifting sands of the estuary. As Captain F. W. Jarrad wrote in a 1907 Report on his survey of the Ribble the previous year, from 1820 to 1836 the South Channel of the estuary had 'undergone almost incredible changes'. The Bog Hole, he wrote, had a minimum width of 500 yards by the mid-1830s and there was no shallow bar at its entrance to the sea, where the minimum depth at low tide was still 12 feet.[33] Even more 'astonishing' in Jarrad's view were the further changes which had occurred by 1850 when the rapid build-up of sand on the Horse Bank cut off the South Channel from the Ribble outflow for much of its ebb. Over the next thirty to forty years, there was little change in the shape of the remaining Bog Hole. In 1882, for instance, the Bog Hole's deepest point at low tide was 52 feet, while it had a stretch of water deeper than 30 feet which extended 1000 yards on either side of the pierhead and was up to 400 yards wide.[34] At this stage, then, the Bog Hole could take vessels of any size, offering deep water safety to boats at anchor even in a heavy storm.

4. Southport Pier 1860 to 1933

The commercial potential of the Bog Hole had been appreciated in Southport for some time. From 1844, there had been several proposals to build a pier into the channel so that ships could unload their cargoes for transport by rail to Manchester. Despite moral support from the town's Improvement Commissioners, the idea of a pier did not attract any financial interest until 1858 when it was promoted as an extension of the town's promenade, aimed not at merchant ships but at the crowds of visitors who came on holiday or, increasingly, as day-trippers, all of whom shared an overwhelming desire to see the sea if not to bath in it.[35] Such was the strength of local confidence in the holiday trade after the railway had linked

Southport with Manchester in 1855, that the Pier Company readily attracted enough capital to launch the project. Construction began in the summer of 1859 and it opened in August of the following year[36] as 'the first of the truly pleasure piers' in Britain.[37] Southport Pier, however, was as vulnerable to the whims of the Ribble Estuary as any of the other local interests dependent on the sea for their livelihood. Even the initial phase of the pier had to be 3,600 feet long to reach the water at low tide.

Most 'promenaders' found it a tiring walk so the Pier Company opened a tramway in time for the 1863 summer season. Then the growth of paddle steamer traffic along the coast led to a further extension into deeper water in 1868 so that they could dock at the pierhead. By then the pier was 4,380 feet long and had also been widened to allow the tramway to operate without risk to those who still preferred the walk. With its characteristic 'T' shaped pierhead standing on the edge of the deep Bog Hole, pleasure steamers could now reach Southport from the Fylde Coast, Llandudno and the Isle of Man[38] and this proved an immense crowd puller which benefited the town's commercial interests as well as the railway companies. Apart from those visitors who simply wished to gaze at the sea, the Pier Company's directors also tried to meet the needs of smaller boats. Before the 1868 extension, they built a narrow access gangway from the first pierhead which extended another 720 feet out into the Bog Hole and was constructed as six stages of 120 feet, each on a different level so that the fishing boats and yachtsmen could have access at any state of the tide. Furthermore, after 1868 the new pierhead 'T' was built on a 180 feet by 30 feet platform with sheltering rooms at each end and eight gangways or landing stages at different levels underneath. These were, eventually, to serve as clubrooms with changing and storage facilities for Southport Corinthians and the WLYC.[39] Furthermore, as explained in the first chapter, the Pier Company supported plans to buoy the channel in the winter of 1883 to 1884. Its directors then provided rented changing rooms and other facilities for the Southport Corinthians in 1884 followed with contributions towards the prizes given at Club regattas.

For all that, the pier was hardly ideal as a base. It was exceptionally vulnerable to storm damage due to its exposure to south-westerley gales and waves moving from the Bog Hole on to the long stretch of shallow beach. A year before the Southport Corinthian Yacht Club began sailing in 1884, for instance, the pier directors agreed with the rowers 'that the Company should allow the Club £1 10/- a Week if their premises were rendered unfit for use for more than 21 consecutive days, by reasons of storms &c'.[40] Within months of this, as explained in chapter 1, the rowers gave up their struggles against the shifting currents and sands, moving to a new lake several miles inland.

The Southport Corinthian sailors who took over could obviously adapt more easily to the sea, but they still faced a threat from storm damage to their club house on the pier which was particularly at risk during the winter months. Usually, the pier directors agreed to pay for any repairs but the loss of property could still be disruptive. A storm in February 1897, for instance, damaged the WLYC staging at the end of the pier and it took a month, including a visit from Edward Baddeley, the club's solicitor as well as its honorary secretary, before the directors agreed that their workmen should 'give every assistance to the members of the West Lancs Yachting Club in repairing the damage done to their staging by the late Storm'.[41] Even then, they took their time, as the *Yachting World* pointed out two months later.

The West Lancashire Yacht Club pier premises will be opened on Saturday, but only part of the staging carried away in the last big gale has been replaced. This is owing to the Pier Company not having got all their new piles in, and until these are fixed it

Aerial photograph of Southport pierhead taken in 1927. It shows the yacht moorings, the distinctive 'T' shape of the second pierhead and part of the Bog Hole surrounded by sandbanks.

is impossible to erect the staging. No doubt, with a little inconvenience, the members will be able to manage for a few weeks.[42]

Storm damage remained as a perennial problem, but a far more serious long term threat stemmed from the notoriety of all piers as fire risks. That was hardly surprising. Piers had vast quantities of heavily painted or tarred timber, with ready made ventilation from sea breezes above or below which fanned the slightest accident into a healthy blaze within minutes. Furthermore, their profits depended on a growing range of theatrical entertainment while their mooring platforms were increasingly used by petrol driven motor boats of all sizes and handled by individuals with varying degrees of competence.[43] As fire engines could seldom reach any pierhead blaze, heavy losses could arise from what began as only a small outbreak.[44]

Southport Pier was no exception in this respect. Much of its rising maintenance costs were related to the physical structure, such as girders, foundations or the tramway, where there might not have been a direct fire risk. But in other cases, for instance involving lighting or wiring, there must have been at least a degree of fire hazard. In 1884 the pier manager reported that the tramway's 'electric signals were very much out of order and has [sic] been a source of much trouble and loss during the past six months'.[45] The directors proposed to remedy this by fitting a telephone but, as the WLYC Committee pointed out in no uncertain terms some forty years later, this work was never done properly and successive managers warned the directors about the need to spend more on maintenance or modernisation.

Serious fires on Southport Pier in 1868, 1897 and 1933 brought home the point, if confirmation was needed. The fire in September 1897 had a direct effect upon the recently formed WLYC. Flames were discovered by the police at 3.00 a.m. by which time it was too late to stop extensive loss. With daylight, the directors found 'the Pavilion, Refreshment Rooms, Covered Way & Shops ... had been completely destroyed, also Tram Tollhouse and

A photograph of Southport pier taken in 1927. It was probably taken from the window of the WLYC's new Promenade headquarters and shows the pier bridge crossing between the North and South Marine Lakes.

the Tram Platforms, Roadway, Pulleys, Rope &c together with the Dock seriously damaged'.[46] The Pier Company had received some £3,700 compensation for the loss from the Commercial Union, by January 1898, and it fully restored the structure.[47] However, the directors were planning to sell the pier and this understandably created doubts over its future until the idea was dropped in July 1898 which, in turn, left the WLYC uncertain as to the tenure of its club rooms and access to moorings for over a year.

This was nothing, though, in comparison with the fire which wrecked 300 yards of the pier's seaward end during the night of 28 to 29 July 1933. Regarded by insurers as the year of 'Britain's disappearing piers', the summer of 1933 also brought major damage or destruction to other piers at Margate, Blackpool, Colwyn Bay, Morecambe, and Worthing. With total claims running to about £90,000, the estimated £5,000 to £6,000 at Southport 'might', as one insurance expert put it, 'have been worse'.[48] The eventual settlement was double this at £12,500 [49] which, if repeated nationally, gives a fair idea as to why insurers were worried. Obviously, the possibility of arson against a background of widespread trade depression and unemployment—especially in the North—had to be taken into account. But there were good reasons for discounting any criminal intent by pier owners, not least because the summer trade for that year was enjoying an unexpected boom.

Even so, insurers pointed to the need for extensive modernisation of all piers in view of their exposure to severe weather and the unusually high fire risk on structures which had virtually all been built during the Victorian and Edwardian period. Southport Pier, more than most, simply lacked the means to improve. A 1934 report on the pier for the Corporation—as the leaseholders it retained considerable powers—shows clearly that the catalogue of complaints were far from imaginary.

It has been common knowledge for many years that the structure of the Pier and more recently the buildings on the Pier have not been maintained in good repair order and condition in accordance with the covenant in that behalf contained in the lease. In August 1925 a complaint was received as to the condition of the Pier on which the Borough Engineer reported. The Town Clerk wrote to the Pier Company directing their attention to the portions of the Pier which we had inspected and we found to be in a rotten and unsafe condition ... and there is no record of the Pier Company having done anything to remedy the condition ... apart from their letter of the 15th August 1925 stating that the defect in the woodwork at the Day Nursery had been made good and that the general condition of both ironwork and woodwork was then under the consideration of the Directors.[50]

The fact that the pier had been allowed to remain in use for almost ten more years in this condition does not seem to have concerned the Corporation. With the Bog Hole almost completely silted up over previous decades, the pier's revenue had declined to the point that the only viable solution was to reduce its length. From the 4,380 feet, which still made it the second longest pier in Britain in 1933, the structure was shortened to 3,633 feet, taking down the prominent 'T' of the seaward pierhead, where most of the buildings in the fire had been destroyed, including the WLYC's pierhead premises overlooking the Channel.

The reduced pier was well away from any remaining deep water in the Bog Hole and the change undoubtedly exposed the yacht mooring areas on both sides of this demolished stretch to a greater risk during bad weather.[51] Compared to its late Victorian heyday, the pier had indeed become Southport's great white elephant, leading nowhere useful and devoid of the numerous entertainments which had proved such an attraction to earlier visitors. The fact that in the 1933 fire 'the ladies' room connected with the West Lancashire Yacht Club was totally destroyed'[52] strengthened the club's growing disillusionment. For its members, the loss was simply a confirmation that conditions in the Bog Hole had deteriorated beyond the point of no return. Any hopes for sea sailing, at least in the foreseeable future, were brought to an end in 1937.

5. Bog Hole Politics

In the history of the WLYC the 1937 decision to end sailing on the sea appears as a marked contrast with the more hopeful days of the late nineteenth century. The marking out of the Bog Hole Channel with buoys in the winter of 1883 to 1884 had been one important factor which gave the Southport Corinthians such a good start when they began racing in 1884. By the time that the WLYC started in 1894, however, the pattern of long term silting in the Southern part of the estuary had become firmly established and the state of the Bog Hole appeared as a main theme in virtually every WLYC commodore's report to the members from the late 1890s through to the 1930s. For the first fifteen years, the WLYC and the Southport Corinthians found themselves in unison over this problem. Indeed, the two clubs simply became part of a wider movement in the town which drew local politicians into a debate about the future of its fishing fleet and the tourist trade. Understandably, these commercial issues had a more immediate relevance than the problems facing yachtsmen.

As the pleasure steamers from Blackpool and Rhyl found it increasingly difficult to reach the pierhead, and the Pier Company faced a future of declining profits, economic and leisure interests combined in what, on paper at least, was a formidible show of strength, well able to finance a civil engineer's enquiry by L. F. Vernon-Harcourt, M. A. and Member of the Institute of Civil Engineers in 1889, with another by him only two years later. The comments in his *Report on the Extension of the Navigable Channel of the Ribble to the Sea, to The Corporation of Southport* formed the core of the information which the Borough used to fuel a lengthy legal battle with Preston Corporation over the future of the Bog Hole.[53]

In fact, the quarrel between the two towns began in the mid-nineteenth century. From 1852 to 1867, a series of negotations between Preston Corporation and the locally controlled Ribble Navigation Company led them into a joint venture aimed at making Preston into a major west-coast port. Convinced that town's nearness to the Wigan coalfield and much of industrial Lancashire offered a basis for trade expansion, they pushed through proposals to enhance the outflow of the river Ribble through the 'Gut Channel' (see map 1). At this stage, the Pier Company and local fishermen at Southport fully realised that there was a risk to the Bog Hole because it was the main outlet for the considerable flow of water which still left the Ribble Estuary through the South Channel, where it performed a valuable part in scouring silt from the Bog Hole. Despite such obvious grounds for a dispute, there was considerable lethargy on both sides and it even took over ten years before Preston Corporation managed to organise its Private Bill securing the Ribble Navigation and Preston Dock Act of 1883.[54]

Under these circumstances the fading political strength of a purely landed influence was all too evident. At Southport the Trustees of the Scarisbrick Estates and Colonel E. Fleetwood Hesketh were by then the principal landowners, with the Corporation holding a significant area in the town centre and on the seafront. Both private landowners continued to wield much influence locally in the late nineteenth century as they enjoyed the benefits of profitable ground rents together with an increasingly 'commercial' approach to their use of restrictions and conditions when granting further leases to local developers, a measure which, in John Liddle's words, kept the town as 'a haven of middle-class respectability'.[55]

As the Borough's Members of Parliament also discovered, however, wealth derived from tourism, retirement incomes and commuting—albeit by the rich—could not provide the cohesion and strength of purpose needed to win against the combined forces of late Victorian and Edwardian trade and industry, especially Lancashire's cotton industry and its closely linked coal interests at Wigan. Indeed one of the lesser ironies of the problems of the Bog Hole was that many of the WLYC and Southport Corinthian yachtsmen who complained about the state of the Channel owed their wealth and influence to the growth of the very industry and commerce of Lancashire which was regarded by the majority of engineers employed to make reports on the Estuary to be responsible for the problem!

Initially, however, alarm subsided at Southport because the ambitious Ribble scheme began to outrun its budget. By the late 1880s, Preston had its own 'party of caution' within the Corporation which was intent upon checking further expenditure. Such doubts inevitably encouraged the opposition at Southport. Their hopes were raised further by an 1889 report from Mr G. N. Aberthny—a past President of the Institution of Civil Engineers and an eminent river and dock engineer—who strongly criticised the Ribble scheme for its lack of foresight. The so-called 'Gut Channel', he wrote, was 'only a swashway' and little or no attention had been given to the many dificulties likely to be encountered when extending the access channel beyond Lytham. In his view, in 1883 'everyone trusted to Providence to make a channel from the end of the walls across the sands to the sea'.[56]

Amidst rising optimism in Southport, a bizarre diversion to the main issues appeared between 1888 and 1894. Proposals from a Mr G. H. Roberts for a ship canal to be built from Preston to the Bog Hole enjoyed much ill-considered publicity and support in the Southport press. Eventually, a more rational analysis of the proposal showed, for a start, that a projected cost of £½ million was ludicrously low, with the likely figure being well over £2 million.[57] Once this had been made clear, the ship canal proposal was never given serious consideration by any of the growing number of civil engineers who had by then gained considerable experience of the Ribble Estuary. As if to confirm its doom, an attempt by Roberts to revive the scheme in 1903 was dismissed by the same local press which had praised him a decade earlier with, in Barron's words, 'scant courtesy' towards 'his supreme delusion'.[58]

Such diversions of attention apart, Southport Corporation actually joined in with a firm proposal in 1891 to create a deepened South Channel bringing the main river access to Preston in via the Bog Hole.[59] In the meantime, though, there was a more strongly backed plan for a shorter Central Channel. The latter was accepted, being the most direct route to that part of the access which had already been built. The Act giving the necessary powers to go ahead was not passed until 1896. Nevertheless, with the opening of Preston Dock as the largest single dock of its kind in Britain in 1892 the seal was set. Any further hopes that Southport's coastline might actually benefit from the development of the Ribble came to an end.[60] From then on, it was a case of opposing wherever possible those aspects of the scheme which could be clearly identified as a specific threat to the Bog Hole.

Ironically, Preston Corporation soon came to regard the dock and training walls as having little or no chance of recovering the large sums spent on their construction. By the time that James Barron took over as the Ribble Engineer in 1901, 'few people', he wrote some forty years later, 'had a good word to say for it'.[61] Certainly, access into the end of the trained wall channel opposite Lytham remained extremely difficult for large vessels because they had to cross an area of shifting sandbanks to reach this point. As a result, when trade recovered and then expanded during the 1890s,[62] the port authorities at Preston had to make increasing use of the Bog Hole as an anchorage from which the larger ships could be lightered. That, in itself, proved an intense irritation to local people. The *Yachting World* made a point that few Southport residents would have disagreed with. The town, wrote the journal's correspondent, had lost control of the Bog Hole. Its two yacht clubs with a total of over 250 members, and the 'enormous fishing interest' were powerless 'to remove the objectionable buoys placed in the Channel by the Preston authorities'.[63]

Even worse, in bad weather, the waiting ships or lightering barges frequently broke loose and—as neither the Southport press nor the yachting journals were slow to point out—the drifting vessels damaged yachts and fishing boats. In June 1905, to take just one example, a 'Swedish steamer waiting in the Bog Hole for large enough tides to go to Preston [had] broken adrift and had fallen foul of Eurynome and Ishtar', two club yachts of 12 and 4 tons respectively.[64] Accidents also happened when these large ships were manoeuvring in the mooring area. In September 1905, for instance, the 31-ton cutter Capri was damaged when the SS Phoenix fouled her moorings.[65] Capri was also a club boat, belonging to William Lawton Hall who became the WLYC commodore from 1910 to 1914. At a less dramatic level, the presence of a fair number of moored ships waiting for their lighters or merely the large mooring buoys, were enough to provoke regular criticism from yachtsmen who resented these obstructions on the best parts of their main racing courses.

Regardless of this, the expansion of trade brought higher revenues into the port of Preston and, by 1903, there were renewed plans to raise the finance for an extension of the Ribble training walls out to 14½ miles from the dock entrance. Southport, Lytham and St Annes renewed their opposition. But St Annes and Lytham were bought off with an expensive diversion scheme and by 1904, when Preston got its power to borrow the necessary money, Southport stood alone. The town had become isolated both physically and politically from the other commercial interests in the Ribble Estuary. By 1910, there was a completely walled seaway, with 26 foot depth at high tide, which ran for 14 miles from Preston Dock to the edge of the shoals.[66] Protests continued in support of the Southport fishermen and, of course, the Pier Company which relied very heavily on the summer trade created by paddle steamers from Lytham, Blackpool, Llandudno and various other resorts.[67] As early as 1895, the steamers were having some difficulty reaching the pierhead and the companies running them were forced to run down their services between 1919 and 1925 as the Bog Hole continued to fill in and safe berthing became impossible.[68] Despite introducing the relatively shallow draft Seabirds in 1898 and the even less demanding Stars in 1906, the WLYC had also faced increasing difficulty in organising races as the area of clear water in the Bog Hole diminished.[69]

It was little consolation to the commercial and recreational interests at Southport that the Ribble works then ran into financial and engineering difficulties. Another twenty years passed, with the World War, the 1926 General Strike and then a severe depression delaying further progress, before the final extension of the training walls began in 1932. By 1937, the Ribble's southern training wall had reached the critical point of 16 miles from the Preston Dock which took the Channel into the deep water of the Irish Sea.[70] But after all the effort and wrangling, it was too late. Lancashire's cotton industry had been devastated by foreign competition in the 1920s and severe losses among what business remained when the depression took hold after 1929. Preston's port revenues could no longer finance its own progress and early dreams of dominating British trade on the west coast came to nothing.

Of course, Southport survived as a resort even though the sea continued to recede. The Pier Company suffered, the Southport Corinthians wound up and the WLYC seriously considered going the same way. Nonetheless, others took advantage of the vast expanses of flat, clean, windswept sands. It was, perhaps, significant that at least one earlier admirer of the pier in its heyday, Thomas Hughes—a judge and the author of *Tom Brown's Schooldays*—disliked the high tide, which yielded 'nothing but very shallow, muddy water', Writing in 1884, he was more impressed by the sands at low tide, when

> the steely gleam of the wet parts, the bright yellow of the dry, and the warm and rich tints of brown of the intermediate, and quaint black line of the pier, running out across them all until it reaches the pale blue of the channel, where the fishing boats lie at anchor round the pier head, are one perpetual feast, even to the untrained eye.[71]

Some fifty years later, with the Bog Hole a shadow compared to this, much of the beauty of the Ribble Estuary's southernmost point at Southport remained. By the 1920s, the massive accumulation of sands on the Horse Bank was obvious to anyone at low tide. Practically cut off from the scouring effects of the Ribble's ebb flow at about half tide since the 1890s, the height of sand above low water had risen markedly from only 4 feet in the early 1880s, to about 8 feet only ten years later and then at least 12 feet when measured again in 1904.[72] Even this, though, offered dangers to yachtsmen and holidaymakers alike which had apparently escaped the notice of the Corporation and Pier Company.

One particularly tragic incident, so far as the WLYC was concerned, occurred in July 1913 when three club members died as their Star class boat, the Cygnet, returning from Lytham was caught in breakers on the Horse Bank and rolled over. The incident certainly marred the club's early history, with the painful lesson that yachtsmen could at times face considerable risks when sailing in the Ribble Estuary.[73] Furthermore, the nature of these risks changed somewhat in the 1920s as sand built up and the Horse Bank increasingly emerged in the form of a large island at low tide which the Bog Hole increasingly failed to isolate from the shore. Foolhardy holidaymakers went exploring only to find themselves cut off as the flood tide swept in at an alarming rate. The almost reckless indifference of the authorities to this hazard led the WLYC committee to warn them in unusually sharp letter to the Town Clerk in July 1926, regarding 'the present dangerous state of the Southport Foreshore and Channel'. The Corporation's reliance upon one 'Patrol Man', even though 'carrying out his duties in a very efficient manner', meant that there was an immense risk of people not being warned in time. 'Our Members, on several occasions have directed people to safety and on Saturday last while the Patrol Man was engaged in rescuing 3 or 4 people at the southern end they went out in a punt and directed some people to safety who had walked on to the Horse bank from the north side of the shore and got into difficulties.'

The WLYC's by then almost total disillusionment with the Pier Company is equally evident from the same letter:

> We would also draw attention to the fact that there is no life-saving apparatus, or life belts on the Pier, and that it is impossible, in case of need, to communicate with the Police for the Ambulance or Medical attention, as there is no telephone at the seaward end of the Pier.[74]

There is little sign of either the Corporation or the Pier Company fully appreciating the dangers which inexperienced members of the public faced when venturing on to the sandbanks. So much so, in fact, that an incident one evening in May 1936, involving the rescue of fourteen youths from the Horsebank by Club members brought well deserved praise from both the Corporation and also the Chief Constable of Southport, Major M. J. Egan, who wrote of his 'appreciations of the great public spirit displayed by the members of the West Lancashire Yacht Club on this occasion and on many occasions in the past'.[75]

Apart from the members, Tom Sutton—'Smiler'—as WLYC boatman became well known locally for his many rescues of stranded visitors, while he was on duty for the club. Indeed, at a special Hot Pot supper to celebrate Smiler's twenty-one years as Boatman in 1935, Leo Garge as vice-commodore, praised his efforts for 'the many lives of people and animals and even motor-cars which Smiler had rescued from the Horsebank'. In a joke which must have had more than a passing significance for the regular sailors, Garge then 'wondered whether he [Smiler] was not included as an asset in the £73,000 valuation of the Pier'.[76] Following the disastrous fire of 1933, the Pier Company was by then in the process of being taken over by the Corporation who, in the event, actually employed Smiler as a patrolman after he retired from being the WLYC boatman in 1936![77]

Meanwhile, the WLYC's willingness to openly criticise the Pier Company from 1926 onwards, in contrast to the private wrangling of previous years, at least partly reflected the club's new sense of security in having a lease on a spacious suite of rooms above Victoria Baths on the promenade which were about to become the club's first proper headquarters. Certainly for the first time recorded, the Committee only agreed to continue their use of the pierhead rooms 'after much discussion' in September 1926.[78] By then, most active sailing members probably realised that the days of their links with the pier were unlikely to last for much longer. In February 1927, for instance, Horace Hatch—Vice Commodore at the time—was discussing the possibility of sailing 12-footers on the Marine Lake again with the Boating Company which controlled the use of this stretch of shallow water. These meetings, together with another attempt in February 1928,[79] failed to establish any compromise between the understandable commercial interests of the Corporation's Lake licensee and the desire of the WLYC to have decent racing free of interference from holidaymakers who hired rowing boats. The same theme cropped up again in 1938, with equally little success, and it was only after the Second World War, when interest in smaller, lighter, but faster dinghies was emerging, that a workable agreement became possible in 1949.

Before the Second World War nobody knew more about the club's long term prospects in the Channel than Smiler. At the special hotpot supper in November 1935, the WLYC Committee made a presentation to Tom marking his twenty-one years' service with the club. The respect and affection shown for him, as an experienced seaman, lifeboatman and craftsman, shows how the very strong Club spirit of the pre–1914 years had survived. Leo Garge made the point in an appropriate tribute.

Sailing has not always been plain at Southport the last few years, but in spite of all the difficulties we have had to contend with, 'Smiler' has always been optimistic as to the possibilities, and has welcomed all newcomers and encouraged them to go on the water and instructed them in the handling of boats.[80]

'Smiler'—Tom Sutton—seen on the left walking along Southport pier with 'Wee' William Sutton in the early 1930s.

As just mentioned, Tom's role in many a rescue was also of more than passing significance. And when he finally decided to retire in 1936 he gave a further signal, if any were needed, that the Bog Hole's days were numbered. 'I hope the sailing will last longer than we expect', he wrote to the Committee, 'and may you have good times with your boats'. [81]

Within a year of Tom Sutton's departure, and well before the start of the 1937 sailing season, the WLYC decided to stop sailing on the sea. The shortening of the pier after its third, and most destructive, fire in 1933 had led to further problems once any protection from storms given by the seaward pierhead had been removed. In March 1937, a meeting of Southport 'Boat Owners & others interested in sailing ... decided that it was no longer safe to moor boats on the shore'. As a result, the WLYC Committee decided over the next few months to give up its pier premises as well as selling the sea mooring chains, the punt and the club boat shed at Crossons. In fact, the shed went as scrap for only £5—half of which was needed to pay for its 'demolition'—a somewhat poignant ending for a building which had been of considerable value to the WLYC for at least fifteen years![82]

Chapter 3

Early Days—'This Young But Certainly Go-Ahead Club'

1. Starting the Club

THE INAUGURAL MEETING of the West Lancashire Yacht Club took place at the Scarisbrick Hotel in Lord Street on Saturday 16 June 1894. Although rumours about the new club had reached the columns of the yachting press some three weeks earlier, no convincing reason was ever given in print for the decision to form the WLYC. Readers were simply assured that the 'now prosperous Yacht Club' of the Southport Corinthians

> could not cater for the large and increasing number of sailing men of the present day. Their premises on the pier were limited and they had no room to extend. Hence the necessity for establishing a new club on some other portion of the pier.[1]

Perhaps there were yachtsmen in Southport who actually believed this. But it is far more likely that the decision to form the WLYC arose from a polite agreement to disagree between leading members of the Southport Corinthians. The latter had increasingly become a club for the owners of large yachts with membership of the Royal Mersey Yacht Club figuring as an additional bonus for those with the wealth and connections needed to gain admission.[2] Sailing for the great majority of these Corinthian members consisted of the occasional handicap race well out into the South Channel or Liverpool Bay, while they also had enough spare time for cruising trips along the coast or across to Ireland and the Isle of Man.

There were other members who preferred the purely 'social' aspects of club life. Neither they nor the substantial offshore yachting element could be ignored because they invariably managed to muster well over a hundred at their 'smoker' and annual dinner events in the early 1890s which were described as having an atmosphere full of ' "go" and enthusiasm'.[3] By and large, though, the average Corinthian member was not particularly interested in becoming a flag officer or playing an active part in the day-to-day running of the club and little change had occurred among the flag officers since its foundation in 1884. It was equally notable that most avoided the regular races in the Bog Hole channel or on the Marine Lake which remained a marginal activity for the small but enthusiastic yachtsmen in the so-called 'mosquito' fleet.[4] This is probably why the WLYC began in an atmosphere of considerable goodwill between the two clubs. Small boat racing—with a one-design emphasis—figured prominently in the WLYC's initial plans whereas an attempt to move the Corinthians in this direction had been resisted early in 1894.

To that extent, the picture of harmony portrayed in the press was correct. At least nineteen Corinthians actually joined the WLYC as well, and they included the leading flag officers of the 'senior' club.[5] Above all, the WLYC gained almost immediate acceptance in yachting circles well beyond Southport because Sir George Pilkington, the Corinthian's commodore, agreed to become the new club's first president. His patronage as a Liberal MP for Southport and the town's mayor proved a vital element in the early success of the club and he remained president until his death in 1916.[6] Another key figure was Frank Coddington, the Corinthians' vice-commodore in 1893, who chaired the inaugural meeting of the WLYC Frank Coddington's son, Dudley, also joined and he eventually took over as commodore soon after Scott Hayward retired in 1903. The family was wealthy and well connected, with a strong cotton textile interest through the family firm at Blackburn led by Sir William Coddington, a strong Conservative and one of that town's local MPs. Consequently, the choice of Sir William's son Reginald, as the first WLYC commodore must also have done much to calm the nerves of any Corinthian diehards.[7]

The choice of Walter Scott Hayward as the WLYC's first vice-commodore proved crucial to its early success. This prosperous Manchester merchant had taken a leading role in creating the Southport Corinthians.[8] He was also an active member of the Royal Mersey Yacht Club and widely involved with developing yacht racing of all kinds throughout the Liverpool Bay area. It is more than likely that an argument about his design for a sturdy 0.75-rater was behind the decision to start the WLYC. Early in 1894 the Corinthians' committee had invited designs for a new class of small estuary racing yachts. However, some club members objected strongly in March 1894 when the committee, chaired by Frank Coddington, unanimously agreed to adopt the 0.75-rater one-design submitted by Scott Hayward.[9] Of course, the adoption of small one-design classes was still something of a novelty for British yacht clubs in the early 1890s. That is why the lame arguments put forward in an attempt to halt the adoption of the 0.75-rater at Southport could have arisen from an excusable lack of technical knowledge or a failure to appreciate the extent to which participation in yachting was gradually widening to include those of quite modest means in the lower ranks of the professions and business. Less charitably, the opposition might have come from members who objected to this change precisely because it promised to make their sport less exclusive.

Whatever their motives, there was no denying their power to block changes if they took a mind to do so. In 1896, for instance, it was reported that there were a total of 250 yachtsmen in the two Southport clubs. By then, the WLYC had about one hundred members so that, even allowing for a considerable growth in dual membership, there must have been well over a hundred Corinthians who had no connection with the WLYC.[10] What is more, over the next thirty years these Corinthians always seem to have found some grounds for complaint. Even before the first 0.75-rater had been built there was a suggestion that the boat would lack sufficient 'body and power' for the Ribble Estuary.[11] Further doubts arose a month later in April 1894, with an objection to the prescriptive nature of any one-design class of small boats 'all to be made to the same plan, the idea being to keep down expense'.[12] To make matters worse, *The Yachtsman*'s Mersey correspondent simply wrote-off Scott Hayward's one-design proposal as a 'mistake' without any explanation.[13] It was almost certainly the same journalist who could still be found trying to justify these misgivings through *The Yachtsman*'s Mersey column nearly a year later in January 1895. By then, the Hoylake Sailing Club members were planning to adopt the Southport Corinthian 0.75-rater one-designs in place of their old handicap class. They ought to take care, *The Yachtsman* warned;

> if sufficient builders come forward, it might be an improvement, but if only two or three boats compete for the prizes, it seems to me that the old plan was the better, as it got a fair number of starters together, and gave the excitement of an occasional race to a lot of knockabout boats that are in the lake (i. e. the wide estuary at Hoylake) and which be shut out of races should the 0.75-rating class be carried.[14]

Most local yachting correspondents remained anonymous but the nature of their reports show that they relied upon regular contacts within each club. In this case, information about Southport had come from the Corinthians since *The Yachtsman* first appeared in 1891 and it is hardly surprising that the Mersey correspondent was still relying on that source four years later. Even so, his comments were out of step with the new ideas then gaining ground in small boat sailing. Although the boat was called the Southport Corinthian 0.75-rater, because that club's committee first selected the design, enthusiaism for the class at Hoylake had stemmed almost entirely from its success with the WLYC. Ignoring the irony, Scott Hayward chose to develop his 0.75-rater in the new club rather than face the risk of at best indifference, if not opposition, from a persistent core of doubters among the Corinthians.

By the close of the 1894 season the WLYC had already gained the keen support of the newly opened *Yachting World* and, with a healthy touch of realism, *The Yachtsman*'s Mersey correspondent gradually changed his mind. As a growing number of Mersey yachtsmen took a liking to the 0.75-rater's combination of sturdiness, good performance and modest costs, his support gradually warmed. So much so, that the journal could be found greeting the 0.75-raters' prospects for 'an abundance of sport' at the start of the 1897 season with what could almost pass for enthusiasm. By then, open series races for the 0.75-raters were not only on offer from the Southport Corinthians and the WLYC, but also at the Hoylake Sailing Club and Menai Straits regatta so that the 'class will have as many as 23 races'.[15] The doubts of only three years earlier were fading, although he was to have one last dig when the WLYC introduced its Seabird one-design at the end of the 1898 season!

While the argument about adopting the 0.75-rater design might have just tipped the scales in favour of forming a new club, the WLYC's early success arose from far more than this. For a start, the club quickly drew in yachting enthusiasts and new recruits of all ages with apparent ease. Many came from local business or professional backgrounds, while others had links with various parts of industrial Lancashire or commercial Liverpool. As chapter 5 explains, the club also drew in its fair share of wealthy and influential yachtsmen, but it was essentially a middle-class membership with an emphasis on young men who were in the professions, retail trade or industry. All of them were well-off compared to the majority of the population, but they were generally far from rich and one purpose of this chapter is to show how the WLYC's policy was clearly aimed at reducing the cost of yachting whenever feasible during the years before 1914. This can be seen in the boat designs introduced by the club as well as in its social occasions, dominated by 'hot-pot' suppers, 'smokers' and lectures on yachting topics. The club also sought to ease initial costs for younger members, with reduced fees and a significant number of crews' races, clearly intended to sustain the interest of those who could not, as yet, afford their own boat. For all that, the WLYC remained very much a male preserve before 1914. The few ladies' races and some crews' competitions showed with embarrassing clarity, at least to the modern eye, that the club had some very good women sailors. But they were effectively excluded from any share in decision making and even from the main social events until the WLYC held its first ball in 1908.

In the meantime, the WLYC's racing on the Bog Hole began with a modest programme from August 1894. Membership had already reached 67 by the end of the season, with twenty boats and a further ten under construction. Confidence was such that the club immediately took over from the Corinthians on the Marine Lake for the winter months.[16] This kept the momentum going and by the following Spring the anchorage off Southport Pier was already being described as nearly 'chock-a-block', with the *Yachting World* adding that

The local fleet is increasing rapidly, and never before in the annals of this now favourite yachting station did a season open with such good prospects of sport. This, no doubt, is largely due to the formation of the new club and its large and increasing membership.[17]

2. The Honorary Secretary and Club Organisation

Although leading figures in the Southport Corinthians helped to get the new club going, there were also many new faces. J. J. Bailey was one of these enthusiasts. While Scott Hayward and Frank Coddington's support gave the new club credibility, James Bailey actually organised the inaugural meeting at the Scarisbrick Hotel. By then, he had also planned the finer details as to how the club was going to start functioning within three months. In fact, a week before the club was founded Bailey had already resolved the space 'problem' at a meeting with the Pier Company's directors, which he attended together with Scott Hayward and Dr Alfred Charlick, a local physician and prominent Southport Corinthian who became the WLYC's first rear commodore.[18] It remained for the meeting to endorse Bailey's nomination as the first WLYC honorary secretary. The post was to prove particularly demanding for much of the time before the First World War because the club operated without a formal system of regular sub-committees until 1911.[19]

Of course, special committees appeared on an ad hoc basis. But these were, by their very nature, responses to particular problems or proposals and they could not produce the continuity needed for good management. Consequently an unduly heavy burden was placed upon a few people, including the flag officers, who usually called themselves the 'sailing committee', while it fell upon the honorary secretary to keep these efforts running smoothly. Little wonder, then, that when J. J. Bailey gave up after three years, there was a fairly rapid turnover in the occupants of this onerous post until things settled down in the remarkably patient hands of George Simpson. He served as the honorary secretary from 1908 until 1942 when he very reluctantly resigned due to his failing eyesight after a record thirty-five years of service as one of the club's officials.[20]

At first, though, it was J. J. Bailey who proved the ideal choice to get the club started as honorary secretary. Described much later on as 'one of life's gentlemen' Bailey was an energetic but also a very diplomatic and popular individual; qualities which undoubtedly helped to ensure the smooth launch of the club.[21] Throughout these early months his efforts and generosity in helping the WLYC were widely acknowledged. For instance, he gave the club a new 17-foot centreboard dinghy, built by the well known Preston firm of Crook & Son.[22] According to the *Yachting World*, this would

> go a long way towards making it [the WLYC] very popular, as it will enable members to enjoy boat sailing who are unable to own boats of their own. Mr Bailey, the Hon. Sec., who is well supported by local yachtsmen, is certainly doing all he can to make it [the club] a success, which I have no doubt he will do.[23]

Originally an engineer, J. J. Bailey had only just moved to Southport from Oldham in 1894.[24] When he met the Pier Company directors with Scott Hayward and Alfred Charlick, his skills as an engineer proved invaluable because he had used them to draft detailed plans for a WLYC clubhouse at the first pierhead in advance of the meeting. 'After considerable discussion' the directors allowed the new clubhouse to be suspended beneath the first pierhead deck, with its changing room connected to the pier's gas and water supplies. A stairway led down from the pier into the club's rooms which, in turn, had a companion way to the jetty for easy access to the moorings. Of course, the directors insisted that their own works superintendant approved the clubhouse before it could be used. But they also agreed that once this had been done the WLYC could occupy the rooms free of rent for the first two years.[25] In this, as in his other work as the club's founding hononary secretary, Bailey's judgement and skills played an essential part in its early success. Later rewards came in his election as a vice-president and a vice-commodore during his thirty-five years of club membership until his death in 1929.

3. The First Clubhouse on the Pier

At least £100 was spent constructing the WLYC's 'old pierhead' clubhouse, as it was known from the start, and the original plan was for the club to pay a fixed rent of £30 a year from 1896. In the event, after the inaugural meeting the membership grew so fast that it reached another agreement with the Pier Company in March 1895. A further £80 was spent to almost double the size of the clubhouse in return for delaying the payment of any rent until 1898.[26] Unfortunately, this smooth working relationship with the Pier Company, which helped so much in the club's initial years, was disrupted by the serious fire in September 1897. After that, the problems arising from the continued silting of the Bog Hole forced the Pier Company's profits into a slow decline, with inadequate investment on repairs and modernisation, and both yacht clubs found it increasingly difficult to gain any further improvements to their rooms on the pier.[27]

Earlier on, though, J. J. Bailey's efforts paid off. The pierhead clubhouse was completed in time for the opening cruise at the end of July 1894. By then the WLYC membership included a solid core of wealthy yacht owners who were more than capable of putting on a good show. In the absence of the commodore, Reginald Coddington, Walter Scott Hayward—as vice-commodore—took charge of the cruise. With a light wind and generally very pleasant weather it was more of a ceremonial event than anything else. Seven of the new club's yachts followed Frank Coddington's recently purchased 23-ton steamer Speedwell some five miles down the Channel to the Jumbo buoy and then back to the pier. As the *Southport Guardian* reporter must have realised, this cruise was more concerned with yachting etiquette than sailing.

> Each boat flew the burgee of the club, a red heraldic rose of Lancaster on a white ground. On arriving back opposite the Pier, Speedwell dipped her flag to the Southport Corinthian Yacht Club. The senior club responded, and the various yachts went to their moorings.[28]

Having displayed its new burgee and observed the social niceties, the new club held its first General Meeting at the Scarisbrick Hotel a few hours later. Here the emphasis changed, with the main resolutions all involving the types of boat to be sailed. Above all, the members immediately adopted the Corinthians' 0.75-rater 'as being a type of yacht well suited to Southport and the local waters'.[29] The meeting also decided to have its own 'mosquito' fleet of 12-foot centreboard one-designs. For the summer season, these were to be stored on the same pierhead platform as the clubhouse, while they later came into use on the Marine Lake during the winter months.[30]

While there was an obvious wish to draw in new members who might not be able to afford to buy a yacht, the club's new premises on the pier showed no signs of penny pinching. It stood on an extensive platform some 46 by 36 feet, suspended beneath the main pier deck. The neatly decorated changing rooms covered about a half of this area with changing facilities for up to thirty members. Presumably they were male only because a separate ladies' room was opened a year later. The club room had good sized lockers for sails and clothing, as well as sufficient room for locker-seats and a table 'upon which the leading yachting literature finds a place'.[31] The rest of the platform was used as storage space for the 12-foot one-designs. As the *Yachting World* correspondent correctly predicted in 1894, the growing popularity of 12-footers among new members, and the need to house their boats, soon forced the WLYC to extend its pierhead premises. Hundreds of members would use this clubhouse, and its later extensions on to the second pier head which included an improved ladies room', before sea-sailing closed down in 1937. Perhaps there were times when members took their surroundings for granted, but there must have been many other occasions when—like the *Southport Guardian*'s reporter—they appreciated that 'from the windows a fine view over the channel in every direction is obtained'.[32]

Quite apart from this view and the pleasant layout of the clubhouse, its situation on the pier placed it near the hub of the town's summer activities. Literally hundreds of thousands of visitors poured on to the pier during each summer season before the First World War and the yachtsmen must have been influenced by the near carnival atmosphere in high season, not least because their own activities, for better or worse, were the object of much attention! They regarded themselves as a cut above most promenaders, even to the point that they expected their right to go on to the pier without paying a toll to be extended to any friends who went along with them to watch the sailing from the clubhouse. This 'visitors' issue became a regular bone of contention between both clubs on the one hand, and, on the other, the directors who never managed to resolve it to the Pier Company's satisfaction.[33] It seems that the possession of a good nerve and a yachting cap could overawe most of the Pier Company's staff, most of the time. For their part, however, both yacht clubs justifiably complained on numerous occasions about the poor maintenance and inadequate safety on the pier. They were also vulnerable to 'petty thefts' because it was quite easy to break into their clubhouses, while their jetties were at times blocked by 'fishermen fastening their Boats and Ropes thereto'.[34]

For all the quibbles about tolls, break-ins, poor maintenance and later the problems with the Bog Hole, the vast majority of club members still had every reason to remember these early days with pleasure. They might go fishing for mackerel from the larger yachts,[35] while the occasional school of porpoises even came close in to the pier for several hours at high tide.[36] Like others before the First World War, no doubt, they sometimes enjoyed the ludicrous risks taken by the flamboyant 'Professor Powsey', whose main stunt involved diving into the sea from a ramp on the roof of the pierhead tea room on his Bamber bicycle, much to the admiration, among others, of the young A. J. P. Taylor.[37] It is equally clear that members were reluctant to leave their clubhouse on long summer evenings. Sometimes, if the wind was light, races ended when it was almost dark. Furthermore, a Pier Company attempt to ban the WLYC selling 'Refreshments among the Members of their Own Yacht Club'—i.e. alcohol—in 1895 proved totally ineffective.[38] Twenty-five years later the directors were still trying to stop the club selling drinks. By then, though, they knew it was a lost cause! As the club pointed out in December 1921, 'it was a privilege that they had enjoyed for some 25 years' and on this issue, at least, the Pier Company had to give in. The directors simply accepted a somewhat hollow promise that club members would use 'the Co[mpan]y's

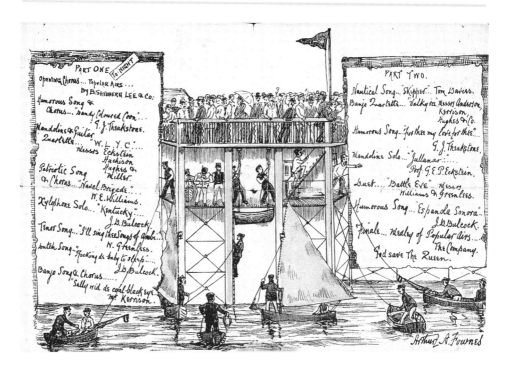

Arthur Fownes' cartoon sketch of the WLYC's Pierhead Clubhouse prepared for the second annual dinner and smoking concert programme sheet.

Refreshment Rooms as much as possible to Compensate the Co[mpan]y for loss sustained in allowing them to sell [drink]'.[39]

From the start, then, it is clear that WLYC members regarded their pierhead clubhouse as far more than just a changing room and a jetty. By chance, the atmosphere was captured in a delightful cartoon drawn for the programme of the club's second annual dinner in December 1895. It shows the clubhouse at the first pierhead, beneath the holiday crowds. Contemporary descriptions of the facilities are also confirmed. A fleet of seven 12-foot centreboarders are in various stages of de-rigging and being hauled up on to their storage platform in what was clearly a joint effort involving many club members.

Meanwhile, during 1895 the WLYC committee also decided to rent its first shore based premises for its members. Initially, the club took a reading room at the Scarisbrick Hotel in April 1895.[40] Only nine months later, though, the Queen's Hotel tempted the club away with an irresistible offer of 'a suite of rooms on the ground floor facing the promenade for their exclusive use ... having a fine sea view'.[41] The Queen's Hotel remained the WLYC's shore base for the next thirty years, after which it rented its own headquarters from the Corporation with a lease on the upper floor of the Victoria Baths also on the promenade and virtually opposite the pier entrance.[42] Until 1926, members might enjoy a fairly discreet drink at their clubhouse on the pier, but they avoided having their own shore-based bar, with regulations about opening times, stock management and the need to employ a steward.

Judging by the amount of extra committee time which these responsibilities occupied after September 1926, it was arguably an advantage to be without them during the club's formative years. The possession of property, including land and a clubhouse, or even an involvement in leasing arrangements, could prove a mixed blessing. The likes of a golf club, with its need for land and generally very large number of members playing throughout the year might be able to weigh the burdens of ownership against its benefits.[43] By contrast, the knowledge that the WLYC possessed nothing beyond the income from its one hundred or so members' annual subscriptions, a 17-foot boat and some mooring chains, could well have served to concentrate minds during these formative years before the First World War. Another, less obvious benefit of not owning property was that the club could avoid potentially costly legal arrangements. Even the agreement to rent the pier premises had to be made through trustees because the WLYC, like the vast majority of 'clubs', did not have a corporate identity and it was not a partnership.[44] There could well have been problems if an attempt had been made to extend this potentially cumbersome legal device into the minefields of ownership, mortgages and leaseholds before the First World War when the club was still in the process of defining its committee structure.

4. 'This young but certainly go-ahead club'[45]

At first, in fact, the WLYC remained content with simply consolidating its position. During the closing months of 1894 the club's very modest racing programme avoided clashes with the Southport Corinthians' events and the year ended in harmony. At the WLYC's first annual dinner in December 1894, Sir George Pilkington was still hoping 'if they did not at some future time amalgamate, that both clubs would go on prospering side by side'. Sir George was, however, much nearer the truth only a few words later when he also 'ventured to predict that the West Lancashire Yacht Club would become one of the strongest clubs on the west coast in a few years'.[46] More than any other member, Scott Hayward had ensured that there were good grounds for such optimism. Reginald Coddington took little part in the club's affairs after the inaugural meeting and his role as commodore seems to have effectively ended once the club was established. In November 1894, for instance, Scott Hayward chaired the end of season general meeting at the Scarisbrick Hotel although he was still the vice-commodore. The term 'annual general meeting' was not used, but the agenda clearly shows that this was the WLYC's first AGM.[47]

It is equally clear that Scott Hayward was firmly in control at this stage. He referred to the success of the 0.75-raters and then announced plans for a new WLYC 10-foot restricted class of single-handed dinghies. At the same time, he recognised the strength of the Hoylake Sailing Club's own 12-foot centreboard class which had opted for restrictions on length and sailing area rather than the rigours of a one-design. He had already made impressive inroads into that class with his remarkable little 12-footer called Slut. Pragmatism therefore won the day, and he secured the WLYC members' agreement to open their own 12-foot racing to retricted class boats in return for an invitation to compete at Hoylake. So as 'to keep the ball rolling', he also arranged for the WLYC to take over the arrangements for winter sailing on the Marine Lake.[48] At the annual dinner in December 1894, still as vice-commodore, he reported a continuing growth in membership and new applicants who were due to be elected. Because he also knew that more boats were being built for the next season, he fully supported the president's optimism by claiming that 'it was a very exceptional position for any club to be placed in'.[49]

The arrival of a 10-foot restricted class produced striking results with little or no delay. It demonstrated Scott Hayward's versatility as a designer and yachtsman who could see what would appeal to yachtsmen at a time of rapid change in their sport. The limits were set to allow variations and yet also to encourage racing upon equal terms. The boats could only be sailed single-handed, with a maximumum length and girth of 10 feet and 10 feet 9 inches

Walter Scott Hayward's prize-winning 12-foot 'Slut' in 1898.

respectively. Sail area was limited to 65 square feet, the centre plate had to be of iron, with a maximum area of 2 square feet and thickness limited to ¼ inch. They also had to be clinker built, with a straight keel and the centre board could not drop more than 1 foot 3 inches below it.[50] No drawings or pictures of this design survive, largely because it quickly produced a wide range of interesting variants despite these restrictions. In 1895, for instance, one WLYC member chose the Hoylake boatbuilder Alex Latta—famed as a right-winger for Everton Football Club until 1893—to build a 10-footer in this class named Jap which was described as 'a marvel of lightness'.[51] Scott Hayward pushed the design rules to the limit with his own boat, named Pogue and built by Crook & Sons of Preston. Pogue was

> a very extreme boat of the 'umbrella midship section type', with a very long fine entrance, and the maximum beam allowed by the rules carried well aft, with short run and low side, and the looks of a very peculiar craft.[52]

By contrast, D. C. Baynes, the WLYC's first official measurer, from 1894 to 1898, went in for 'a more wholesome looking boat' with a good freeboard and generally more stable appearance. There is, said *Yachting World*, 'nothing of the machine about her'.[53] The variations on these simple rules provided considerable local interest. Dudley Coddington got Crooks to build Little Gill into the same fleet and she turned out 'quite unlike any of her class'. And yet he proved her sea-going qualities when he sailed her around from Crooks at Preston to Southport Pier on a September evening, 'making quite an ocean cruise of it'.[54] While the introduction of 12-foot one-designs at Southport proved popular with younger members, however, these 10-footers were clearly a more costly experiment. Baynes, like Coddington, was a wealthy Blackburn cotton spinner—also a member of the Royal Mersey since 1881[55]—and these boats provided such members with a chance to try their hand at something new on the Marine Lake in the winter months. As a class, though, they were rapidly overhauled by the support given to the various WLYC one-designs during the next ten years once the club had become established.

Scott Hayward chaired the next WLYC general meeting in March 1895 as commodore, thereby confirming his own role as the guiding hand behind events.[56] With the WLYC's first full season just starting, it needed his strong influence among other local clubs more than anything else. Respect for him had been considerably enhanced by the growing popularity of his 0.75-raters which had 'without doubt proved themselves fine little sea boats with a good turn of speed'.[57] Although he still continued to develop his interests as a merchant, he was clearly moving over to becoming a near professional boat designer and yachtsman. With his own restricted model 12-footer Slut, designed by George Harvey Wilmer, he had won an impressive string of prizes around the Mersey between 1891 and 1894. Many younger members first got on to the water due to crewing opportunities in these early 12-footers and this was helped by the WLYC's decision to allow the restricted class to race alongside its one-design boats. As just one example, Edward Baddeley, a Manchester solicitor and founding WLYC member played a key part in the club's early history. Among other things, he served for a time as honorary secretary, in 1897 and 1898. In the latter year, his 12-footer Tartar won the class prize for the one-designs, after which he changed over to Seabirds.

No boat and no helm, however, seemed a match for Scott Hayward's Hoylake design 12-footer Slut. Built by Crooks in 1892, he had gained no less than 165 prizes in this elegant little dinghy by the turn of the century. Of these, 100 were first places and Slut was renowned throughout the North West and along the coast of North Wales. Unlike many small yacht sailors, who often had their boats towed or taken on the decks of fishing smacks, Hayward normally either sailed her to racing venues or used his own 0.75-rater Queer Girl to tow her.

Sometimes he had another club member as a crew. More often than not, though, he sailed her single-handed fully justifying reports that she was an excellent sea-boat despite being 'in appearance a fine-weather craft'. If he had achieved nothing else, Scott Hayward would have earned a place in the local record books for this achievement as a yachtsman. Naturally, the WLYC members took full advantage of their new commodore's contacts in the Mersey region and gained a great deal from his expertise and efforts to promote more racing. Compared with 'the usual stagnation' of the winter months at Southport, his 'go ahead'[58] policy continued into the early months of 1895 when it brought the first signs of a rift with the Southport Corinthians even before sailing began on the Bog Hole. In the meantime, though, the club also had to take a second look at its burgee.

5. The 'Golden Lion'

The choice of the Lancastrian red rose as the WLYC's first burgee emblem was certainly highly appropriate in symbolic terms. Unfortunately, however, it closely resembled the international flag code then used to signal the letter 'C', which was a red ball on a white triangular background. Consequently, the WLYC emblem did not stand out as a distinctive club flag. Another problem arose because it was fast becoming the fashion in the booming seaside holiday resorts for trippers and other 'non-boating men' to wear yachting caps. Naturally, the Southport hatters had been as quick as their fellow tradesmen elsewhere to spot the potential for new business. Not suspecting this looming threat to their dignity, the WLYC's founders had overlooked the need to register their original emblem as a coat of arms. By the 1895 summer season there were many more yachting caps with WLYC badges about the town than there were club members! That simple fact probably influenced the committee's decision to alter the WLYC emblem just as much as any desire to avoid confusion between the club burgee and the international flag code for 'C'.

In choosing the 'golden lion' on a blue burgee in November 1895, the club remained true to its Lancastrian origin. The lion was a direct copy of part of the Lancashire crest, being described as 'statant, gardant' against the azure background. However, the *Yachting World* immediately pointed out in a light hearted way that the Royal Harwich Yacht Club had an 'identical' flag and an unusually sensitive WLYC committee seems to have risen to the bait. The honorary secretary took considerable trouble to explain that the journal had got the wrong idea because the heraldic details of the two clubs' emblems were significantly different. Of course, both had golden lions on azure backgrounds. However, the new WLYC burgee would bear a lion standing on all four legs, full faced, with a collar around its neck, whereas that of the Royal Harwich was reared up on its hind legs and side faced.[59]

Being mid-winter, with little sailing to write about, the *Yachting World* decided to apologise at some length in a manner which showed that nobody is safe from a bored column writer. The WLYC explanation, he said,

> shows that there is a difference in the attitude of the respective 'lions', and that the West Lancashire animal is enriched with a collar and three drops (of any particular fluid?) and a coronet, while the East-country lion is unadorned. Such little differences, though doubtless readily noticeable to those well versed in heraldry, will, I fear, escape the ordinary eye, and I am still of opinion that some more distinctive burgee might have been adopted by that young and vigorous club, the WLYC.[60]

Unimpressed, the WLYC committee responded by hanging on to its new 'golden lion', which has remained the club's emblem ever since without there having been any obvious confusion with the Royal Harwich flag. Indeed, it appeared for the first time in the annual dinner programme for 1895 as part of a cartoon! More seriously, however, the WLYC had also taken the trouble to register this badge with the YRA. Although a modest armorial bearings tax had to be paid annually until the Second World War, when the government abolished this charge, the WLYC enjoyed the security of knowing that its new emblem could not be copied for commercial or other reasons.[61] When coupled with the fact that the WLYC had just been granted official YRA recognition six months earlier,[62] the 'golden lion' became a tangible symbol of this enhanced status both in the eyes of members and among the yachting community beyond the club.

6. Corinthian Tensions

The WLYC's early success clearly took the Southport Corinthians by surprise. Most yachtsmen who belonged to both local clubs kept up this dual interest but the initiative in planning a racing programme and developing the sport passed to the WLYC. Despite the Corinthians' earlier indifference to small boat racing, their committee responded by announcing a full racing programme unusually early in the 1895 season and without any discussion with the new club. An immediate result was that each committee acted independently with no attempt to coordinate their racing programmes on the Bog Hole. The inevitable clashes led to postponements and poor turn-outs which, in the event, hit the Corinthians far more seriously than the WLYC for a number of reasons. For a start, there would have been far less trouble if the Corinthians had kept to their area of strength, the larger yachts, and offered a sensible handicap race programme. Instead, they tried to run races for everything, including the new 10-footers, the 12-foot one-designs and, of course, 'their' 0.75-rater class. In doing so, they did not take into account the fact that most small boat owners were also planning to race at Hoylake and Rhyl, and then in the show-piece August regattas at Anglesey. Whereas the WLYC left free slots in their programme when they knew that their small boats would be away, the Corinthians failed to do so and the numbers at their starts fell off as those members who belonged to both clubs enjoyed themselves in North Wales.[63]

Quite apart from this, some Corinthians now took what can only be described as a petulant attitude towards the WLYC which contrasted sharply with the comfortable paternalism of the previous season. Occasionally, latent resentment emerged as a public difference of opinion which most neutral observers regarded as daft. The Corinthians, for instance, still used their 'senior club' status to control the Southport Regatta. In June 1895 they took their authority to ridiculous lengths when they insisted upon excluding boats belonging to those WLYC members who were not also in the Corinthians. Their dubious grounds for doing so lay in the claim that the WLYC was not a yacht club 'recognised' by the YRA and that it must therefore be excluded from competing in events other than those organised by its own committee. The result was that several yachts moored off the pier had to miss the handicap race for 3-rating and under. To take such a decision at a purely local event was dismissed as an 'arbitrary proceeding' by the *Yachting World*.[64] As if to reinforce the point, the journal went out of its way only a week later to anounce that the YRA had actually recognised the WLYC.[65] The YRA Council's decision was clearly a boost for Merseyside racing because the New Brighton Sailing Club was granted recognition at the same meeting, whereas applications from the Great Yarmouth, Forth Corinthian, Salcombe and Cambridge University clubs were deferred.[66] In his 'Southport' article, the *Yachting World*'s correspondent welcomed the WLYC's new status.

> As the membership is now large, and the matches sailed under their flag are both numerous and well contested, it can but give general satisfaction to yachting men of the district, that this new and sporting club has been recognised by the association.[67]

Morale among those Corinthians who cared about sailing fell to a new low point. There is every sign of participation in the club and at their races falling off sharply. They did little to help themselves. For instance, in the early 1890s they actually adopted the 12-foot centreboard one-design class which later proved so popular with the WLYC. But the latter club had immediately realised that they needed competition with the Hoylake Sailing Club if the racing was going to be worthwhile and so they modified their strict one-design rule to let the Hoylake boats in. Meanwhile, the Corinthians kept to one-design only and hardly anyone turned up to race! Even Dudley Coddington, whose father was still the Corinthians' vice-commodore, deserted the dwindling fleet by taking his 12-footer over to Hoylake when the Corinthians held their own races for the class.[68]

Bad luck and poor preparation seemed to add to these woes. One can only imagine the irritation felt by those Corinthians who disliked the WLYC when they heard that only two 0.75-raters had turned up on the line in September for their club's first race of the season in this class. Even worse, these two—Imp and Queer Girl—'found there was no official from the Corinthian Club to start them; had it not been for the kindness of Mr Hutchinson, who has so well filled the office of starter for the WLYC this year, giving them the gun, a

very awkward delay would have occurred'.[69] Doubtless some Corinthians would have
preferred the 'awkward delay' to this type of press report! Indeed, they must have wondered
if the *Yachting World* had it in for them because a separate account of their seventh handicap
race for yachts of 6-rating and under—still one of the club's strengths—was nearly as bad.
There was at most a 'fresh breeze' when eight starters began their twelve-mile course out
into the Channel and

> the yachts got away well together, but soon got divided. Hazard's skipper understanding
> it was the usual long course, sailed away down the channel and so was out of the race,
> Millie carried her mast away in the confused sea off Birkdale. Mollie and Sheila not going
> well; the latter having some trouble with her jib, left the fight to Dot and Imp.[70]

Only one other boat finished out of the eight in what can best be described as a fairly dismal
end to the Corinthians' season because they did little else after this. On the other hand, the
0.75-rater fleet at Southport was going from strength to strength with newcomers to the class
joining the WLYC as a matter of course. Despite the Corinthians' difficulties, the boat itself
proved increasingly popular. These 'little racing cruisers',[71] as they were now labelled, were
proving themselves more than able to cope with lengthy coastal passages in rough weather.
Besides, they became the means by which some of the 10- and 12-footers were towed from venue
to venue around the coast at the height of the summer season. In one particularly notable voyage
in April 1897, for instance, the 0.75-rater Lancashire Lass made the passage from Latham's yard
at Crossens, near Southport, to Beaumaris, Anglesey, in 10½ hours.[72] Gone were any doubts as
to their seaworthiness and due credit for their success went to the WLYC.[73]

Behind the scenes, Frank Coddington—then vice-commodore of the Corinthians—had
done his best to revive the club's racing. At a Southport Corinthians General Meeting in
November 1895, he had chaired the club's Sailing Committee which proposed

> to allow non-members (if members of a recognised yacht club), owning either 0.75-
> raters (one-model) or 12-footers, to compete in the club class races, and so secure
> better entries and give more sport than they did in the past season.[74]

The members rejected the proposal outright. That might have been reasonable if it
had been quite easy to get into the Corinthians. But they appear to have remained far
more selective than those clubs in the North West like the WLYC which were trying to
boost small boat racing. Inevitably, entries to their races fell sharply and remained low
throughout the Edwardian period, despite a brief and unsuccessful attempt to revive interest
in 1911.[75]

Signs of Corinthian resentment about their lack of success emerged briefly in 1896 when
the WLYC invited them together with officials from the clubs at Rhyl, Lytham, Hoylake
and Fleetwood 'to confer as to dates for matches for the coming season'.[76] Only the
Corinthians failed to appear at the meeting in the WLYC's new clubrooms in the Queen's
Hotel. In the event, it was a costly slip of protocol because this turned out to be the first of
the regular meetings between those clubs in the Liverpool Bay area with small one-design
and restricted classes. The meetings did much to avoid the clashes which had arisen in 1895.
Fixtures were set for both the 12-foot class and the 0.75-raters. In the latter fleet, matches
were arranged 'as follows: six at Southport, six at Hoylake, four at Rhyl, and two at Lytham,
as no representative attended from the Corinthian Club, nothing could be done with regard
to their fixtures for this class'![77]

To their great credit, the Southport Corinthians took the point and had the sense to
realise that some change was inevitable. The threat to the Bog Hole and the condition of the

pier were, in themselves, potentially very good reasons for the Southport clubs to cooperate with each other. Even when grounds did exist for resentment, a gentlemanly if somewhat token politeness was always maintained during the next thirty years. Their flag officers attended each others functions with good grace, while there remained some overlap in membership right up to the eventual winding up of the Corinthians. Dudley Coddington actually served as commodore to both clubs from 1906 to 1910, while George Cockshott—the Corinthian vice-commodore in this period—was also a key figure in the WLYC who designed the Star class boats in 1906.[78] Just as significantly, it is clear from local reports and surviving correspondence between officials in the Corinthians and WLYC that the conduct of most inter-club business remained very friendly and informal.

One immediate benefit of this accord was that the Southport Corinthians did take part in subsequent joint meetings of the Merseyside clubs and there were no further fixture clashes to compare with those of 1895. In fact, through the efforts of George Cockshott, the WLYC and Corinthians actually agreed in 1903 that they would run all 0.75-rater class races jointly in the future.[79] This partly reflected the growing popularity of the WLYC's new Seabird fleet which had been going from strength to strength since 1898 and was beginning to threaten the 0.75-rater's survival. But the agreement did confirm that relations between the two clubs had warmed considerably since 1895. It is just possible that this also played a part in Walter Scott Hayward's decision to resign as commodore in December 1903, but he certainly left without rancour and, indeed, was happy to become the club's earliest 'honorary life' member the following year.[80] This was a rare privilege and Scott Hayward was clearly delighted to receive such a special form of recognition. A measure of its significance can be seen from the fact that the next honorary life membership on record went to Lieutenant Commander Percy Dean VC—a WLYC member since c. 1900—in recognition of his wartime bravery at Zeebrugge in April 1918.[81]

Meanwhile, George Cockshott was simply happy to have made some progress towards closer ties between the two clubs, although he did admit that 'he was sorry it had not been found possible to extend it to all the classes in Southport'.[82] Firm proof that genuine goodwill now existed between the two clubs appeared in 1908 when the continued silting of the Bog Hole was already starting to leave the WLYC's first pierhead jetty stranded at low tide. The Corinthians agreed to give up a part of their premises at the second pierhead to the WLYC,[83] even though the latter also kept its original clubrooms. Without this help, which allowed the WLYC continued access to water at all states of the tide, the club's sailing in the Bog Hole would have become severely restricted far earlier than the 1930s when it gave up until after the Second World War.[84]

For all that, the Corinthians remained determined to hang on to their independence as a club. The existence of so much space on their part of the pier was a measure of the club's decline since 1894 when they had filled all of the large and very distinctive 'T' shaped platform at its seaward end. Even by 1920, however, when the Corinthians were virtually defunct as an active yacht club there were at least some committee members who refused to tackle, as Howard Sandbach explained to the WLYC committee, 'the difficulty of *any* scheme of amalgamation giving equal representation'[my emphasis]. And this diehard attitude persisted despite the best efforts of Sandbach, who was the Corinthians' honorary secretary, a WLYC member and former vice-commodore and, due to his standing as a prominent local architect, the only yachtsman to ever serve as a pier company director. If he, of all people, could see no hope of a last minute compromise between the two clubs, the position was truly hopeless.[85]

Chapter 4

'Principally Sailing Members'

1. Club Life with the West Lancs, 1894 to 1914

CHANGES OF COMMODORE between 1903 and 1914 had no obvious influence upon the emphasis in club activities which continued to focus upon racing and the expectation that the vast majority of members would actively participate in some form of yachting. Chapter 5 looks at the personalities of some of these early leaders in more detail. The main changes followed when Scott Hayward decided to resign in December 1903. He was nominally replaced by J. E. Latham, the vice-commodore. However, Dudley Coddington had clearly become *de facto* commodore before the following spring and he continued up to 1910, when William Lawton Hall, a Southport jeweller took over. Like his predecessors, William Hall was a member of the Royal Mersey Yacht Club, having been elected in 1908. His family were also closely involved with club racing, owning two Seabirds by 1910 with which his son, William, and daughter Maudie regularly entered the club prize lists. The family's 31-ton cutter Capri, built by Gibson & Sons at Fleetwood in 1902, had also become a familiar sight in the Channel and at various regattas in the Mersey where WLYC boats were taking part.[1]

Meanwhile, in a notable contrast with the problems of the Southport Corinthians, there was a steady growth of WLYC membership until the turn of the century, with 100 members in 1896, rising to about 130 five years later. More significantly, the club ensured from the start that a high proportion of its members were active sailors. Herbert Baggs, in a brief spell as honorary secretary, emphasised the point with characteristic directness at the 1900 annual dinner.[2] Walter Scott Hayward left even less room for doubt in his commodore's speech the following year. He made it clear that the WLYC had little room for purely 'social' members when he discussed the turnover of membership which was to be expected in this as in any club. 'Those who were resigning', he said, 'were non-sailing men' and those joining 'were principally sailing members'. To applause, he added that 'it was something they had long worked for, and he considered it a healthy sign'.[3]

In fact, the Workman's Compensation Act of 1906 and the 1911 National Insurance Act, Part I, led many large yacht owners to look again at the merits of employing paid hands. This put something of a premium on the talents of willing young amateur, or 'corinthian', crews who could afford to meet their own travelling expenses and had the time to go by rail at the weekend to one of the main coastal yachting venues. That certainly helped some 'sporting' young clubs, like the WLYC, which had made very little use of paid hands from the start. The outstanding victory of Zulu's crew of WLYC amateurs in the 1908 Midnight race from Liverpool to the Isle-of-Man showed just what could be achieved. When coupled with the club's sustained and diversifying enthusiasm for small one-design yacht racing, it also helps to explain how membership rose from the 130 of 1901 to 184 in 1913 despite the economic pressures facing the sport generally.[4]

Another factor in the WLYC's early success was its lively social life. Lowerson has described the Humber Yawl Club's membership of 123 in 1913 as drawn from local solicitors, merchants and other commercial men. In that respect, this by the then thirty-year-old Yorkshire club was very similar to the WLYC. There was another parallel in its 'annual round of smoking concerts, dinners and festivities to foster out-of-season spirits'. Reports of these social events convey an obvious sense of fun and enjoyment which, as Lowerson puts it, 'was almost as far from that of the Royal Yacht Squadron as it is possible to imagine'.[5] Of course, these clubs were like any others in yachting so far as their conformity to basic codes of conduct was concerned. No recognised yacht club would dream of missing its male-only formal annual dinner with loyal toasts, visiting clubs and main speeches. But the tone undoubtedly varied from club to club.

The appearance of 'Sir George' at virtually every annual dinner from 1894 to 1914, for instance, was genuinely popular with the members who seem to have regarded his presence as essential for the success of the evening. Sometimes his tone was supportive, with the Bog Hole a hardy annual throughout. At others he amused members with some mild ribbing which was taken in the spirit intended. The odd surprise could easily occur; as in December 1901 when Arthur Campbell, the WLYC honorary treasurer who was about to be married, found himself receiving 'a daintily decked toy cradle' from Sir George, who had hidden it beneath a serviette before handing it 'to the astonished and blushing treasurer'. True to form, Campbell responded 'in the best of humour and returned his thanks in a short and effective speech, quite in keeping with the occasion and provocative of much mirth'.[6]

Apart from the round of social functions, the WLYC members initiated key technical and educational measures during this period. From at least 1896, for instance, the club ran regular evening classes during the winter. They began in 1896 with a series of navigation classes at the Albany Galleries on Lord Street.[7] Horace Hatch was probably behind this choice of venue. He was a founder member of the WLYC and an auctioneer, whose father, John Hatch had built the Albany Galleries as the offices for the well-known firm of J. Hatch, Sons & Fielding which remains as one of the main estate agencies in Southport today.[8] Topics such as 'Tides', 'Weatherology and the Law of Storms', or 'How to Choose a Boat' all appeared between 1896 and the early 1900s and were well attended. One meeting in 1900 at which the well-known Mersey yachtsman J. F. Jellico led a discussion on the YRA racing rules 'was not particularly well attended'. But it was a Saturday evening three days before Christmas, so one can only wonder at the dedication of the few who spent 'a very pleasant evening' at the meeting![9] Less than a month later the lecture programme attracted far more interest when Professor Hele Shaw demonstrated the 'Stream Line Theory, and its Bearing on the Actual Flow of Water Round the Sides of a Ship'. Hele Shaw was a WLYC member, owner of the 0.75-rater Molly which he sailed regularly, and a professor at the University College Liverpool. He gave his talk at the university so that 'elaborate models' could be used.[10] The evening was opened to all other local sailing clubs and the WLYC received considerable praise in the yachting press for encouraging yachtsman to learn more about his research which was at the forefront of early twentieth century marine science.[11]

2. The Arrival of the Seabirds and the Twinklers

Walter Scott Hayward, Herbert Baggs and the Liverpool yacht designer G. H. Wilmer were also among the numerous lecturers who made these evenings such a success. Club members obviously believed in the value of learning more about the technicalities of their sport and it is, therefore, hardly surprising that the WLYC also adopted two new one-designs in 1898 and 1906 which maintained the pace of change within the club. The origin of the Seabird one-design class suffers somewhat from a long-established, but unconfirmed, tale that the draft plans were drawn at midnight under a lamp-post in Southport.[12] In one respect, this was perfectly possible because the Seabird can be broadly described as a scaled down version of the 0.75-rater. The latter had an overall length of 23 feet 5 inches and about 255 square feet sail area, while these dimensions in the Seabird were reduced to 20 feet and 182 square feet. They also looked very much alike on the water except for the stern where the overhanging 'counter' of the 0.75-rater was not used for the Seabirds. Furthermore, Walter Scott Hayward designed both, although Herbert Baggs shared in the credit for the Seabird.[13] That much said, the Seabirds proved a long term success while the 0.75-raters did not. The reasons for this were partly down to personalities and partly to the success of cost controls for the Seabird as an effective one-design class when compared to the increasingly expensive 0.75-raters.

So far as personalities were concerned, Herbert Baggs typified the WLYC's strong connections with Manchester before the First World War. Born in 1870, he served a technical apprenticeship and was soon 'acknowledged as a very good engineer and drafts-man'.[14] Baggs was still only twenty-four years old when he became works manager for the Salford electrical engineering firm of Dorman & Smith. Further successes followed as he became one of the company's managing directors in 1914 and its chairman between 1930 and his retirement in 1937. Virtually all of the many new patents gained by the firm originated from his ideas during this period. He was said to have a passion for good engineering although he showed much less interest in the 'commercial' aspects of the company's business and subordinates feared his impatience. Like many other yacht club members, Herbert Baggs came to regard sailing as an ideal way of escaping the pressures of work.[15] He is not mentioned in any of the press reports about the WLYC until September 1898 when he is listed as one of those planning to build a Seabird.[16] Possibly, he first came to Southport on business because there was a great deal of new contract work in electrical engineering in the resort during the late 1890s and his firm had been involved previously with the electrification of the Winter Gardens.[17]

Whatever, the reasons for his involvement with the WLYC and then the design of the Seabird, the new boat truly reflected his skills as a draftsman with an eye for the simple and yet elegant. Scott Hayward was the obvious source of the design features carried over from his 0.75-raters. Equally, it could have been the younger and less wealthy Baggs who first saw the potential for a slightly smaller and less costly boat with the same sea-going qualities as the 0.75-rater. His keenness to become one of the first Seabird owners suggests that he viewed this as more than simply another technical problem and it certainly led to a lifelong involvement with sailing. Furthermore, Herbert Baggs was a popular club member, con-firming reports that he did not carry his notable abrasiveness in business over to his private life. His winter lecture on 'How to Choose a Boat' went down very well in March 1901 and he also took his turn briefly as honorary secretary and official measurer.[18]

Meanwhile, he was doing well above the average on the water, taking Seamew up to second place out of six regular competitors in the 1901 WLYC Seabird Class championship. However, he sold the boat to Percy Dean in 1902 and he appears to have spent less time at the club during the next few years.[19] At this early stage in his career, Baggs was undoubtedly preoccupied with business. Even so, he continued to visit Southport from Salford at the weekends and after 1902 he was still happy to have a go in the 'mosquito' fleet on the Marine Lake, as a report on his well publicised capsize in Flirt in October 1904 testifies! By then, there are clear signs of his increasing wealth as well perhaps as a little more spare time. He was elected into the Royal Mersey Yacht Club in 1907 [20] and at some stage during the next five years, he actually moved to Southport and purchased the 5-ton sloop, Corona. He later made a further change to the 11-ton auxilliary cutter Iere which he sailed as a WLYC member during the 1920s.[21] Having made his mark in the early years, Baggs was an obvious choice for the more sophisticated committee system which drew far more members into at least some aspects of club management after the First World War than previously. That apart, though, his inspired contribution towards the Seabird design in 1898 gives him a deservedly more prominent place than most members in the history of the club.

When the WLYC announced its plans for a Seabird fleet the emphasis was upon their very modest cost and the intention of keeping firmly to the one-design principle. The idea was that the boats would be bought by younger members 'whose pockets are not quite long enough to enable them to build a boat costing so much as a 0.75-rater'.[22] That aim led to a strict cost limit of £35 which even included the boat's ground tackle in what was described as an 'on the water' price. Immediate opposition came from some 0.75-rater owners who, correctly as it turned out, predicted that the new boats posed a threat to the survival of their own class.[23] It soon became obvious why this was so. Eight Seabirds were built by Latham's yard at Crossens and these could only be balloted for after all of the boats were complete, which was as good a method as any of ensuring strict compliance with the one-design rules. To that extent, the original plan held good.

The other idea that Seabirds would be taken up by younger members with less money never came to much. The original owners included Scott Hayward and R. C. Standring, who had been successful in the 'mosquito' fleet of 12-footers for several years. It was in the likes of their capable hands that the Seabird immediately proved to be an excellent racer and a good sea-boat in heavy weather. The number of boats and clubs adopting the class grew at what contemporaries regarded as a remarkable speed largely because 'crack helms' like these took a liking to it. Walter Scott Hayward played the key role in the development of the class until 1906. During this period, the Seabird spread to Northern Ireland, the Mersey and Welsh clubs and to Scotland. By 1907 the total fleet had risen to thirty-one boats[24] and they were organised by a thriving class association. Steady growth continued up to the First World War, when there were forty-one, and the class retained its attractiveness as a small sea-going racer during the difficult inter-war years.[25] Although the 1939 total of seventy-two might seem small by modern dinghy class standards, it was certainly a tribute to the Seabird's resilience.[26] Moreover, despite the depredations of storms and neglect, the class survived until the 1960s when new boat construction was revived and the fleet recovered much of the lost ground so that today there are still sixty-six Seabirds in existence.[27]

At their peak in the late 1890s, there were about a dozen 0.75-raters on the water in the North West. However, the boats cost about £60 and had been built to individual orders at several local yards including Gibson & Sons at Fleetwood, Latta in Hoylake, as well, of course, as Latham at Crossens.[28] Furthermore, by 1897 the class had already started to breach its own one-design principle by introducing the first of a series of modifications which by 1903 had amounted to significant alterations of the ballast and rig. In 1897, for instance, the internal 6½ cwt iron ballast had to be replaced with lead. Then, the following year saw rig changes. Complaints of 'rather strong' weather helm resulted in trials at Hoylake in October 1898 and the adoption of a bowsprit with a larger jib. At the time, a gaff-mainsail was also considered as a replacement for the existing lug. But this was delayed until 1903, when the class also introduced a small topsail. The overall sail area appears to have been kept at about 255 square feet, while the balance of the rig was said to have been further improved. The hope was that it would 'tend to make the little boat easier to handle from a cruising standpoint'. That change was coupled to the forlorn hope expressed in the view that 'a revival of the class racing is expected at Southport'.[29]

There was, in fact, little chance of such a revival. Each alteration to the 0.75-rater class required a considerable outlay over and above routine maintenance costs simply to keep a boat competitive. By contrast, the rules for the Seabird class controlled initial costs very firmly. Their owners then maintained a fleet of strictly one-design boats which yachtsmen clearly preferred to the more costly 0.75-rater. Whereas the WLYC and Southport Corinthians 'joint' 0.75-rater series in 1904 only brought three boats on to the water on the best of days, the Seabirds had a regular fleet at Southport alone of ten to twelve competitors. Another WLYC decision at the close of the previous season, which introduced races for both classes each week instead of on alternate Saturdays, hit the 0.75-raters severely. The idea had been to get more members to race regularly. However, members with an interest in both classes simply confined their efforts to Seabird racing because they knew that there would always be a good fleet in that class.[30] And if there had been any lingering hopes for the 0.75-raters, these had clearly come to an end by August 1905 when the two top boats *Gaiety Girl* and *Imp* were sold out of the club through J. F. Jellico's yacht agency in Liverpool.[31]

Meanwhile, the Seabirds also drew interest away from the club's two smaller classes. Nothing more was heard of the single-handed 10-footers after the Seabirds had become established. Admittedly, the 12-footers did manage to hang on. They offered good racing for a crew of two on the Bog Hole and also at the Marine Lake during the winter months. Scott Hayward actually took his prize winning 12-footer *Slut* over to Northern Ireland in the late 1890s, while he raced Sir Naylor Leyland's 0.75-rater regularly at Southport and other local clubs. Nevertheless, he had *Slut* shipped back in 1902 for yet another go at this type of single-handed racing 'after three years' rest'.[32] His example revived the 12-footers' fortunes for a while. By 1906, though, interest in them had slumped again and the WLYC took this as the cue to introduce a new two or three-man centre-boarder with strict one-design rules. The resulting Stars were 16 feet 9 inches overall and their immediate success put paid to any further local revival of smaller dinghy classes until after the Second World War.

Each boat was named after a star or other 'heavenly body' and the idea was that they should become the first yacht which newcomers to the sport would normally buy and sail in. It was welcomed by the *Yachting World* with the comment that 'The West Lancashire Yacht Club seems to have hit upon an admirable scheme for promoting yachting interest "among the young", as one might say'.[33] Of course, the Seabirds began with similar intentions. But this time the club went out of its way to ensure that the Stars continued to meet the needs of those relatively inexperienced yachtsmen who were keen to race. For a start they were designed with this in mind by George Cockshott, a local solicitor who belonged to both Southport yacht clubs. He deliberately kept the cost of these part-decked vessels even lower than the Seabird by setting an 'all-in' ceiling price of £32. Furthermore, the lug and jib sail area of 160 square feet could normally be easily managed by a competent crew of three. Initially, seven boats were built by Latham & Co. and they were given turkey red sails to 'impart a distinctive character to the little ships',[34] while the very prominent star shaped symbol on each boat's lug mainsail soon earned them the name Twinklers, which further enhanced this impression. By August 1907, the Twinklers were racing on the Bog Hole with a rule that only novices were allowed to steer the boat.[35]

There is every sign that the class was immediately popular with a core of members who then kept to them until at least 1914, while other helmsmen moved on after learning the basics. Within a few months, the Stars were already being described as 'handy and able' little boats which were able 'to carry their stuff as well as the "Seabirds"'.[36] Furthermore, the Stars then took over from the 12-footers on the Marine Lake during the winter months. Apart from continuing to offer the less experienced yachtsmen good sailing on these waters, they were used for a regular inter-club event which became an essential part of the social calendar for the leading clubs in the North West. It was basically a race in WLYC Stars between representative helms from up to eight local clubs outside of Southport but the chief aim was to create an excuse for a good social evening. The 1907 effort went badly because fog caused a postponement in December. Then another delay due to the Marine Lake freezing over the following January seems to have put paid to the idea until the next autumn.[37]

However, the WLYC got in before the bad weather at the close of the 1908 season by arranging their open invitation race for mid-October. Leading helms were entered by seven local clubs including the Royal Mersey Yacht Club, while the renowned Splicers also put someone in. The latter were a group of former merchant service masters whose performances of sea shanties was very popular at yacht club suppers. Their performance on the water was far less impressive but nobody seemed to mind because the Splicers made the evening afterwards a great success. Indeed the relatively new Blackpool and Fleetwood Yacht Club appears to have been almost overwhelmed by this 'subsequent hospitality' which figured more prominently in their honorary secretary's letter of thanks to the WLYC than any reference to the race itself.[38] From then onwards, the race became a highlight in the pre-war Mersey yachting calendar with the WLYC playing the host and allowing the other local clubs to enjoy themselves. After the October 1910 event, for instance, over 100 guests attended an excellent post-race supper at the Queen's Hotel.[39] To that extent, these were undoubtedly 'golden years' for the club. Membership continued to rise with both the Seabird and Star classes thriving. New arrivals included the 'aquatic parson'—the Rev. C. C. Marshall, vicar of Headingley in Leeds—whose skill at the helm of his Seabird named Chila led to his well-earned nickname when he won the half-rater series at the 1910 Straits Regattas.[40] Certainly, the thriving Seabird class association had by this stage become an excellent example of how cooperation between clubs could raise the level of competition and standards of seamanship within the sport generally.

3. Offshore; from Jullanar to Zulu

Even the keenest of the club's small yacht sailors enjoyed a trip on one of the larger vessels in the club if the opportunity arose. Sometimes their main interest was fishing, or simply cruising, while on other occasions they raced. One trip of more than usual interest occurred in May 1898 when J. H. Lees took 'some of the most prominent members of the West Lancashire Yacht Club for a cruise to Ireland in his SY Nellie'. The 150-ton Nellie called at Douglas and then continued to Donaghadee, where it remained a few days before returning.[41] It could hardly be a coincidence that Scott Hayward had moved to Donaghadee and restructured its sailing club within two years of this trip which marked the first of a series of valuable links between the two clubs. For his part, J. H. Lees was a generous patron to the club. He provided a WLYC 12-foot challenge cup which was, in fact, won by Edward Baddeley in 1898, while there was at least one other club cruise in the SY Nellie two years later. Furthermore, in keeping with a custom among many large yacht owners, Lees generously helped other club members in emergencies. In August 1898, for instance, Frank

Nellie, off Southport pierhead in the 1890s.

Coddington's SS Speedwell got a hammering when her propellor fouled a trawl net and she was driven ashore at Beaumaris 'during the sudden gale'.[42] Nellie immediately went over to recover Speedwell and tow her in for major repairs.[43]

Sir George Pilkington's earlier venture into the costly world of offshore yachts is particularly notable for his choice of Jullanar. This 126-ton yawl had been designed and built in 1875 at Heybridge on the river Blackwater in Essex by Edward Bentall who was a successful agricultural implement maker. Her name was taken from a tale in the *Arabian Nights* about the 'Princess Jullanar of the Sea'; an appropriate choice because during the next three years she gained a near magical reputation as a racing yacht. In fact, Bentall had Jullanar fitted out with what seems even by the standards of the time to have been a luxurious interior, including a central heating system, main quarters of pitch pine and mahogany, and satin wood with Hungarian ash for the ladies' cabin. Meanwhile, Jullanar was a remarkably solid vessel built of oak, with a main boom of Oregon pine and other spars made from Norway white pine. All of her deck metalwork was bronze, while sections of her internal flooring were made of cast iron weighing some five hundred-weight at each level.[44]

Edward Bentall did not race Jullanar. He was highly satisfied with her performance as 'a very fine sea-boat',[45] but that was all. However, he sold her to A. D. Macleay within two years of launching and it was in his hands that Jullanar shook the comfortable world of large yacht racing. According to the so-called 1730 rule of yacht handicapping, a boat's penalty was determined by the length between perpediculars at the bow's entry to the water and the stern-post supporting the rudder. Until Jullanar appeared, this rule effectively measured the racing yacht's waterline length and gave a reasonable system of handicap between vessels.[46]

Jullanar.

But Jullanar broke the mould because she had a very large counter—or submerged over-hang—at the stern and her vertical rudder post stood about 10 feet forward of the actual waterline length. This meant that she was handicapped on a measure of 90.8 feet, while her actual waterline length—which determined her speed—was 100.2 feet. Add to that, an appearance which the more conservative and undoubtedly jealous observers regarded 'as passing everything afloat in ugliness'[47] and it is hardly surprising that she proved a yachting sensation. Macleay took Jullanar to a string of victories in 1877 and 1878 which completely silenced her critics. Looking back only ten or so years, *The Yachtsman* could describe her in 1893 as a 'bold foreshadowing'[48] of design changes which eventually forced the newly created YRA to reconsider the entire rating system.

Even so, by 1893 Macleay had just sold Jullanar—shown above—to the then Dr George Pilkington who brought her up from her base on the Thames to Southport and the Royal Mersey Yacht Club. There is no record of Pilkington racing her and even his cruising was restricted by his growing civic duties. Indeed, he sold her after only a few years and wryly admitted to the WLYC members at their annual dinner that his ventures with Jullanar had been a costly experience![49] In those few years, though, Jullanar became part of the WLYC's history, achieving in the minds of some members a near mythical significance; not least because of her past history as an extremely successful racing yacht. After Sir George Pilkington sold Jullanar, she returned to racing but proved no match for the new designs of the late 1890s. Very few yachts have enjoyed such a brief period of near total success before becoming effectively obsolete. Quite apart from her special significance to the WLYC, the

Zulu—B. A. Percival's 19-ton winner of the 1908 'Midnight' race.

Yachting World's reports of her sale for scrap in 1905 probably brought a twinge of nostalgia to more than a few older yachtsmen as they read; 'Gosport, Jullanar, yawl is now hauled up on the upper slip, and the breaking up of the once-famous vessel has been commenced'.[50]

However, neither the offshore cruises nor the nostaligia surrounding Jullanar could in any way compare with the near euphoria which greeted Baden A. Percival's Zulu when she won the Midnight race from Liverpool to the Isle of Man in June 1908 with a WLYC crew of six members and two paid hands. They included two of the club's most experienced yachtsmen in W. S. Moore, Zulu's skipper on this occasion, who later became club president from 1936 to 1940, and Charles Henry the WLYC's sailing captain. Described locally as 'more important than any other yachting event except the America Cup',[51] Zulu's victory in horrific weather earned her crew widespread and well-deserved admiration. In 1990, Baden A. Percival's son, Tom, completed a fascinating research report on the history of the boat, entitled *From Zulu to Zulu Chief*. As Tom Percival explains, Zulu was built by Gibson & Sons' yard at Fleetwood in 1901 on similar lines to the sturdy local fishing boats known as 'nobbies'. At 39 feet on the waterline and 19 tons she was small compared with most offshore racers. The boat was a gaff-rigged cutter with a distinctive retractable bowsprit, shown extended in the photograph of her opposite. She had originally been called Zara, but Baden Percival renamed her Zulu when he bought the boat in 1905. He was certainly a popular club member, who also supported the Star class and became known as the 'Admiral'.

Zulu had set off on the 75-mile course from New Brighton to Douglas at 6.45 p.m. on 5 June 1908 in what the *Yachting World* described, with a degree of understatement which suggests that its correspondent was on the shore, as 'rather unfavourable conditions', although he did add that there was 'a strong breeze NNW with a lot of sea, which made the prospects of a dead thrash to windward all night anything but enticing'.[52] Other reports suggested that the race would have been postponed but for a mistaken reading of the weather forecast by the official starter who had received it by telegraph from Holyhead. In the event, only six of the fifteen yachts entering the race actually reached Douglas, with the majority of those who dropped out having done so before leaving the Mersey Estuary. Doubtless, the crews of the six surviving yachts all wondered if the effort was worthwhile at some stage in the race. Zulu, for instance, actually sailed nearly 150 miles to reach Douglas at 9.31 the next morning. On arrival at Douglas, Zulu's crew told the *Manchester Guardian*'s correspondent that by '2 a.m they had had enough of it and did not care where they went, as all had by now foresworn yachting, intending in future to keep hens instead'.[53] Needless to say, it merely took an enjoyable after-race dinner and evening at the Villiers Hotel in Douglas to dispel such feelings. Indeed, Zulu celebrated with a 'very fast run back' to Southport and a place in local yachting history.[54]

It was against the rules of the Midnight Race to allow paid crews to take the helm. With only two paid hands and six amateurs—who were all WLYC members—Zulu had a clear advantage in this respect over her nearest rival Walleroo which had only two amateurs and six professionals. That was a true reflection of the WLYC as a club for amateur yachtsmen who made very little use of paid hands in races. Moreover, unlike many offshore yacht owners, Baden Percival—who lived at Brooklands in Cheshire—only held a membership with the WLYC and he was clearly delighted with this success for his club as well as for his boat. At the annual dinner in December 1908, he took the unusual step of presenting his entire 'amateur crew with silver and enamel match-boxes in commemoration of the Liverpool to Douglas race won by Zulu this year'.[55]

Zulu never won the Midnight again, although she did well with a fourth out of fourteen starters in 1909 to prove that her victory the previous year was no fluke. Besides, *The Yachtsman* did seem to capture the spirit of this particular race better than anyone else before the First World War when a 1911 article about the event said,

> it must not be overlooked that in 1908 in a storm the like of which will not readily be seen again in the summer, the little Southport boat Zulu most brilliantly won. Sporting prophets are supposed to predict eventualities—but the 'Midnight' is beyond them.[56]

As Tom Percival explains, his father sold Zulu in 1913 and she had a 'paraffin motor' fitted two years later. During the inter-war years she changed hands several times while continuing to distinguish herself as a racer in the Irish Sea. On one occasion during the 1934 annual Whit race from Fleetwood to the Isle of Man, she gave up the near certainty of victory to rescue her old rival Wallaroo and tow her home in very bad weather. Zulu was then rewarded with a victory in the same race in 1938, when she achieved a record time of 6 hours 52 minutes which stood unbeaten for thirty years. Her own remarkable record as a survivor has continued. In 1944, she was renamed Zulu Chief and stayed in the North West until 1965 when a new owner took her to the Mediterranean. The boat was then purchased by two United States Navy officers who shipped Zulu Chief across the Atlantic. After further changes of ownership, which nearly led to her being left to rot away, Zulu Chief was bought by Robert Sikkema of Florida. By 1989, when Tom Percival visited him, Sikkema had restored the near ninety-year-old yacht from Fleetwood to a fully seaworthy condition.[57]

4. The End of a 'Charmed Life'

From 1894 to 1913, the WLYC avoided the accidents and drownings which were an all too familiar aspect of Edwardian yachting. The yachting journals for any month in the 'season' between April and October reveal the extent to which amateur yachtsmen were frequently drowned. Although a regulation Board of Trade life-jacket was readily available by the 1890s, there is little sign of them being used for either cruising or racing. A glance at any of the hundreds of photographs in the yachting press is all that is needed to make the point. Furthermore, in a modern age of radio, helicopters, mini-flares and very fast inshore rescue boats, it is all too easy to forget just how isolated the average small-boat sailor was before the First World War. Once a yacht had left her moorings, there was very little immediate help available if things went wrong unless there was another, preferably larger, boat nearby.

This is why Frank Coddington's 25-ton yawl rigged steamer Speedwell had been so popular with WLYC and Southport Corinthian members. After his death in 1903, Speedwell was sold and nothing similar took its place. And yet there were clearly dangers and the Stars turned out to be particularly vulnerable. In their first year's sailing, several Twinklers were rescued by Baden Percival's Zulu 'during a fearful passage from Lytham to Southport'.[58] 'A Few Admiring Friends' were so grateful for Percival's help that they presented him with 'a two-handled cup of old Irish pattern' at the next annual dinner in December 1907.[59] Percival was known affectionately in the WLYC as the 'Admiral' and he was clearly a very popular member. Even so, such gestures were rare and the rescue had obviously made an impression upon the club as a whole. Furthermore, Percival owned a Star named Iris which was frequently sailed by other club members. As if to emphasise the hazards of the Channel, his boat was also involved in an incident two years later, when it was reported that

> Iris capsized at Southport last week just before a race. She was endeavouring to carry a whole lug, while the other boats were either single or double reefed, and paid the price for her temerity. Her crew were at once picked up and the boat has since been raised.[60]

Regrettably, the warning signs were ignored. Even though the Stars were sailed by owners who built up a fair amount of experience of racing and cruising on the Bog Hole, they do not seem to have been as good as the Seabird owners. In several cases, at least, it seems that Star owners and crews actually moved up to a Seabird after a few years. The history of the Star yacht Cygnet is a case in point. On Sunday 20 July 1913 she sank off the Horse Bank during the return leg of a round trip between Southport and Lytham accompanied by the Seabird Whaup. Three of the four WLYC members aboard Cygnet died in the worst incident in the club's history. Quite apart from the immediate sense of loss, the incident cast a shadow over the WLYC's sailing during the inter-war years and removed any lingering confidence about the long term future for yachting on the Bog Hole.

Owned initially by William Lawton Hall's family, Cygnet gave his son, William junior, and daughter Maudie an excellent start from 1907 to 1909. After that they moved on to the Seabirds Goshawk and Seahawk. William Hall junior sailed Seahawk successfully from 1909 onwards.[61] Meanwhile, Maudie Hall had already won a Seabird ladies race with Kittiwake in 1908 and she was regularly taking Seahawk to the front of the club fleet by 1911. Having served its purpose for the Hall family, Cygnet had been sold to Henry Newton in about 1911.[62] Newton lived at Southport and was an accountant in Liverpool. He still appeared in club races as a 'novice' at this stage, while for the next two years he had Stanley Hargreaves and George Grundy as his regular crew.

The distance across to Lytham from the pierhead at Southport was six miles as the crow flies, and WLYC yachts made the round trip at spring tides on 'scores of occasions' each summer. Nonetheless, the Ribble Estuary with its shifting sandbanks, short seas and breaking waves could become an immense hazard with little or no advanced warning for even experienced yachtsmen. Doubtless, Cygnet's crew were well aware of this when they set out for Lytham on Sunday 20 July 1913 accompanied by the recently built Seabird Whaup.[63] Whaup was owned jointly by J. C. McGuffie and Henry Gascoigne, the managing director of the Prince of Wales Hotel on Lord Street. On this occasion it was helmed by Edward Baddeley, the Manchester solicitor and founder member of the WLYC who had done his turn as honorary secretary in the late 1890s. He had C. E. Emmet for a crew. Both men had appeared regularly in the WLYC prize lists for over fifteen years and, as events during this cruise were to show, they were highly competent yachtsmen. They also took their wives and another woman, which reinforces later reports that the weather gave absolutely no cause for concern on the morning of their cruise to Lytham. The nine people aboard Cygnet and Whaup were in every sense a true cross-section of the membership on the eve of the First World War. One sympathetic journalist reported that until 1913 the WLYC had been unusually lucky to have had no loss of life in nearly twenty years of sea-sailing. He added that members and locals alike had felt that the club led a 'charmed life' in this respect. Cygnet brought that to an end.[64]

By 7.30 a.m. on Sunday 20 July 1913 Stanley Hargreaves had left his parents home at Marshside, two or three miles to the North of Southport, and was heading for the WLYC clubhouse at the second pierhead. Hargreaves at twenty-one was in his fourth season with the club. The son of a Southport leather merchant, he had been educated at Hulme Grammar School in Manchester and he was now employed as a clerk for a firm of estate agents in Hulme. Meanwhile, by 8.00 a.m. George Grundy a thirty-nine-year-old Manchester provisions merchant had left his home in Coudray Road in Southport to join Hargreaves. As just explained, both men had been crewing in the Star class yacht Cygnet for about three years with Henry Newton as their skipper.

There was certainly nothing wrong with the boat, which had been one of the original eight built by Latham's yard at Crossens. William Hall junior had sailed it successfully during the first season and Maudie Hall had also helmed Cygnet 'extremely well' to win the club's Ladies race on the Marine Lake in October 1907.[65] Cygnet then appeared regularly in race reports during the next four years, including the invitation events and one for novice helms on the Marine Lake in November 1911, when it was actually helmed by Stanley Hargreaves.[66] George Grundy appeared in the same race at the helm of Iris. Both boats were at the rear of the fleet of eight boats, but the race report shows them to have at least been competent as helms in calm water. A week later, Cygnet was being sailed in a single-handed race on the lake by Henry Newton, who did well in the 'brisk breeze' to come third out of the eight boats.[67] Even so, Newton had only just started sailing on the Bog Hole the previous summer, when he raced in another Star, Vega, in a match for 'novice helmsmen'.[68]

The three men sailed regularly together in Cygnet during the 1912 season and they had clearly gone some way beyond the novice stage by the following year. For all that, they did not have a great deal of experience of sea-sailing and, in particular, of the Ribble Estuary beyond the Bog Hole. Possibly that is why they were joined by forty-three year old William White when they set off for Lytham. 'Billy' White was a Southport wine merchant and long standing club member. He originally came to work in Southport at a branch of the Preston Bank in 1888 after being educated at Wigan Grammar School. Since then, he had become very popular in the town as a local football player and charity shield organiser, a Freemason—being Secretary of the Unity Lodge in 1913—and an experienced yacht crew. Within the WLYC he had served as honorary treasurer for eight years until he resigned in November 1912. At the time, Sir George Pilkington had presented him with an oak barometer and silver tea service in recognition for his work as treasurer. Furthermore, three years earlier the members had given him a silver tea tray 'on the occasion of his marriage'.[69] As a regular and well-liked sailing member, he had almost certainly been invited to join many previous trips across the Ribble Estuary to Lytham.

But Edward Baddeley and C. E. Emmett were far more experienced than the crew of the Cygnet and this was to become all too obvious when conditions deteriorated on the return trip. At first there had not been a hint of trouble. At about 10.00 a.m. both yachts left their moorings near the pier two hours before high tide and caught the flood which helped them over the Horse Bank towards the Foul Naze Channel. From there they sailed easily in a north-westerly moderate breeze of perhaps 15 knots to arrive at Lytham by 12.15 pm. The entire party of nine then went into the Clifton Arms Hotel for a sandwich lunch which lasted less than an hour. There was no hint of concern when they left in 'good health and cheerfulness' just after 1.00 p.m.[70] However, the wind was increasing and although this would not have been immediately apparent on the sea off Lytham which was sheltered from the North and North West, an experienced yachtsman would have been aware of the likely effects in the Ribble Estuary. An official report at the subsequent inquest said that a windspeed of 16½ knots had been recorded at Southport at 2.00 p.m. and this had risen to just over 27 knots by 4.00 p.m. This covers the time when Whaup and Cygnet returned from Lytham. It would explain why Baddeley decided to put two reefs in Whaup's mainsail. Regrettably, the less experienced Newton thought this unnecessary and Cygnet left for Southport with her full rig. Baddeley later explained to the Coroner that he had reefed because he had three ladies on board, but even when pressed he was not prepared to wholeheartedly support Newton's decision to go off without doing the same. This mistake on Newton's part led to the disaster. It was difficult to reef a Star once it was in trouble and he was never in a position to do so off the Horse Bank.

On the return from Lytham, it was usual for yachts heading towards Southport to sail with the ebb tide. They then faced the relatively difficult task of entering the Foul Naze Channel, cutting across the northern edge of the Horse bank and sailing up the Bog Hole to the pier. Thirty or so years earlier, pleasure steamers had regularly used the same route without difficulty and it had been very clearly marked with buoys. The silting had long since stopped that traffic and the only reliable means of navigating through the shoaling sandbanks was by taking bearings from conspicuous landmarks on the shore at Southport and Crossens. On this occasion, visibility was good and and any of the club's experienced yachtsmen would have been able to follow a course set by the very prominent buildings on the flat Southport coastline. They must also have been aware that even their shallow draft centre-boarders could only reach the Bog Hole with safety if they avoided the northern edge of the Horse Bank.

The return journey by Whaup and Cygnet was observed through a powerful telescope by Mr Squire Platt, a local auctioneer who lived on the promenade near the northern end of the Marine Lake. He had already seen the prominent red sails of Cygnet leaving Lytham with Whaup nearby. He thought no more of it because there was no racing on a Sunday and club yachts often cruised over to Lytham and back. When he next looked through his telescope at 2.20 p.m., Cygnet was some 2 to 2½ miles from the shore and sailing directly towards his house, with Whaup about a ½ to ¾ of a mile behind. Platt immediately noticed that Cygnet was in severe difficulty 'having a rough time of it and seemed to be steering in the direction of the Convalescent Hospital on the Promenade'.[71] Now, the hospital stood about a hundred yards to the South, or pier side, of Platt's home. This meant that Cygnet was on a dead run before the north to north-west wind and cutting very close to the northern edge of the Horse Bank in the fast ebbing tide and high wind.

On Cygnet, the crew had become extremely alarmed by this stage. Indeed, as soon as they sailed clear of the shore at Lytham they had hit very rough water caused by the ebb tide running against the freshening northerly breeze. Before reaching the edge of the Horse Bank, Cygnet was apparently moving through this water at about 7 or 8 knots. That was when Squire Platt saw her for the second time. A pitching wave caught Cygnet, pushing the bows under and filling the cockpit just before another wave broke over her stern. Newton was by now desperately looking for Cygnet's life-belts, but they had already been washed overboard. The boat gybed, broached and rolled over on its side, throwing Newton into the water where he kicked off his shoes and jacket and managed to swim. His three crew were up on the gunwhale as Cygnet started hitting the sand on the Horse Bank in the trough of each wave.

Whaup had now caught up and recovered an exhausted Newton who collapsed into the bottom of the Seabird and remained unconscious for some minutes. With considerable skill and no small risk to his own boat, Baddeley circled several times and in one 'pass' got within 3 feet of Cygnet's crew. Each time, he told them to leave Cygnet and swim or jump into the water where he could pick them up. But they hesitated, not least because there was a great deal of wind and sea noise and understandable confusion. Before they could respond, Newton recovered and peered above the Whaup's coaming. That appears to have encouraged the three stranded crew who immediately cheered and assured Baddeley that they were alright. Baddeley was also growing concerned about his three lady crew members, so he sailed off to put them ashore at the pierhead. At this stage, he was obviously worried, but nobody aboard Whaup believed that the three men remaining with Cygnet were in serious danger. Yachts had grounded on the Horse Bank quite often in recent years and the their crews had simply waited and eventually walked off as the tide went out. Their boat could then be recovered at the next high tide. Baddeley therefore got to the pierhead at about 3.15 p.m. and dropped off his three lady crew members. Meanwhile, Squire Platt had cycled to the pier entrance and telephoned a warning to those WLYC members who were at the pierhead. By 3.30 p.m., at least two yachts and several punts were heading back up the Bog Hole, still in the belief that they were simply going to pick up the three stranded crew members. As they got into the shallow end of the Bog Hole some men jumped from the yachts into the punts, but they soon found it quicker to leap out and drag the boats along.

It was only then that the alarm was raised by the rescuers. They found Stanley Hargreaves drowned and laying face down beside Cygnet in a pool of water. The boat had been holed in the battering after her capsize but she was now on her keel with Billy White sitting inside supporting George Grundy. Grundy, however, had died from exhaustion and White was unconscious. Every effort was made to revive Billy White with artificial respiration and a doctor was waiting on the pierhead. He never regained consciousness and he died on the electric tramcar as it was carrying him from the pierhead to the entrance. Even then, few people beyond the pier realised what had happened. The police were not informed until 5.00 p.m. and there had been no attempt to call the lifeboat.

Mr S. Brighouse, the Coroner at the inquest held the following day was also a local yachtsman. He conducted the investigation with considerable tact and skill. Henry Newton was questioned with particular care and he was given an opportunity to deny rumours that he and his crew had been drinking. Cygnet did have a small bottle of spirits on board, he said, but that was all and the jury were left in no doubt that Newton and his crew were fully sober when the incident happened. The fact that the Cygnet's life jackets were stowed away also passed without criticism because it was normal club practice. The evidence was less clear on Newton's decision to sail without a reef. Edward Baddeley was prepared to say that he would have done so if he 'had been sailing in a race'.[72] But this was not a race and the club courses did not go across the northern tip of the Horse Bank on the ebbing tide. The jury decided not to pursue that line of questioning. Without retiring, they gave a verdict of accidental death, expressing sympathy for Henry Newton as well, of course, as for the bereaved. Cygnet was recovered but never raced with the club again. Newton remained with the WLYC, returning after wartime service and buying the Seabird Kittiwake in 1920, when his wife also joined as a lady member. Certainly, he was in no sense blamed for what happened and there is every sign of his having been given sympathetic support by club members in the immediate aftermath of the incident while he played a full part in the WLYC committees in the post-war years.

For all that, the incident tarnished the optimism which had been such a feature of the club's early years. The 1913 annual dinner was a dismal affair with barely seventy members and guests attending.[73] There were absolutely no references in the local press reports of the dinner to the July accident, although there was also none of the usual light-hearted fooling and jokes which had been so typical of WLYC social evenings. Indeed, as war approached the club had clearly gone through a watershed. With the return of peace, there was to be an impressive 'victory' regatta and much of the old spirit and enthusiasm returned. But the winter races on the Marine Lake stopped and in 1922, as mentioned earlier, the club sold its remaining fleet of five Stars to the West Kirby Sailing Club, where they still race on their Marine Lake and the River Dee. After that, the WLYC only raced Seabirds on the Bog Hole at Southport and the inter-war years were marred by considerable uncertainty about the future as the silting in the Channel intensified.

Chapter 5

Figureheads and Leaders before the First World War

1. Introduction

THE WEST LANCASHIRE YACHT CLUB of today is a true reflection of the changes which have occurred in the sport nationally. Those who serve as flag officers are elected for a set period and the club's affairs are conducted by an efficient system of committees. External audits and safety requirements as well as the influence of bodies like the RYA and representation on behalf of various dinghy class associations all contribute towards the accountability of club management. Such a position emerged gradually. The post-Second World War years have seen by far the greatest changes, but the WLYC had by then already made significant organisational improvements during the inter-war years. By contrast, it is fair to say that in the early phases of its growth up to 1914, the club was dominated by certain personalities who exerted an influence far in excess of what would be regarded as acceptable today. Beyond that, the lingering influence of Victorian deference towards the rich and especially those with aristocratic connections was felt just as much in the Southport yacht clubs as any others. That much said, there were also some interesting contrasts between the WLYC and the Southport Corinthians which might help to explain why the former survived while the latter did not.

2. Corinthian Figureheads

In part, the Southport Corinthians' attitude stemmed from those wealthy owners who still preferred the club's old-fashioned air of exclusiveness to the WLYC's more openly competitive style. Even during its fading Edwardian years the Southport Corinthian Yacht Club bridged the subtle divide between the old Lancashire gentry families and the professional and business élite of the North West.[1] The tone had been set by the first Earl of Lathom, formerly Lord Skelmersdale, who served as the Corinthians' president until his death in 1898.[2] His son, the second Earl, took over as the club's president. He was well-known nationally as the owner of the 80-ton yawl Onyx and he belonged to the Royal Yacht Squadron, the Royal Thames, Royal Welsh and Royal Mersey Yacht Clubs, serving as rear commodore of the latter in the 1900s. Like his father, though, he never took part in the Southport Corinthians' sailing activities and he seldom appeared at their social events.[3] Neither did that other bastion of local wealth Charles Hesketh Bibby Hesketh (1871–1947) who took up yachting in a 5-tonner in 1895 when he was twenty-four and who then bought a 59-ton yawl before giving up the sport temporarily in favour of polo. By the early 1900s Hesketh had returned to yachting with the purchase of the 130-ton Elfreda,[4] which only made the occasional, fleeting, visit to the Bog Hole even though he was the Corinthians' vice-president.[5]

Patronage of this sort brought the Corinthians prestige but it was of little practical help. When it came to fighting the Ribble Navigation Company's work in the estuary, for instance, these families were as powerless as Southport's business and political leaders and the Channel became virtually useless for their large yachts long before the small craft which raced regularly on the Bog Hole were forced to withdraw.[6] Even so, the relationship between the Corinthians with their remote figurehead leaders, and the WLYC with a president who was clearly liked and regarded with affection by the members reflects in microcosm the wider changes in Lancastrian society. Despite being well past its best and lacking the 'go' needed to recover, the Southport Corinthians still appealed to the snobbery of a local élite which emphasised it's landed and aristocratic connections.

By contrast, the WLYC drew its élite support from the more progressive and less remote leaders in business and commerce. They were often every bit as wealthy as the older country gentry families and certainly not lacking in confidence as social leaders. Nonetheless, the differences were there. It would explain why wealthy Liverpool merchants like William Bibby, Aristides Bersi and Domingo de Larrinaga were quite happy to join the WLYC while Charles Hesketh Bibby-Hesketh and the Earl of Lathom kept to the Corinthians. Of course, the overlap in membership at most levels ensured that the such differences were concealed in the day-to-day running of each club. But when it came to new ideas, new boats and, increasingly, new members the WLYC was obviously far more in tune with the times than its 'senior' partner on the pier. Even the fact that 'Sir George' virtually always turned up to club functions, while the Corinthians usually had to make do with apologies from the Earl of Lathom and Bibby-Hesketh must, over the years, have given the morale of the WLYC members a boost at times when they needed it most.

3. 'Sir George', WLYC President 1894 to 1916

'He knew that he himself was only an ornamental figurehead, but … he occupied the post of president with very great pride and pleasure'.[7] Sir George Pilkington's contribution to the early success of the WLYC could have no more appropriate introduction than this, his own modest assessment of his role. At the time he was speaking to the members after their 1895 annual dinner. However, it remained one of two recurring themes in nearly all of his highly popular speeches as the WLYC president. The other, of course, was the state of the Bog Hole. With the South Channel gradually silting up between 1894 and the First World War, the long term prospects for yachting were hopeless. For all that, Sir George Pilkington provided a strand of continuity and encouragement through twenty two years during which the club had six different commodores. On any one of several occasions, such as when Scott Hayward or Dudley Coddington resigned, or after the 1913 accident, the WLYC membership could easily have slumped dramatically. It did not do so because the members had developed a club spirit which went beyond their immediate interest in yachting. Rather than simply 'an ornamental figurehead', their 'Sir George' became a public expression of that sense of identity.

He was, of course, initially welcomed by virtue of his local prestige which helped to get the WLYC started in 1894. Furthermore, although he was never a yachtsman in the sense of, say, someone like Walter Scott Hayward or Dudley Coddington he did take a genuine interest in the sport. He was a founder member of the Southport Corinthians and served as their commodore, while in 1884 he had also been elected to the Royal Mersey Yacht Club. At this stage, he was still Dr Pilkington, 'Surgeon' of Southport and he owned a 15-ton

'Belle Vue'—Sir George Pilkington's impressive house on Lord Street. This photograph was probably taken in about 1900 and shows the glass tower from which Sir George could watch the racing in the Southport Channel.

yacht Stella.[8] By 1893 when he was knighted, though, he owned the magnificent 126-ton yawl Jullanar which was to bring him the temporary yachting fame of a full-plate photograph in *The Yachtsman* supplement for June 1893, a privilege reserved for only the best or most interesting boats.[9] Ownership of this famous yacht had its costs, however, as Sir George made clear in a humorous and typically frank annual dinner confession in December 1896 just after he had sold Jullanar. To the amusement of the members he said that his own limited yachting experience was

> what he termed the family cruiser style, but after several years of yachting in the cruiser he had come to the conclusion that there was a great deal of money to be spent that way, and a great deal less fun to be got out of it (Laughter).[10]

Only the briefest of glances at Sir George Pilkington's career is needed to show why he had little time to become an active yachtsmen.[11] Born in 1848 in Cambridgeshire, his father was a surgeon and he followed the same path through private education to Guy's Hospital. His family name was Coombe, and it was as Dr Coombe that he practiced medicine in Southport from the age of twenty-two. He acquired the name of Pilkington from his marriage to Mary, daughter of James Pilkington, after the death of her only brother in 1882. By then, Dr Pilkington had already become a well established local figure. He was the house surgeon at the Southport Infirmary, while he fulfilled various civic and charitable duties.

He was still in his thirties when chosen as the Mayor of Southport in 1884. As Walton has explained, during the late Victorian period the office of mayor in one of Lancashire's numerous wealthy boroughs, 'carried a special mystique, an impression of special citizenship'.[12] George Pilkington's attainment of that social peak at a relatively early age is in itself an indication of his local significance. He was elected for the Liberals as Southport's first MP in 1885 following the creation of this new Lancashire constituency the previous year. His brief venture into national politics ended only a year later when G. N. Curzon won the seat for the Conservatives and retained it for the next twelve years until giving it up to become the Viceroy of India in 1898. However, Pilkington's status as an influential local figure remained unchallenged. He became the mayor of Southport for a second time in 1891 and was the first citizen of the borough to gain a knighthood two years later.

Meanwhile, Sir George showed little enthusiasm for the rough and tumble of national politics and he stood down as Liberal candidate in favour of Sir Herbert Scarisbrick Naylor Leyland, grandson of Charles Scarisbrick and reputably one of the wealthiest men in the country. Sir Herbert Naylor Leyland's appearance as a Liberal was a remarkable political about-face beacause he had previously been the Conservative MP for Colchester. He unsuccessfully contested Southport against Curzon in 1895 when he took up the cause of land reform and even criticised his own family's past activities, as owners of the Scarisbrick estates, for 'seriously retarding the growth and development of the town'.[13] However, when Curzon resigned in 1898, Naylor Leyland won the seat for the Liberals. His critics accused him of political opportunism and claimed that he had not the least intention of reducing the Scarisbrick estate Trustees' hold on the town. Before these claims could be put to the test, though, he died suddenly in 1899 at the early age of thirty-five.

Whatever his political opponents might claim, Naylor Leyland could count the members of the WLYC among his many friends in Southport. He had been a member and an active supporter of the club for at least a year before his election. He actually bought a new 0.75-rater from Latham's yard which he named Wenonah at the start of the 1898 season and when he was elected an MP *The Yachtsman* commented that he 'will be well known to yachtsmen of that West Lancashire district by his Southport one-model 0.75-rater Wenonah, which has been much in evidence on those waters of late'.[14] As the MP for Southport, he was also elected a vice-president of the WLYC and he would undoubtedly have retained his interest in the club over a long period. At the start of the 1898 season, in fact, Walter Scott Hayward and R. C. Standring had sold their 0.75-rater Queer Girl to Thomas Rowe who raced it successfully in the club series over the next few years. Initial rumours that Scott Hayward was dropping out of the class were ended when it became clear that he would be racing Wenonah for Naylor Leyland.[15] The addition of a new boat to the 0.75-rater fleet was the most suitable way in which Naylor Leyland could support the WLYC at a time when the costs of this class were rising and younger members could not afford them. Furthermore, Wenonah was bought by J. Acton and remained in the club after Naylor Leyland died. Various members raced it successfully over the next few years. Apart from Scott Hayward, for instance, the Manchester solicitor Edward Baddeley who handled the Seabird Whaup so well in the 1913 incident, sailed Wenonah throughout the 1900 season to win the club helmsman's cup for 0.75-raters.[16]

In the meantime, as the undisputed leader of the Liberals in Southport, Sir George Pilkington had immediately taken Naylor Leyland's place to become the MP for Southport at the 1899 by election. He lost the seat to the Conservative candidate, Edward Marshall Hall, at the general election the following year and he did not put himself forward as a candidate again. This brief return to national politics was purely an expression of his local influence as a patriarchal figure[17] and he certainly had no ambitions in that direction beyond representing Southport when asked to do so. Within a local context, of course, he was extremely concerned about the state of the Ribble Estuary and he became an acknowledged expert on the political and civil engineering disputes surrounding its use. Beyond that, though, his few political statements were far from radical and his approach to liberalism was in line with the generally conservative tone of public life in Southport.[18] In 1885, for instance, he said that the new Board School in Birkdale was not 'an unmixed blessing', even though the creation of these non-denominational schools formed a key part of the Liberals' progressive education policy.[19]

The truth was that in a wealthy town like Southport the local élite enjoyed a common social round of clubs and an affluent lifestyle which all but ignored differences in politics between the leading Liberals and Conservatives. Indeed, Sir George purchased and improved a large villa known as 'Belle Vue' which occupied a suitably prominent position at the southern end of Lord Street. Among WLYC members it was also noted for its prominent glass tower, from which Sir George often watched the yacht races in the Channel. Civic and social leadership at this level was financed by his wide range of business interests rather than from his prominent local role in medicine. For instance, he owned a substantial tea plantation in Ceylon,[20] while he was a director of the Lancashire and Yorkshire Railway as well as for the Manchester and County Bank.

Many Southport residents could claim to have business connections and wealth on this scale and beyond. None, however, could match the popularity which Sir George Pilkington enjoyed among all levels of local society before the First World War. He obviously liked being a civic leader and he had a rare talent for becoming involved in local activities without patronising people. Local fisheremen, lifeboatmen, footballers, athletes and swimmers were among the many who welcomed his support and genuine interest in what they were doing. Within the WLYC he always seems to have known what was going on and he gave practical as well as moral support. In 1898, for instance, he helped to establish the Seabird fleet by purchasing one of the initial batch of eight boats. He clearly had no intention of sailing it himself, but his Seabird Kittiwake figured regularly in WLYC races with various members at the helm, including Walter Scott Hayward,[21] until he sold it to another club member— J. C. McGuffie—for the 1904 season.[22] The *Yachting World* commented on Sir George's decision to buy Kittiwake with what was perhaps one of the most fitting tributes to his contribution to the club during his many years as its president.

> The popular president, by building for this class has given great satisfaction to the members ... it is indeed satisfactory to see what are often termed ornamental officers take such a keen interest in a sport [i.e. racing] that is the very life of a club.[23]

In fact, Sir George 'was always pleased to do all he could to promote the success of the West Lancashire Yacht Club'.[24] And he did so with a style that was hard to follow. Indeed his death in 1916 marked the passing of his own brand of Edwardian paternalism. As if recognising his unique contribution, no attempt was made to choose a successor to 'Sir George' until well after the war. Then, in 1920, the club began the logical practice of electing its president from among former flag officers, most of whom had served as WLYC commodore and who had substantial experience as yachtsmen. There were to be some exceptions to this during the inter-war years. Nonetheless, Harry Spurrier's election as commodore from 1915 to 1918, and then as the second WLYC president between 1920 and 1924, was clearly a step towards the current practice and away from that of the club's late Victorian and Edwardian years. In 1992, for example, David Hewitt became the twenty-third WLYC president after having served as the club's commodore for 1985 and 1986.

4. Walter Scott Hayward: 'The Best Known Yachtsman in the North of England'

Sir George Pilkington was a true 'gentleman amateur', a corinthian in spirit who supported the WLYC to the full. His presence at social events greatly enhanced the club's prestige even though he was not an active sailor.[25] By contrast, Walter Scott Hayward was one of the growing number of near-professional yachtsmen who took the sport into the twentieth century. He combined wealth, business acumen and a talent for innovation with an irrepressible enthusiasm for yacht racing. Scott Hayward was born in London in 1855 and, although little is known about his origins, his family were probably from a mercantile background in the City. They were certainly wealthy enough to enable him to join the Temple Yacht Club when he was about sixteen. At the time, it was still based on the Thames and enjoyed a reputation as a 'rising and prosperous little club, specially devoted to the training of amateur sailors'.[26] He probably took part in the club's move in May 1871 from Charlton down the Thames to Erith. The day was organised as an event in which

> Yachts will rendezvous at Charlton and sail in company down the river, members and friends dining in the evening at the Crown Hotel, Erith.[27]

A report written in 1910 claimed that he had owned and raced a cutter named Rover from 1871 to 1873. But it is far more likely that he was a young amateur crew at this stage, and that he bought his first boat Blanche in 1873 at the age of eighteen.[28] Over the next ten years he was gaining experience in business and as a yachtsman. Some of this time was spent racing on the south coast before moving to Manchester and joining the New Brighton and Cheshire Sailing Clubs. Then in 1879, at only twenty-four, he became one of an élite group of top yachtsmen who gained a full Board of Trade certificate as a master.[29] Some idea of his importance in this respect can be gained from Lloyds Register of Yachts. The certificates were first issued to yachtsmen in 1873, with Scott Hayward gaining the sixty-third of these awards six years later. Just before he died in 1910, the list shows a total of only 241 certificates ever having been issued, with 122 of these currently valid. Scott Hayward certainly made immediate use of his certificate because he chartered the 50-ton schooner Resolute for a trip to the Moroccan coast in 1879. Four years later he was elected as a member of the Royal Mersey Yacht Club, with the New Brighton yacht builder and designer W. H. Wilmer proposing him.[30] His proposer described him as a 'merchant' of Manchester and he clearly had the resources needed to develop his interest in yachting to the full.

As explained in earlier chapters, like many yachtsmen from Manchester he was probably attracted to Southport because it offered a direct rail link from the city to the nearest and most accessible coastal water. By 1884, he was playing a leading role in local yachting as the first vice-commodore of the Southport Corinthian Yacht Club. From then until the start of the WLYC ten years later, he was continually involved with attempts to promote racing on the Bog Hole in ever-smaller and less expensive craft. His role as the designer of the 0.75-raters and the direct part which he played in the foundation of the WLYC more than confirmed later reports that he had 'a very decided genius for organisation'.[31] In fact, by 1894 he was already being referred to in the yachting press as that 'well-known yachtsman, Mr W. Scott Hayward'.[32] To that extent, his significance as commodore of the WLYC from

1895 to 1903 is beyond doubt. He also became commodore of the newly founded Rhyl Yacht Club in March 1895, while in the late 1890s he bought a house at Omeath in the north of Ireland and then moved to Larne Harbour where he joined and reorganised the declining Donaghadee Sailing Club, becoming its commodore in about 1900.[33]

His interests in the Seabird fleet were coupled to this and it was due to him that the class spread to Ireland, as the Seashell, and WLYC members enjoyed the experience of more competition away from home.

Because he found a need to spend an increasing amount of time in Belfast where he was establishing a new business, he moved his family once more and settled in the wealthy suburb of Greenisland overlooking the Lough. By then, he and his wife, Louise, had a daughter and five sons. He must have been particularly proud of his daughter, Gladys, who was rapidly establishing herself as a respected yachtswoman on the Belfast Lough. Scott Hayward had taught her to sail in the WLYC 10-foot one-designs, probably on the Marine Lake, while she crewed for him in Sandpiper for all of the club's Seabird races during the 1900 season. She had ended that very successful summer by helming Sandpiper to first place in the Seabirds' crews race on the Bog Hole.[34] Scott Hayward's own commitment to the two clubs, at Southport and Donaghadee, resulted in the successful 'inter-club' races for Seabirds, Seashells and Cariads, which received considerable praise in the yachting press. The WLYC's role in promoting the Seabird—despite local variants in name—could be seen by the arrival of seventeen one-design yachts at the starting lines of a week-long series of races on the Belfast Lough. At the time, this 'international' one-design event was regarded as very impressive and a pointer towards the future direction for the sport.[35]

As commodore of both the WLYC and the Donaghadee Sailing Club at the time, Scott Hayward rightly enjoyed a large share of the credit for this success. At first sight, then, his sudden decision to resign as WLYC commodore just over a year later appears, to say the least, surprising. Of course, he did accept that he was becoming 'an absentee commodore'. But that was an afterthought aimed more at quelling any differences within the WLYC over his decision. He still spent a great deal of time in the North West and even gave his full support to his friend William Bibby's efforts to establish another Seabird fleet with the rejuvenated Liverpool Yacht Club from 1906 onwards. Indeed, he bought a half share in Bibby's highly successful Seabird Curlew and continued to sail regularly.[36] Nevertheless, his business and sporting interests were moving towards the new world of motor boats and this, rather than having a home in Ireland, is probably why he felt that it was time to leave the WLYC to go its own way after the differences of opinion at the 1903 AGM.

By the 1900s, in fact, Scott Hayward had already gained a sound reputation as a designer of motor boats. As early as 1896, Roberts' yard at Chester were building the powerful motor launch Nemo which he had designed for Charles Maden of Southport. With an overall length of about 50 feet she was described as 'by far the largest motor yacht in or about this district' and attracted much local interest.[37] By the early 1900s, there are increasing signs of this having become his main business activity as well as taking up most of what passed for 'spare' time in his life. In 1905, reports began to appear of his efforts in a motor boat called Iarracht, which is Gaelic for 'trial', powered by a 10-h.p. Gardner petrol engine. He won a race at Port Dinorwic in August 1905 during the Straits Regattas.[38] Through his influence, the Liverpool Yacht Club hosted a motor boat regatta the following year and then in January 1907 he tried to establish a Liverpool branch of the British Motor Boat Club. That idea failed because 'motor boating in Liverpool had not yet attained such importance as to warrant the election of flag officers'. Undeterred, he went ahead a week later with the purchase of a 25-foot launch from the Belfast Marine Motor Company which he intended racing on the Clyde. Named Irish Adamate and fitted with a 45-h.p. engine he had gained enough experience by September 1908 to enter her in the British Motor Boat Club's Annual Regatta at Burnham-on-Crouch. With over 160 entries, he could not have expected much from this, his first venture into the top league of the British sport. Even so, in the class for boats up to 25 feet, he achieved a sixth place from fifteen entries in one of the sixteen-mile sea races and this encouraged him to go further.[39] By the end of the year he was reported to be 'building a 6½ metre racing motor cruiser for racing at the chief English regattas'.[40]

Scott Hayward was clearly aiming at becoming a national figure in motor boat racing. With his sons, he had established the Belfast firm of Messrs. W. Hayward & Co, marine motor engineers. He was also gaining wider recognition as a motor boat designer with a particular talent for applying technical ideas about nautical engineering in a simple but effective way. This had already opened up another source of business when the Congested Districts Board of Ireland commissioned him to develop the use of motorised fishing boats on the west coast of Ireland. From 1906 to 1909 he drove hundreds of miles in his motor car, visiting these poverty stricken areas to advise on the modernisation of local fleets. Others clearly recognised his value because in 1910 he was invited to travel to Vladivostock to advise Russian fishermen about the use of motor boats. Only someone like Scott Hayward would have accepted and, perhaps equally typically, arranged to fit this in with a visit to two of his sons in Hong Kong where they were setting up a car dealership. He travelled on the trans-Siberian railway to Vladivostock but then he caught influenza during the journey from Russia to Hong Kong. If he had paused to rest, all might have been well. Instead, he took a partial improvement in his health as the cue to return home with one of his sons on the Royal Mail Packet Steamer Pembrokeshire. He died as the ship passed through the Red Sea on 15 August 1910 and he was buried at sea.

Yachtsmen from clubs around the North West and in Ireland paid tribute to his tireless contribution to yachting and the development of motor boats. In an appropriate gesture, 'four of his old friends and former pupils of his small boat racing' asked the captain of the Pembrokeshire, Richard Hayes, to lay an evergreen wreath in the Red Sea near where Scott Hayward was buried. On the outward voyage, Hayes complied fully with their wishes as his letter to the editor of *Yachting World* from Penang on 26 November 1910 confirmed.

> At 3.20 p.m., November 8, the Pembrokeshire was steamed over the position, viz., lat. 22 deg. 17 min. N and long. 37 deg. 26 min. W.; the engines were stopped, the wreath deposited in the sea, the ensign 'dipped', and the ship proceeded on her voyage.[41]

Such a fitting tribute marked the end of a career in which the successful creation and leadership of the WLYC for ten years was certainly a high point among Scott Hayward's many achievements. He was truly an individual with the ability to identify when and where to initiate changes. Of course, he had the wealth and social background needed to fit in at any yacht club in the country. In 1910, for instance he was a member of at least ten yacht clubs and the YRA. He had also joined the Scottish Motor Boat Club and the Motor Boat Club of Ireland as well as being the honorary secretary for Ireland for the British Motor Boat Club. There were doubtless many wealthy 'yachtsmen' who were members of numerous clubs and did little or nothing about it. Scott Hayward stood apart from that type. The *Belfast Newsletter* said, in 1910, that he had done 'a great deal to popularise marine motoring in the country'. In this case the compliment applied to Ireland. Others in England, not least in Southport, praised the way in which he had applied his skills and technical knowledge as a yachtsman to push through the kind of changes which did so much to widen participation in the sport during the twenty or so years before his untimely death.

5. The Coddington Family and the WLYC 1894 to 1910

Walter Scott Hayward had obviously been the driving force behind the WLYC's early successes and it was due to him that the club earned such a high reputation for its competitive racing. The Coddington family played a different but arguably just as significant part in the history of the club before 1914.[42] Their position as a wealthy and well respected Lancashire family has been referred to earlier. Reginald Coddington's passive role as the first WLYC commodore was significant simply because he was an uncontroversial figure with the sort of connections needed to establish the club's credibility. By contrast his cousin, William 'Dudley' Coddington (1872–1928) brought the WLYC through a potentially difficult period from 1903, when Scott Hayward resigned unexpectedly, to 1910 when he also stood down. These were hardly 'golden years' for the average yachtsman. Many in clubs like the WLYC must have been feeling the pinch from rising costs. This became a recurring theme in the yachting press, which also became nervous about the competition for new recruits from equally exclusive sports like golf, motoring, tennis and shooting.

The Coddington family's interest in the WLYC therefore added another strand of local wealth and influence in these early years. As mentioned in previous chapters, their roots lay in Blackburn where their strong cotton spinning and weaving interests provided the means to gain a powerful local political base. Its focal point was the Victorian partnership between Francis Henry Coddington and his brother, Sir William Coddington, Bart, who became a Conservative MP for Blackburn. Francis Henry, known as Frank, Coddington (1847–1903) was Dudley's father and a good yachtsman in his own right. Born in 1847, he entered the family firm in the 1860s after studying at Oxford. Like others of similar social standing he fulfilled a range of near obligatory social duties including service on the bench at Blackburn, from 1887, while also becoming first a Conservative councillor and then an alderman in 1897. Even so, the latter could only have been a token role. Unlike Sir George Pilkington, his interest in yachting overshadowed politics and business and he had retired from the family firm to live in Southport by 1892. Nevertheless, he retained some links with the cotton industry by entering into a partnership with a Samuel Lamb at Manchester to create a successful firm of cloth merchants and shippers.

Frank Coddington was commodore of the Southport Corinthians in 1894 when he took the chair at the WLYC inaugural meeting and became the first person to be elected as a vice-president of the club. Despite his obvious financial links with the cotton industry at Blackburn, his connections with both Southport clubs put him in a prominent place alongside Sir George Pilkington during the campaign against the Port of Preston's activities in the Ribble Estuary. Furthermore, in 1894 he bought a small steamship, the 21-ton SS Speedwell, which more than proved its worth to local yachtsmen. In the hands of its master, Captain Spencer, this little 'boiler boat' became a familiar friend when there was no wind or on the many occasions during the next ten years when she served as the club transport by towing the 0.75-raters and later the Seabirds to regattas at Lytham or along the Welsh coast.[43] The SS Speedwell apart, Frank Coddington also achieved impressive results as the owner and helm of various yachts. His early boats included the 40-ton cutter Silver Star and, then, the locally built 10-tonner Katie which did well in the mid-1880s. However, neither could match his successes with the 'celebrated' 3-tonner Millie which won over fifty prizes in races throughout the North West and North Wales during the late 1880s and 1890s.

Although Frank Coddington remained a staunch Conservative and member of the Southport Unionist Club, local politics played a minor part in his life after he moved to Southport. In fact, his most notable interests beyond yachting were football, horticulture, motoring and shooting. As a one-time president of Blackburn Football Club, he was always welcomed as a keen supporter of the Southport F. C. on Scarisbrick New Road. For others, the gardens of his large house on Lord Street—known as The Lawns—were a source of interest, with some 80,000 crocuses which were 'undoubtedly the admiration of horticulturalists from far and near'.[44] An enthusiasm for motoring, and a reputation 'throughout the North of England as a crack shot', complete a picture of a man who could obviously afford the time and money needed to maintain such a style of living.

Dudley Coddington—Commodore of the WLYC 1906–1910.

When he died in 1903, Frank Coddington's business interests passed to his son, William Dudley Coddington (1873–1928) who had also been a founding member of the WLYC. By this stage, Dudley Coddington already had a string of yachting successes to his credit, while he had been elected to the Royal Mersey Yacht Club, as a 'cotton manufacturer' of Birkdale in 1897.[45] Motoring was another of his interests and he possessed that ultimate status symbol of the wealthy young batchelor a 30-h.p. Daimler.[46] Unlike his father, he took an active interest in local politics 'as one of a group of young conservatives who formed the spearhead' of a successful attack on the Liberals' hold over Souhtport. In 1907 they gained control of the borough from the Liberals with Dudley Coddington becoming the Conservative councillor for Marine Ward, which included the area along the promenade. Meanwhile, his marriage in 1903 to Ella, daughter of William Birtwistle who was also a wealthy Blackburn cotton manufacture, had confirmed his position within Lancashire's industrial élite. Through this and his own interests in Messrs Coddington and Lamb at Manchester, he could clearly afford the kind of lifestyle expected of his position in society. Even in 1928, after the near devastating years of post-war recession in the cotton trade he was still worth some £60,000.[47]

When Scott Hayward resigned in December 1903, he was nominally replaced by the vice-commodore J. E. Latham. However, Dudley Coddington emerged as the most prominent member of the club. Only two months later, in early March 1904, a *Yachting World* report of his marriage referred to him as the 'popular commodore of the West Lancashire Yacht Club',[48] and Thomas Rowe—a former honorary secretary—had become the vice-commodore by the end of that year. Dudley Coddington's position had certainly been confirmed by the following season when, as the commodore, he became the butt for some good-natured criticism from Sir George Pilkington at the WLYC annual dinner in December 1905.

There was a danger that yachting might be superseded by motoring, but he hoped not. Yachting was a nuisance to no one; it was the sport of kings, the noblest, purest, and best of any they enjoyed, while motoring was an infernal nuisance—(laughter)—except to the man who sat in the car and left the stink and dust behind him. In their commodore, Mr W. Dudley Coddington, they had a gentleman who was both a yachtsman and a motorist, but he hoped the motor would not be permitted to drive yachts out of favour.[49]

Dudley Coddington sailing the Seabird class one-design yacht 'Seasnipe' off the pierhead in about 1899. The WLYC member crewing on the left was probably E. Winder, while the man in the centre would have been a club boatman.

Coddington certainly lived up to what was expected of him in this respect. During the 1890s he had taken his 12-footer Millie to no less than 200 prizes of which 145 were wins.[50] He subsequently owned and raced a variety of boats, including his half-rater Sea Snipe, with which he had dominated the Seabird fleet in the early 1900s and, according to the *Liverpool Courier*, 'won so many races that the class was endangered if he continued'. In fact, he switched to a Royal Anglesey Class boat named Red Spider which he took to victory in the 1910 Straits Regattas. But he had also purchased a half share in the 7-ton Royal Mersey one-rater Ikinoo the previous year. Until he bought her, Ikinoo had reputedly been a 'bad performer' but Coddington showed what was possible when he steered her to no less than nineteen wins out of twenty-five races during the 1909 and 1910 seasons, which was said to be a record for any class in the Royal Mersey Yacht Club.[51]

Against this background, his decision to resign as WLYC commodore in 1910 might have surprised some members. However, it clearly made sense. William Lawton Hall was more than capable of taking over from him and Dudley Coddington was above all a yachtsman who found the day-to-day routine of any club responsibilities tiresome. That is why he also decided to resign as a Conservative councillor in the same year and he does seem to have preferred the trials of the sea to those facing him as commodore and councillor. The WLYC portrait photograph of him suggests an aloof, if not cold, individual. Yet as a yachtsman he was genuinely liked and often to be found in the 1900s wearing 'a rough red tam o' Shanter'. One story has it that when he beat one ardent rival he celebrated by lending him his motor car 'out of pure sport'.[52] He remained a life member of the WLYC after 1910, but failing health led him to move across to Beaumaris in the early 1920s. It proved a choice which he regretted and he returned to live in Southport in 1926 where he died two years later at the relatively young age of fifty-five.

All of the key figures in the early history of the WLYC were colourful individuals in their own right. Sir George Pilkington was one of the last of the wealthy local patriarchal figures who had ruled the boroughs of Lancashire virtually unchallenged during the late Victorian period. His perhaps unique brand of paternalism certainly helped the WLYC to survive its early years. Meanwhile, Walter Scott Hayward and the Coddington family shared common roots in the middle-class wealth of industrial Lancashire, which ranked second only to London in this respect during the late Victorian and Edwardian years.[53] In Southport they found an accessible and attractive location to pursue their interest in yachting. Had it not been for Walter Scott Hayward's single-minded enthusiasm for small boat racing in the 1890s, the Coddington family could well have stayed within the élitist confines of the Southport Corinthian Yacht Club. Fortunately, they backed his efforts to break new ground with the WLYC and in giving the new club their patronage and practical support they proved themselves far more than just 'figureheads'.

Chapter 6

Years of Doubt

1. Introduction

A T THE END OF THE First World War the WLYC enjoyed a remarkable spell of success in the sense that its total membership rose to a peak of some 250 in 1920. It took well over forty years to regain this level and that recovery reflected the boom in the design and construction of lightweight sailing dinghies which emerged as a remarkable feature of British yachting during the 1960s. Indeed, the 1960s proved highly significant for the WLYC which responded to national trends without forgetting local interests. After many years of talking about it, for instance, there was a revival of racing on the sea in 1962. The widening of the Marine Lake began during the same year and this obviously contributed to the club's decision to move into its modern headquarters. Competition from the newly formed Southport Sailing Club undoubtedly provided a further impetus within the WLYC which helped those members who were arguing the case for changes. With the start of the first 24 hour race on 16 September 1967, it was clear that the WLYC had entered a new and more promising phase of its history.

Just as striking in terms of the history of the club, however, is the simple fact of survival between 1919 and the 1960s. Few members would have taken that outcome for granted in the mid-1920s, with the Bog Hole silting up and the Marine Lake more or less out of bounds. And who could have blamed the members if they had decided to wind-up the whole affair in 1937? The next ten to fifteen years, including the war, produced little more than a holding operation. In fact, the members had become engrossed with the club's move to a comfortable new 'headquarters' on the promenade as early as 1927. After that, they simply worried about how it was going to be paid for. Committees became absorbed with lengthy discussions about the steward's wages, the state of bar profits, the organisation of dinner dances and, later, of snooker or billiards exhibition matches.

All this was far removed from the preoccupation with sailing, and above all else racing, which had dominated the club's activities from 1894 to 1914. Even the post-First World War surge in membership can probably be attributed to the WLYC committee's under-standably generous attitude towards membership subscriptions during and in the immediate aftermath of the conflict. In one respect, they obviously had no wish to offend members on active service—of whom there were at least thirty by 1918—by pressing for subscriptions. Another point is that the club was used to having members who enjoyed secure business or financial backgrounds. The idea that a member would be unable to pay his subscription or meet any boat repair costs does not seem to have arisen in the prosperous days before 1914. Even after the war, Lancashire's industrial base remained more resilient than those of North-eastern England or South Wales. Nevertheless, in the early 1920s, there is every sign of local trading conditions having been affected by the blow to the cotton trade which hit the whole region severely once the brief post-war boom in overseas demand had petered out in the face of competition from the Far East and India.[1] Anyone connected with local industry, the building trade or shipping felt the pinch to some degree even if they were cushioned by income from investments in overseas bonds or reliable home securities.

For the WLYC, which still relied on subscriptions for the bulk of its income in the early 1920s, non-payers remained by far the exception to the rule. Even so, the committee found it increasingly necessary to take steps which would have been unnecessary before the war. Failure to pay a subscription or boat repair and storage bill on time was met with a curt reminder followed by removal from the club list. Enough evidence from minuted records of reminders and warnings exists to confirm that this was more than just a temporary problem in the early 1920s. By 1926, the immediate post-war peak of some 250 members had slumped to only 138. Could it have been that the middle classes in the North West were no longer able to afford to spend so much on yachting as in earlier years? This was possibly true immediately after the war when everyone felt the effects of inflation followed by the shock of a recession from 1921. It is, for instance, of particular note that the sharpest fall came in 'outport' membership which suggests that among those who lived away from Southport there were at least some who decided that the subscription costs were too high in the tight business conditions of the 1920s. As one remarkably frank member who was a building and quantity surveyor put it in his resignation letter to George Simpson, the honorary secretary, in 1926:

> I have no explanation to offer beyond the fact I cannot get paid for the work I have done myself, therefore I am unable at the moment to meet my obligations. In the meantime will you please ask your Committee to accept my resignation, and further-more will you please inform them that I shall pay what I owe at the earliest possible moment.[2]

This was an extreme case, and the committee could therefore afford to be generous in accepting his request which involved a total debt of £17. Even so, the near halving of the membership total from 1920 to 1926, must have included many others who were at least facing the need to economise. That much said, the membership then settled to a steady core of around 160 to 180 members between 1927 and 1939. Despite the closure of sailing on the Bog Hole from 1936, the WLYC retained a loyal following throughout these years largely because the Committee encouraged a greater diversity of activities 'off the water'. Membership certainly recovered slightly, when the WLYC leased its own clubhouse in an impressive suite of rooms above the Victoria Swimming Baths in 1926.[3] From a vantage point opposite the pier entrance, the new clubrooms occupied one of the most prestigious sites in the town. They had been completely refurnished and were now 'thoroughly up-to-date, replete with everything that is likely to enhance the comfort and pleasure of the members'.[4] Certainly, the move to the club's own shore based 'headquarters'—as it was invariably called—opened up new vistas of brushed green billiard cloth and bar receipts in what was from the start an exclusively male preserve.

2. Life on the Pier

Organised regattas and similar yachting events came to an end for the duration of the First World War and even local matches were few and far between, although the YRA recognised that they were acceptable 'amongst those ineligible for military service'.[5] Even cruising was effectively restricted to small boats and most yachtsmen did little if any sailing during the war years. The WLYC's 1914 Yearbook, produced at the end of 1913, shows a full racing calendar of local matches and open events throughout the North West. By contrast, its spartan 1915 edition had no racing calendar and those club members who were not directly involved with the war confined their activities to a routine of committee work aimed at planning for better days. These included proposals for improving the pierhead premises which were kept open throughout the war. In fact the Pier Company directors did what they could to maintain an air of normality about life on the pier. In response to a letter from the Deputy Chief Constable of Southport in February 1915, they had to ensure that any lights shown on the front of the pavilion were 'subdued: the object being to prevent such lights serving as a guide to hostile aircraft'.[6] And there was the slight risk of the odd zeppelin raid in the North West. But this was nothing compared with the Second World War, when the pier was sealed off and occupied by a searchlight battery to combat the much greater threat from bombers.[7]

In that respect, the real problem for the Pier Company in 1914 was not so much the war but the continued silting of the Channel. The paddle steamers had found increasing difficulty in approaching the landing stage on the second pierhead before 1914 and when they returned after being requisitioned during the war it was soon clear that they did not have long to go. That is probably why the relationship between the yacht clubs and the Pier Company went downhill during the war years. By the end of 1917, the WLYC committee had prepared plans for some very modest improvements at their pier head premises. These included the removal of some changing lockers from the first pier head, which had by now become virtually isolated from the sea for most of the time, and locating them 'on the Steps adjoining the Dressing Room at the Second pier Head—the same to be suitably weather-proof'.[8] However, the Pier Company's directors were far from cooperative. At first they simply ignored George Simpson's letters and then, in April 1918, they concluded that the 'Directors see great difficulties in the proposed scheme and regret that they cannot grant the concessions asked for by the Club Committee'.[9]

The signs were not promising! Indeed the Southport Corinthians were facing the same kind of stone-walling and when George Simpson raised the question of the WLYC's tenancy on the pier, a month later, the response was worrying, to say the least. The Pier Company's secretary was told to 'write to Mr Simpson asking him to state on what points in the Agreement they wish to discuss as they do not consider any interview is requisite on the subject'.[10] At least the yacht clubs continued to pay their rent on time, which could not be said for all of the Pier Company's tenants, and this enabled them to hang on. Even so, the correspondence from the Pier Company was distinctly cool and uncooperative. It soon became clear that the directors were fed up with both clubs and that they wanted more rent from them, while also having a tighter control over the activities of yachtsmen on the pier. In September 1921, the Company's patience had run out and their solicitor was 'instructed to give notice to the West Lancashire Yacht Club to terminate their tenancy on 31st December 1921'.[11] A similar notice was sent to the Southport Corinthians[12] and the two clubs had little choice but to seek a new agreement. They decided to act jointly and, a week before their tenancy ran out, they met with the Pier Company to agree new terms which had been drafted in considerable detail.[13] Rightly or wrongly, the WLYC committee had clearly been shaken by what it saw as the unreasonable new demands. On 12 December 1921, the committee held an emergency meeting 'specially called to consider the terms of a new agreement with the Pier Coy—some of which were very drastic'. Charles Henry, then the club captain and George Simpson agreed to join two Southport Corinthian representatives at an eleventh-hour meeting with the Pier Company directors on 22 December.[14]

In fact, what the Pier Company wanted was quite reasonable when one remembers its own perilous financial situation. By October 1920 its bank overdraft had reached £5,400 and there was little chance of raising fresh capital; few people were interested in investing in a pier which was rapidly becoming stranded on a sandbank.[15] Therefore, they tried to squeeze more rent out of the yacht clubs, while they also wanted members to pay tolls and to stop running their own bars, which seem to have been quite profitable! To their credit, both clubs accepted that the demand for extra rent was fair. The WLYC had paid a modest £30 a year until 1909, when it moved onto part of the Corinthians' second pier head premises and the rate had been increased to £44. With wartime and post-war inflation, the Pier Company now wanted £60 and the WLYC representatives agreed to that without further ado. The fact that the Southport Corinthians agreed a new rent of £14—which was also an increase— gives a very clear indication of the extent to which that club's membership and use of the pier had by then declined.

The discussion then moved to other points which say much about the way in which local yachtsmen treated the pier. Although both clubs agreed to these new 'terms', there is every sign that they actually continued to carry on much as before! It was agreed, for instance, that 'heavy Weights & Materials together with Hand Carts are subject to the discretion of the Manager & subject to other Traffic'. Meanwhile, 'All Handcarts to be paid for at usual rates'. The latter was simply an extension of an old issue which was revived in the agreement that; 'All members and Staff to pay all Pier Tolls'. It had always been obvious that the members regarded themselves as tenants on the pier and that, having paid their rent, they did not see why they should then fork out a toll every time they went to the clubhouse. In practice, they seem to have continued to ignore this request for payment whenever they could get away with it. They also agreed that, in future, 'both Clubs close not later than 10.30 each evening'. Again, there is anecdotal evidence to suggest that members were in no hurry to leave on summer evenings during the inter-war years.

On two other issues, though, both clubs dug their heels in and more or less got their way. The directors clearly disliked the use of a signal gun for races and wanted it replaced with some other means of signalling. However, the yachtsmen 'urged that it was most necessary for a Gun to be used, & after discussion they promised as a compromise to Minimise it as much as possible by reducing the charge in Cartridges used'. Possibly, some effort was made to do so. But by all accounts this was another agreement which was not taken too seriously. Finally, though, there were no grounds for a meaningful compromise on the question of the WLYC's long-standing practice of selling drink in their pierhead clubhouse. The Pier Company wanted yachtsmen to use the bars on the pier and it is clear that they had no intention of doing so. This, more than anything else, must have been why the WLYC found the Pier Company's proposals 'pretty drastic'. The Corinthians were virtually pushed aside on this issue, which was reduced to an argument between the WLYC and the directors. The latter caved in, with the mildest of conditions, which could in effect be ignored at will.

> Offers were then made suggesting to them that all drink should be purchased from the Pier Company at a small Commission, but after further discussion upon the proposal of the Chairman it was agreed to Continue as before subject to the Club using the Co[mpan]y's Refreshment Rooms as much as possible to Compensate the Co[mpan]y for loss sustained in allowing them to sell.[16]

Except for a higher rent, which was justified, the end result was that the WLYC carried on its life on the pier much as before the war. Of course, the sailing gradually deteriorated as the Bog Hole silting worsened but this was the last occasion upon which the Pier Company threatened the WLYC's tenure. Disputes continued, largely because the Pier Company was simply unable to maintain the structure and facilities, but the club's tenure of its premises at the first and second pierheads remained secure until the 1933 fire. Meanwhile, the Corinthians actually benefited as well because the Pier Compnany conceded in August 1922 that they could retain the same type of bar arrangements as the WLYC.[17] By then, though, the Southport Corinthians' days were numbered as any hope of an amalgamation with the WLYC had just disappeared and membership was declining.

3. Amalgamation or What?

For many years the two Southport yacht clubs had settled for a gentlemanly truce in which both lived side by side without excessive friction. After the war, the Southport Corinthians' position seems to have been weakened by a further decline in membership. It was therefore logical for the two clubs to amalgamate and share faclities. Unfortunately, logic was the last thing which influenced the discussions towards this end between 1920 and 1924 and it is fair to say that a diehard element in the Corinthians preferred oblivion to what they saw as a take-over by the WLYC.

Howard Sandbach, a local architect, was a member of both clubs and widely respected as a yachtsman and yacht measurer. He also acted as honorary secretary to the Corinthians. At one stage, between 1922 and 1924, the honorary secretary's role was taken over by G. M. Cottam, who actually joined the WLYC in June 1923 at a time when it was clear that any hope of an amalgamation had gone.[18] Other well-disposed and influential members of both clubs included Aristides Bersi and Leo Garge.[19] At this level, then, there was clearly a strong desire to secure a fair agreement and the WLYC accepted that in good faith. In December 1920, for instance, Howard Sandbach sent copies of a Corinthian resolution to George Simpson. 'For the information of your Committee', wrote Sandbach,

> below is a resolution passed at a Committee Meeting of the SCYC held 8.12.1920, 'That this Committee favours joint racing next season, and after the SCYC Jubilee year is completed would be prepared to consider any equitable scheme of amalgamation put forward by the WLYC'.[20]

Ignoring the haughty tone and dubious ancestry, which relied upon the existence of a Corinthian Rowing Club prior to the foundation of the SCYC, the WLYC agreed to joint racing and waited for the rest.[21]

A modest joint racing programme then continued for two years and developed into fairly close links so far as sailing courses and start times were concerned. Meanwhile, the WLYC had long since drafted out its long term intentions. A unanimously approved series of resolutions in November 1921 had outlined three options. The second and third were for various degrees of joint activity in sailing. Both were rejected as permanent measures by the WLYC committee. However, the committee then discussed the first option of 'amalgamation' at great length. The arguments against it were seen as being based on sentiment, the removal of 'friendly competition', a vague 'difference of policy generally' and, the one which probably mattered most, 'difficulties of equal representation'.[22]

While, therefore, the WLYC merely saw the joint racing agreement as a courteous pause during which the SCYC celebrated its 50th anniversary, the latter had yet to make up its mind. When the Corinthians did get round to serious discussions, they were still unwilling to let go of much. They wanted a scheme which gave them 'equal representation' in the new club—nobody seems to have mentioned a name for it!—and it became quite clear that the WLYC had no intention of agreeing to that. In the end the Corinthians came up with a series of proposals which they probably knew would be turned down. Details have not survived, but the WLYC spent months considering these and making its own. By December 1921, for instance, it had approved the 'suggested first 18 Rules of a new Club formed by the amalgamation of the WLYC and the SCYC', which was then sent to Sandbach.[23] At least another four lengthy meetings followed early in 1922. On one occasion, the committee had to postpone due to the 'lateness of the hour', and there is every sign of a genuine desire to resolve things fairly.[24] In the end though it all hinged on 'Clause 5', which seems to have been the impracticable 'equal representation' requirement. By that stage, in April 1922, the WLYC committee were fed up. They resolved that it was 'useless to proceed any further' and dropped the question of an amalgamation entirely.[25]

Relations between the two clubs deteriorated after that. In February 1923, for instance, the Corinthians suggested the usual joint races and were told curtly that the WLYC 'would fix their own courses'.[26] By 1924, the Corinthians were clearly out of the picture. It had become customary since the war for the two Southport clubs to share the cost of their contribution towards the Seabird Association's major racing trophy, the Gibson Cup. But in September 1924, the WLYC heard that the Corinthians' Committee

> has discussed the matter of the Gibson Cup and has come to the conclusion that it cannot pay a share towards the days racing as the Club has not arranged a racing fixture this season.[27]

That, in effect, marked the end of the Corinthians. They had given up their impressive clubrooms above the Victoria Baths on the promenade to the Catholic Club. They had, instead, taken a room at the Queen's Hotel, which was still the WLYC shore base as well. In fact, the Corinthians retained a shadowy existence for a few more years, with its last entry in Seeds Southport Directory appearing in 1931. By then, of course, the WLYC had taken over the clubrooms above the Victoria Baths, which had become its own new 'headquarters' in December 1926.

Ironically, in his official opening of the WLYC headquarters the mayor, Councillor Hibbott, said that 'it took one back to the days of the old Corinthian Club, who used to have these rooms, and it was very fitting that they should follow in their steps'. That such a comment should be a cause for satisfaction is in itself a measure of the degree to which the WLYC had itself lost much of the zest for new ideas which had dominated the earlier years before 1914. No new yacht designs, no Zulu, few invitation races, but plush new leather armchairs and a smart billiard table! Of course, the assembled members and local dignitaries took a different view. Another official guest, Alderman Potts, 'congratulated the club on acquiring these fine premises'. He added that 'they were comfortable and beautifully appointed, and he was sure that it would be an influence in increasing the membership of the club'.[28]

A slight boost in membership of about twenty in the late 1920s gave some grounds for optimism on this score. But any lingering hopes of an early revival were dampened by the club's experiences in the 1930s. The end of sea-sailing was a problem specific to the WLYC, while its impact was undoubtedly compounded by the general sense of uncertainty still prevalent in the cotton and shipping sectors which held an immediate relevance for many members with business interests beyond the town. Even in the more prosperous South of England, the YRA found that yachting activities at all levels during the inter-war years were 'clouded by the national financial crisis'.[29]

4. The National Scene

Elsewhere in Britain, though, this was also a period of innovation in small boat design and racing organisation despite, or maybe in response to, the problems facing most clubs at the time. Tentative trials with the Bermudian rig had established its overall superiority with the Americans taking a firm lead in its development.[30] At the small boat level this influence was reflected in the Bermudian rigged Snipe, which appeared in 1931. The design began as the Florida Trailer Class on a restricted format controlled by the Florida West Coast Racing Association. In that respect, its immediate popularity reflected the far more widespread use of the motor car in the United States, compared with Europe. However, as the one-design Snipe, it rapidly achieved international recognition—with the Manchester Cruising Association adopting it for instance—and it was to remain the world's largest one-design class for the next thirty years.[31]

Meanwhile the YRA was also taking positive steps to repair its relationships with two separate small boat organisations, the Boat Racing Association (BRA) and the Sailboat Association. Both had arisen before the First World War when the YRA rather stubbornly dug its heels in and refused recognition to a growing number of purely 'small-boat' clubs. Yachtsmen of all kinds more than proved their worth during the war and by the 1920s new attitudes had gained ground within the YRA which were, doubtless, partly spurred on by financial realism.[32] J. F. Jellico, a member of the Royal Mersey Yacht Club since 1883, played an important part in bringing about this changed outlook. Jellico was a Liverpool merchant who also became very prominent in the North West as an official yacht measurer and handicapper as well as a trusted broker.[33] He was well known within the WLYC as a valued outport member who had contributed to the club's regular winter programme of talks before the war, and he retained his membership in the early 1920s. Furthermore, he had proposed or seconded leading WLYC members, such as Harry Spurrier in 1910 and Aristides Bersi in 1919, for election into the Royal Mersey Yacht Club; which is doubtless one reason why none of them were ever turned down![34]

At the YRA, Jellico was credited with having originally proposed that the Association should create recognised classes for dinghies just as it had been doing for large yachts since its foundation. His idea led ultimately to the YRA's successful 14-foot and 12-foot dinghy classes.[35] Such new ideas, though, took time to gain ground. At first it seemed that older designs would prevail and there were promising signs for the WLYC. In 1922, for instance, the first Marine and Small Craft Exhibition was held at the Royal Agricultural Hall in London and the Seabird Association was well represented. George Simpson wrote an account of the class for the exhibition and the WLYC lent its photographs of Seabirds which were displayed in its pierhead clubhouse.[36] Meanwhile, a model maker named Jack Heaton had made a half-cut of the Seabird for Messrs Rowlands—a recognised builder for the class—and this had been used in the display. The WLYC committee were, therefore, particularly pleased when Jack presented his model to the club when the Smallcraft Exhibition was over and it still occupies a prominent place above the bar in the new clubhouse.[37] This was recognition at the national level which reached well beyond the specialist columns of the yachting press. If taken with the unprecedentedly large Seabird fleet moored at Southport, any WLYC member who chose to look on the bright side at the end of 1922 could be excused for at least a degree of optimism about the future.

5. Local prospects

Southport was certainly far from dying on its feet. After the shock of the early 1920s, there is every sign of an at least partially successful effort to stem the loss of tourist trade to Blackpool. In a sense, Southport even enhanced its attractiveness for middle-class visitors and residents during the inter-war years. By 1926, for instance, there were already 10,000 motor vehicles registered in the town, which placed it well above the national average per head of population and gives a fair indication of the existence of local spending power.[38] Since the Southport Motor Club had been founded by and for the wealthy in 1902, it had certainly worked hard to attract far more than a purely local interest. In 1926 it organised races on the sands which drew in such outstanding competitors as Major—later Sir—Henry Segrave who established a new land speed record of 160 m.p.h. and earned Southport Motor Club a national reputation as the 'Premier British Beach Racing Club'. With no less than 100,000 turning out to watch Sir Malcom Campbell race in 1928, the club confirmed a well deserved prominence in the racing world and it continued to organise major events on the sands throughout the 1930s.[39]

Meanwhile, the sandhills were proving ideal for golfing. With seven well established links, the Borough of Southport possessed more clubs than any other town in the country. Local confidence in the sport was so high that the prestigious Birkdale Golf Club had already responded to the new opportunities by completely reconstructing its course in 1931 and opening 'a magnificent new up-to-date Club House'.[40] Furthermore, the resort's international status as a golfing venue was confirmed when it hosted the Ryder Cup contests in 1933 and 1937 at the Southport & Ainsdale Club.[41] Inter-war golfing drew its support from the same kind of middle-class social background as yacht clubs and the rules of etiquette, both on the course and in the clubhouse, were if anything more demanding than those expected of the average yachtsman who seemed to like drinking, singing and playing billiards when not on the water.[42] Many WLYC members, however, were also enthusiastic golfers and their new headquarters on the promenade undoubtedly reflected a wish to develop a haven similar to the 'nineteenth hole' of the golf course. It became even more likely that this would happen once sailing had ended on the sea in 1936. Attention switched to social life in the clubhouse which tended to overshadow the original purpose of the WLYC and dampen enthusiasm for new ideas. Indeed, when the Walker Cup was held at the Birkdale Golf Club in 1951, an admiring WLYC committee went so far as to make the captains and members of the US and British teams honorary members 'during their stay at Southport', a privilege which was denied to the club's own lady-members for another fifteen years![43]

The existence of select clubs for those who could afford to play such games as golf or lawn tennis helped Southport to retain its up-market image. Even the crowds who turned up to watch such well organised events as the Ryder Cup were fairly exclusive, not least by virtue of 'the use of gate money not only to meet expenses but to exclude social undesirables'.[44]

The inauguration of the Southport Flower Show in 1924 had much the same effect, creating a serious amateurs' rival to the professionals at Chelsea, while a growing number of national organisations also chose the resort as the venue for their annual conferences, especially after the large Floral Hall had been built alongside the North Marine Lake in 1930.[45] Such events drew in revenue, filled hotels and put Southport on the national map. Indeed, jokes about the disappearing sea meant little to such visitors. The mayor in

1934—Councillor Ashton—made this point as guest of honour at the WLYC annual dinner. 'The problems of the sea', he said, 'had been disastrous to the yachting fraternity—(hear, hear)—except to those connected with model yachting (Laughter)'. But he then admitted that the changes had also produced benefits for the town because they 'had enabled foreshore developments to go forward by providing space for various schemes'.[46]

Few club members could have objected to such realism. Unlike many resorts crammed in by cliffs on the South coast and in Wales, Southport Corporation was actually gaining ground along the foreshore. Despite the setbacks on the pier, after the 1933 fire and the loss of any worthwhile fishing trade, the town was doing quite well as a resort during the inter-war years. Furthermore, the vast majority of Southport's residents began to enjoy the benefits of the new national electricity grid and the all too easily ignored growth in wireless and bicycle ownership, cinema attendances and other leisure activities. Indeed, the town's tourist industry proved remarkably resilient and all local traders must have gained some benefits from the continued influx of visitors. Of course, the realities of the depression were still obvious to those who cared to see them. Southport had its share of poverty, unemployment and ill-health beneath the surface gloss.

For all that, the Corporation attempted to improve many of its facilities and avoided the depressing run-down of municipal spending which occurred in the worst hit industrial towns of Lancashire.[47] While employment in coal, cotton and shipping declined, Southport went against the regional trend by taking its share of the working class holiday trade which grew faster in the late 1920s and 1930s than before the First World War.[48] Population figures for Southport in this period hardly suggest a town in distress when compared to many parts of the North West. The total number of residents increased from about 76,000 to 79,000 in the 1920s and then far more rapidly over the next ten years to some 85,000.[49] Meanwhile, the Corporation continued its efforts to clean up the North Marine Lake and kept the retaining walls in reasonable repair during the 1920s, with more ambitious plans for an expansion in its area by the end of the next decade.[50] The £60,000 spent by the Corporation on a massive new Sea Bathing Lake at the southern end of the Marine Lake left little doubt as to the town's confidence in the future. When it opened in 1928, it ranked as 'probably the finest in the country', and it certainly introduced safe and clean bathing for the great majority of local people and holidaymakers for the first time.[51] The huge crowds around this very impressive pool showed little concern about the loss of the sea and for them the accumulating sands were, if anything, an added attraction.

6. Watching the World go by

If these local developments are taken into account, the severe impact of silting in the Bog Hole upon the morale of the WLYC members becomes even more obvious. There really was no other reason why sailing should have folded up in the way that it did during the late 1920s and the 1930s. Incidents like the pier fire of 1933 only accelerated what was in any case happening gradually. Coupled with access problems on the Marine Lake, it dealt a final blow to any hopes of a revival of local sailing in the near future. Developments in small boat sailing at the national level only served to heighten the sense of crisis for the WLYC. In 1921, for instance, the BRA had become part of the YRA. Over the next four years the YRA then established its rules for a recognised 14-foot racing dinghy class.

Full acceptance at the national level came in 1927, with the first Prince of Wales Challenge Cup event being held for the 14-footers.[52] Meanwhile, very good progress had also been made with a 12-foot class. Acceptance of a 12-foot dinghy event in the 1928 Olympics certainly kept the momentum going. Safety was also improved, with far stricter rules about the need for effective buoyancy tanks,[53] and there is every sign of a genuine official enthusiasm emerging for small and relatively light dinghies which contrasted sharply with the less than welcoming attitude of the Edwardian period. Quite apart from these national classes, which were organised by YRA dinghy committees, the Association also began to support other new designs when it 'recognised' Sydney Cheverton's lightweight British Moth single-hander in 1932. At 11 feet in length with a Bermudian rig and skimming dish hull, this dinghy was far lighter, more manoeuvrable and had greater buoyancy than the pre–1914 single-handers. It remained the most popular British single-hander for at least twenty years.[54]

Some WLYC members, at least, must have watched these events with considerable disappointment. The club's success at the 1922 Smallcraft Exhibition had obviously been shortlived. For all their many attractions the Seabirds and Stars were no match for such new designs. Compared with the heady days of the 1890s and 1900s, the club seemed to be devoid of new ideas and the sale of the Stars to the West Kirby Sailing Club in 1922 could hardly have been regarded as a good omen for the future of yachting at Southport.

7. The Twinklers depart

No serious efforts were made to revive winter racing in the Stars on the Marine Lake immediately after the First World War. Perhaps understandably, there was opposition to the WLYC's later attempts during the inter-war years to introduce a new series for 12-footers on the still relatively confined area of the North Lake. Another forty years passed before the lake was extended to its present width of some 500 metres, with the two 'islands' marking the limits of the original stretch of water. In the meantime, the WLYC's activities would have clashed with the Southport Boating Company's summer interests which grew into a substantial commercial venture with more sailing as well as rowing boats for hire during the inter-war years. In any case, year-round club racing on the lake was an altogether different proposition to the WLYC's earlier out-of-season events for the Stars.

The committee's inability to reach an agreement with the Boating Company needs to be judged in this context. With a heavy seasonal demand upon a local amenity which figured prominently in the Corporation's own efforts to boost the town's tourist trade, the WLYC never had a realistic chance of gaining clear water for racing in the summer at times when its members were likely to take part. Even during the post–1945 revival, when lighter and less expensive marine ply one-design boats prompted a much greater public interest in sailing throughout Britain, the club faced difficulty in gaining the regular access needed for any decent racing programme on the North Lake. In that respect, then, the WLYC had virtually no choice but to use the Bog Hole during the summer months. The pre–1914 concerns about silting and its related hazards in the channel soon overshadowed the optimism underlying the committee's plans for an impressive 1919 'Victory' season.

Unanimous support for a decision by the WLYC committee to organise the sale of the remaining Stars to members of the West Kirby Sailing Club in 1922 was an early sign of the many uncertainties which overshadowed the club's sailing activities during the inter-war years. If they had really wanted to do so, the handful of remaining Star owners could easily have revived their out-of-season racing on the Marine Lake in 1919. But they showed no interest in supporting either the very popular 'invitation' lake races or even a modest 'winter' series of their own. Barely more than ten years earlier, the Stars had been welcomed as a one-design yacht which would allow new members to gain experience in safety and at a relatively low cost. Their plate-down draft of 4 feet 3 inches was just about acceptable for the Marine Lake which approached this depth throughout. That is why lake sailing became part of an informal training route to sea-sailing during the Edwardian period. Many club novices began sailing Stars on the lake and then ventured on to the Bog Hole in them during the season. Progression into either a Seabird or possibly a larger yacht for cruising and some handicap racing had done much to build successfully upon Scott Hayward's earlier efforts.

Enthusiasm had obviously been dampened by the tragic incident in 1913. Following that, the need to suspend the club's sailing activities during the First World War can hardly have improved the prospects for a revival of interest in racing Stars on the sea. Nevertheless, there were hopeful signs that the WLYC had every intention of at least maintaining the existing fleet of Stars after the war. When it came to planning the 1919 'Victory' season's midweek and Saturday series on the sea, for instance, a new Star Committee was elected and given the same standing as the members chosen to represent the, by then, far larger Seabird fleet. Just as many prizes were then offered in the Star class as for the Seabirds and 'Restricted' handicap events for larger yachts. From the WLYC committee's point of view, the aim was very clearly one of encouraging the six remaining Stars to take part in races. Aristides Bersi gave his full support in March 1919 when he provided a new Commodore's Cup for the Stars to be competed for over three 'Victory' races during the season. Several other new Star trophies then appeared in the spring of 1921, including another Commodore's Cup from Aristides Bersi for the regular midweek and Saturday Star series.[55] Indeed, when another club member, E. H. Taylor, offered the Star owners a 'Cup—value £10 for a race to Lytham and back under the rules of that class', the response was one of immediate enthusiasm in which the WLYC committee 'had much pleasure in accepting his kind offer'.[56]

The previous year, Commander Percy Dean VC—who had been a keen club member in the early 1900s—had also presented the club with a 'Cup for a race to Lytham and back'.[57] When coupled with E. H. Taylor's prize specifically for the Stars, there could hardly have been a clearer sign of the club's wish to face up to the memory of the 1913 incident rather than trying to forget it. The sheer scale of the wartime loss of life which hit the North West as much as anywhere else in Britain, certainly overshadowed everything connected with the Edwardian period and encouraged such an attitude of realism. Besides, the Star still managed to attract the occasional young recruit despite the prevalence of older yachtsmen among the post-war Twinkler fleet. It opened the way for John Batten junior (1901–1954)—known as Jack Batten—who joined the WLYC as one of the club's first 'junior' members in June 1918 at the age of seventeen.[58] Like many other club members, his family had firm links with Manchester where his father, John Batten senior (1872–1937), developed a successful business producing glues and resins. As in the club's early years, the Batten family's prosperous middle-class background remained typical of the members who joined in the 1920s. In the case of the Battens, it led to a connection with the WLYC which has spanned three generations to grandson John who is still a club member.[59]

John Batten senior had decided to sell up his share in the family firm at Manchester and move to Southport when his wife became ill during the First World War. He joined the WLYC in about 1917, while his wife and daughter both became members in April 1918 to be followed only months later by Jack. Being only about sixteen years old when the family moved to Southport, Jack Batten was too young for wartime military service and he had to settle to the routine of learning the family business. At this early stage in his career, he spent some time living in rooms at Manchester while he travelled by motor car and rail around

Early post-war optimism: WLYC Seabirds off the pierhead in about 1921. The pierhead can be seen behind Seabirds No. 2, Goshawk, and No. 4, Kittiwake. There are also two Star class one-designs sailing nearer to the pier. The size of the crowd on the pierhead confirms that yachting continued to attract public interest in the post-war years. The second photograph of No. 2, Goshawk, shows the elegant design of the Seabird's hull. Note also that the crew, at least, is wearing a life-jacket, whereas nobody aboard Seasnipe in about 1899 was doing so.
(Photographs by courtesy of Mrs Davies.)

the North West gaining experience. But he still regarded the family house in Southport as his home and there must have been many mornings when he joined the mass of 'white-collar' commuters who caught the 8.10 a.m. train to Manchester. Of course, Jack Batten's mother was too ill to sail and she unfortunately died in 1921. Furthermore, neither Jack's father nor his sister Peggy took much interest in yachting and they appear to have been principally 'social' members. Even so, they were obviously keen that Jack should become a yachtsman because they bought him the Star Vega as a birthday present in time for the 1919 season. He more than justified their faith in him by winning both the midweek and Saturday race series in that year.[60]

Regrettably, Jack Batten was not a typical Star owner during the immediate post-war years. Gone were the days when the fleet met the needs of young members and novices. Its reduced support came from older yachtsmen who could just as well have owned and raced a Seabird and the future of the Stars as a WLYC class was clearly in doubt even by 1919. Of the five remaining boats, only four—including the Batten's Vega—actually raced in the Victory series. Of course, it was much to his credit that he won races against other helmsmen who had competed in at least several years of the Stars' series before the war. But that was hardly the point. The purpose of the class was to provide a regular training fleet for newcomers who were novices and Jack Batten had been the first new recruit for many years while there were no others in prospect to maintain interest if he moved on to Seabirds.

The committee were well aware of the problem. They made a last ditch effort to revive the training function of the class in April 1921, when the Star owners were 'invited to offer a series of three races to Novices for prizes to be offered by the Club'.[61] But these good intentions were overtaken by events and, after a poor season for the Stars which included some uncharacteristically bitter wrangling about a protest committee decision arising from a midweek race,[62] the WLYC negotiated the sale of all five boats in the class to the West Kirby Sailing Club. The offer was one which the owners could hardly refuse because their boats fetched £40 apiece in a heavily oversubscribed ballot for them among the members of West Kirby Sailing Club.[63] By contrast, the going rate at Southport seems to have been considerably less, with the most recent valuation on 'the Star class boat Iris' being set at 'a sum not exceeding £30' in 1920.[64] Jack Batten certainly had no regrets because he used the money to buy the Seabird named Fleetwing and he joined the racing in that fleet for the 1922 season. In fact, he held on to Fleetwing until the WLYC stopped sailing on the sea in 1937.

Why, then, did the Stars leave Southport? Doubtless, an intangible and near superstitious memory of the Cygnet disaster discouraged many would-be new owners. And who could blame them? The Bog Hole was certainly getting worse and any fears about the seaworthiness of a particular class were bound to be magnified with the passing of time. Despite the fact that a well handled Star is perfectly safe in a rough sea, memories die hard and most club members were probably glad to see the red sails of the dwindling fleet depart for West Kirby in 1922. Emotions apart, there were logical reasons for the sale because, at £40 a boat, it was simply a good deal. The Star owners were—like all yachtsmen—facing rising repair costs during the immediate post-war years and the offer therefore came at the right time in this respect. Furthermore, except for Vega and George Simpson's Carina, the Stars were jointly owned. Of course, joint ownership had for some time offered one route by which a person with limited means could get on to the water. Not surprisingly, these early syndicates were common in most yacht clubs and they usually served their purpose well. It went without saying, though, that each part-owner was expected to pay their share of maintenance, laying up and mooring costs.

From 1894 to 1937, when sailing was suspended, the WLYC hired boatmen who went on to winter wages after the season.[65] During the winter months they would lay up, repair and maintain any member's yacht if asked to do so. The honorary treasurer would then invoice the owners before the boats were launched the next season. Regrettably, the two part-owners of at least one Star had quarrelled when one of them refused to pay his share of a repair bill and the boat was not, in fact, allowed to sail in 1921, even though the committee expressed every sympathy for the other member who had paid his share. In this case, at least, the receipt of payment for the Stars from the West Kirby Sailing Club solved his problem. It also helped the harassed WLYC honorary treasurer who was only too pleased to offer a £40 cheque in return for one paying off the £14 still owing to the club. It was left to the two former part-owners to sort out the rest![66]

Overshadowing these possible motives for the sale of the Stars were some obvious long term changes at Southport. The first, as mentioned, was that the WLYC had given up its use of the Marine Lake. More seriously, the continued silting in the Bog Hole had increased competition for mooring spaces in the remaining patch of deep water which enjoyed some shelter from the pier. And here the Star owners ran up against the root cause of their dwindling influence in the club; the growth of the Seabird fleet. Whereas interest in the Stars had declined since 1914, the Seabird fleet had gone from strength to strength. On the eve of the First World War, there were sixteen Seabirds in the WLYC of which twelve raced regularly on the Bog Hole. All of these boats returned after the war for the 1919 Victory

The Star class one-design yachts Carina, No. 4, and Sirius, No. 8, sailing in the Menai Straits in 1963.

season. As soon as it had become obvious that the Seabird numbers were going to hold up, further boats joined the club fleet. During the next twelve months the WLYC Seabird fleet grew to twenty-four boats, of which no fewer than twenty joined the midweek and Saturday series for the class in 1920.[67]

Some of this increase occurred because former joint owners split up and bought an additional Seabird. Dudley Coddington, for instance, sold his share in Skua to Howard Sandbach and became a part-owner of Fansy, with J. Heaton junior. He then left the racing in Fansy to this new member when he moved to Beaumaris. A few others were probably owned by Southport Corinthian members who had accepted the inevitable and joined the WLYC. Certainly, the rapid growth in the WLYC fleet prompted the Seabird One Design Class Association, to organise a special meeting of all Seabird owners at Southport including a handful who remained with the Corinthians. By December 1920, they had agreed upon a joint racing programme at Southport which would, in effect, be controlled by the WLYC.[68]

With numbers on their side, the Seabirds obviously stood up well in comparison to the Stars. Of course, both classes had supporters who believed that their one-design was vastly superior to the other and by all accounts this argument continues today! In reality there is probably little to choose between them in terms of performance. The Seabird's profile, with its carvel construction and sweeping bow and stern is perhaps more elegant and 'yacht-like' in appearance than the Star. Even so, few could dispute the attractions of a Star under full sail. The two Stars shown here in a photograph taken at the Menai Straits in 1962 are proof enough on this count. Their canvassed decking, sturdy bowsprit, solid clinker design and lug rig epitomise an element of continuity in British small boat sailing which has ensured the survival of this and similar classes such as the 18-foot Essex One Design. The nearest Star in the picture is Carina which was one of the eight original boats built for £32 apiece by Latham & Co. at Hesketh Bank. From 1907 to 1915, George Simpson had owned a share in her with other members. Then he remained as Carina's sole owner until she was sold to the West Kirby Sailing Club in 1922. Some fifty years later, she was actually purchased by another John Batten—son of the Jack Batten who was given Vega as a birthday present in 1919—and his late wife Pauline. Indeed, John and Pauline Batten only purchased Carina as a second choice after trying unsuccessfully for Vega, which had also survived as a West Kirby boat since 1922. They owned Carina until 1977 when it was sold to a syndicate of four West Kirby Sailing Club members.[69]

In striking contrast with Vega, the other Star in the photograph is number 8. It is named Sirius and was built in 1948 as a replacement for the original number 8, Mars, which had been lost off Hilbre Island in the Dee Estuary twenty years earlier. It cost £250 to have Sirius built by Williams & Nixon of Deganwy. But this near eightfold increase in building costs, which itself reflected the severe shortage of timber after the Second World War, was to be overshadowed by the inflationary years which followed. Undeterred, two more of these boats were built in 1981—at a cost of £5,000 apiece—so that there are currently twelve near identical Stars sailing with the West Kirby Sailing Club ranging between twelve and eighty-five years old. Largely through the strong support at West Kirby Sailing Club, Star owners have in the meantime resisted several attempts to 'modernise' the boat's design. Except for the inevitable arrival of man-made fibres for sails and rigging from 1956, there have been no significant changes. Indeed, a Star Class Association was also formed in 1988, just over eighty years after the first boats sailed with the WLYC, and if anything this will further strengthen their position as West Kirby's senior class.[70]

Perhaps the most fitting comments about the Star's viability and attractiveness as a one-design class on the modern yachting scene appears in John Millar's fascinating history of the West Kirby Sailing Club. After emphasising their sturdiness and ability to withstand the 'countless gales that can strike at our moorings with the force of a hammer', he turns to their aesthetic appeal and writes that there is 'no lovelier sight on a fine morning than to see those familiar boats with their red sails bobbing along the Dee Estuary'.[71] Those WLYC committee members who decided to sell off their club's entire fleet of Stars in 1921 undoubtedly made a wise choice. It is equally fortunate that they were taken up by another club which had the foresight to retain the strict one-design principles of the class. Purely in terms of location, also, the River Dee proved an ideal base for their new owners to sail the Twinklers in regattas at home as well as throughout the Mersey and along the coast of North Wales.

8. Inter-war doubts?

In fact, the modest success of the West Kirby Sailing Club during the inter-war years is in itself a sign of what the WLYC might have achieved if it had not lost access to the sea. Like the WLYC, West Kirby yachtsmen had to deal with the immediate post-war effects of inflation and then the slump in trade in 1921. However, the West Kirby Sailing Club had more success in retaining members. In 1919, it had 151 members compared with over 200 at the WLYC By the eve of the Second World War, numbers had declined to just under 140 at West Kirby, but they had a very active sailing programme—with no less than fifty-two 'junior members'—and Jock Wallace, the commodore, had just announced plans to build a new clubhouse.[72] By contrast, the decline in the WLYC's membership to a core of about 140 to 150 largely 'social' members by this stage was hardly a promising sign for the future. As if to intensify the sense of gloom, the committee also decided to deposit all of the club's sailing trophies at their bankers, Williams Deacons & Co., in 1937. They were to sit in the bank's Lord Street vault for no less than ten years as unpolished symbols of a club waiting for better days.[73]

Obviously, the silting in the channel played its part in this stagnation. In the early 1920s, for instance, as much as a third to a half of the membership still took part in the racing and cruising on a more-or-less regular basis. By the end of the decade, however, there had clearly been a sharp decline in participation. In the early 1930s, only six Seabirds were racing off the Bog Hole and there were no other trophy events. Nothing, of course, replaced the Stars, but support for the larger yacht handicap events had also faded. The outcome was that the season's prizes awarded at each annual dinner went to a depressingly small group of three or four helmsmen which usually included Leo Garge, Jack Batten and Harold Hall.[74]

For all that, at least some of the old enthusiasm and club spirit survived. It appeared, for instance, during a memorable pair of invitation races with the Royal Windermere Yacht Club which took place for the first—and last—time in July 1934. Behind the customary inter-club courtesy, it degenerated into something of a grudge match for the WLYC. The irritation began at the start of July when a group of WLYC members went up to Windermere in their motor cars only to find a chilly reception. 'As the name may imply', wrote one cynic later on, 'that Club was what might be termed "posh"'. And he added that their 'boats are indeed "posh" being more in the nature of furniture than sailing craft'. Things then took a further turn for worse. While the 'sailing members' of the party were ushered away and treated as guests, the other visitors were not even allowed in the clubhouse and after the race they were not offered a meal. To cap it all, the Royal Windermere won, with the first three places, while the WLYC trailed in 4th, 5th and 6th. This, of course, was entirely due to the 'light and fluky' conditions and their unfair advantage of 'knowing the slants of wind through the gaps in the hills'![75] Although, the WLYC committee formally wrote to 'the RWYC thanking them for their hospitality on 8 July', the aggrieved WLYC members privately viewed their return match with the 'snooty lakelanders' in this 'head in the clouds' yacht club as an opportunity for revenge! Using six Seabirds, it became 'a full blooded affair and not like sailing in a bath with toy craft'.[76] The WLYC race committee chose a conveniently long course from the pierhead four miles down the coast past Ainsdale and back. The resulting victory, with WLYC boats coming in first, second and third was greeted with considerable pleasure; 'the home club ... thus avenged their defeat at Windermere a few weeks ago', recorded the *Southport Visiter* with disarming clarity.[77]

Whatever the long term prospects, then, there can have been few regrets about the way things had gone up to that time. These days off the pierhead could still be remembered with more than a hint of pleasure. For instance, Joe White was one of several pre–1914 members who moved overseas after the First World War to become a factory manager in South Africa. 'Time passes so quickly and imperceptibly', he wrote in a letter to George Simpson in 1941, 'that it is difficult to realise that it is thirty years since I sailed on the Bog Hole.' Apart from one day's visit in 1932, Joe White had not been back to Southport since then and yet for him, like many other members, it seems that the notorious Bog Hole was at least memorable.[78] The club, in fact, recognised his long standing loyalty in 1953 when he was elected an honorary life member and he was one of several overseas members who liked to keep in touch. Joe White, in fact, did so until he died at Capetown in 1966.[79] And such memories were rooted in far more than nostalgia. Even the keenest yachtsmen were content to make the best of the advancing sandbanks when the weather was right. It was, for instance, not uncommon for Seabird owners to beach their boats on on the Horse Bank at ebb tide and stay there with their family for a picnic until the flood enabled them to sail back to moorings. Others liked to go on cockling excursions, returning to the pier with 'these shellfish being gathered and contained in old trousers tied at the bottom of the legs'.[80]

Even the trials and hazards of the Bog Hole could generate grim humour at times. By the early 1930s, the Channel had become so confined that the six remaining Seabirds were forced to moor on the northern side of the pier. Furthermore, the ebb tide now flowed very rapidly under the pier itself which meant that it was no mean feat for a crew to pick up a yacht's moorings successfully. Harry Leigh, later to become commodore from 1951 to 1956, discovered this when he was helming Sea Swallow. He finished the race too late to get back to moorings in comfort. Totally undaunted he swept down to the mooring on the rapidly ebbing spring tide with his spinnaker flying. Unfortunately, he missed, and with a rendering crash sailed straight under the pier. 'It was', he said, 'a spectacular sight to see one's sails, spars and rigging left impaled on the cross bracing of the pier'. Thirty seconds later Sea Swallow emerged on the south side of the pier with oars at the ready!. But what hurt Harry's pride most was the reaction of two young Liverpool lads who had viewed the whole incident. Leaning over the pier rail, one of them said 'Hey! That's bloody clever he's turned it into a rowing boat now'.[81]

Others in the WLYC would remember the snooker exhibition given at the clubhouse by Joe Davies only months before the outbreak of war in 1939.[82] And on at least one memorable occasion, in July 1927, the WLYC organised a return cricket match against the Southport & Birkdale Cricket Club which was actually played 'on a pitch in close proximity & opposite the Pierhead on the Horsebank'. Doubtless the cricket was abysmal. But the Games Committee emphasised that the match, which hopefully had a time limit, 'attracted much enthusiasm both on the Pier and the Horsebank & a most enjoyable game ended in the Cricket Club winning by 7 runs'.[83] It was this ability to enjoy taking part in a round of often competitive and always sociable activities when the club's racing days seemed numbered, which ensured that the membership held up reasonably well even during the late 1930s and then the war years. Despite the Bog Hole, the problems with the pier and the limitations of the Marine Lake, morale seemed to remain high. So much so, in fact, that the WLYC was still around to take advantage of the opportunities in the new world of dinghy sailing which emerged after the war.

It is equally fair to emphasise that many other yachtsmen in the North West were supportive and wanted the WLYC to survive. Certainly, Jock Wallace from West Kirby was among those who wished the club well. He attended the WLYC annual dinner in 1938 and paid tribute to the club's earlier work in creating small yacht designs which 'had been an inspiration to Merseyside'. Quite apart from the Stars and Seabirds, he added that the West Kirby Sailing Club 'had benefitted from that in the class for their 12-foot dinghies which originated from Southport'.[84] His club's sturdy 12-foot Dreadnought dinghies had been racing on the Marine Lake at West Kirby since 1913. They were popular with helms of all ages who found the 100 square feet of sail area manageable, while the centreboard could be raised easily, making the boat particularly suitable for the shallow waters of the lake. That is undoubtedly why several WLYC committees considered them for the Southport Marine Lake during the inter-war years and were put off by the attitude of the Boating Company rather than by the Dreadnought's design. Wallace's comment about the WLYC's contribution probably refers to the 12-foot forerunners to the BRA dinghy, including the near unbeatable Slut. Certainly, the BRA had commissioned its own design just before the First

World War, and this was the one adopted by West Kirby where it survived until the arrival of Cadets and Firefly dinghies after the Second World War.[85]

Unfortunately, the WLYC had by then lost any remaining influence over small boat design. The appearance of the Seabird at the 1922 Small Craft Exhibition proved more of a last fling than a sign of future trends. The emphasis gradually switched to far lighter Bermudian rigged boats designed for the YRA's new dinghy classes. The advent of the National 14 during the 1920s was one success story. Another arose in the 1930s, with the origins of the highly successful National 12-foot class dating from 1936 when boats conforming to the YRA rules competed for the Burton Trophy for the first time. When Sir William Burton—then YRA vice-president—presented his trophy for the National 12-foot class its status as a racing dinghy was assured. After nearly sixty years, competition for this cup remains today as the high point of the National 12-foot class racing calendar.[86] It might well have offered one route by which the WLYC could have retained a sailing programme of sorts if access to the Marine Lake had been even marginally easier. Instead, those club members who still wanted to sail responded with ideas which spanned everything from the feasible to what was little more than a grim reflection upon the hopelessness of the WLYC's position.

On the positive side, for instance, it is fair to say that the WLYC never completely gave up sailing during the inter-war years. When things stopped off the pierhead, a hard core of enthusiasts took their Seabirds across to New Brighton and the Menai Straits. In 1938, for instance, a total of eight WLYC members were reported as having raced their boats at these venues and Leo Garge, then commodore, added that they 'had been welcomed wherever they had gone during the last season, and had been asked why there were not more boats coming'.[87] By then, the Corporation was also beginning to regret the loss of a well handled yacht fleet which had undoubtedly attracted many visitors in better days. During the 1920s, the advance of the silt had become a source of guarded amusement. At the 1925 annual dinner, for instance, the mayor—Councillor Hadfield—raised a genuine laugh when he commented, as a non-sailor himself, that he felt safer on the sea as it became shallower. He must have been sure of his ground when he ventured a step further.

> Somebody had told him that the members of the club were not quite so keen on sailing in the Channel as they used to be but that they were very keen yachtsmen down the Pier (Laughter). He was sorry the Channel was silting up but they still had the Marine Lake, which was very much safer (Laughter).

The truth was, of course, that nobody really liked the idea of trying the lake even if the option had genuinely been available. Members who actually wanted to sail preferred to speculate about the prospects for sailing off Ainsdale or Birkdale, even though 'they had nowhere to keep their boats'.[88] The prize for sheer impracticality, though, must go to the jokers who suggested that the club sail off Wigan Pier 'when there were a lot of craft in the Bog Hole, and it was blowing very hard'. Yes, said Leo Garge in 1938, 'it was a joke, but really there were some attractive sheets of water at Wigan'! In fact, the mayor—Councillor Gedhard—was able to reassure the members

> he had the authority to assure them that when the Marine Lake was considerably enlarged, as it would be in the near future –(hear, hear)—officials of the club would be consulted in order that facilities could be given to them, as a yachting club, to indulge their particular pastime.[89]

During the following year, there are signs of the WLYC preparing itself for this opportunity. In July 1939, as mentioned in Chapter 2, Basil Monkhouse persuaded members to re-establish a sailing committee with the task of preparing a report on how they could start sailing on the Marine Lake again.[90] But there was little prospect of anything being done. Two months earlier, the committee had already decided that with war threatening, it was 'inopportune to seek any reduction' in its headquarters rent from Southport Corporation.[91] And with the declaration of war against Germany on 3 September 1939 all thoughts of sailing were forgotten.

9. A Different Kind of War

During the Second World War the club focussed on its social role and opened its doors to 'any commissioned officer in uniform … as a temporary member during the duration of the war'. Ever cautious, the resolution added firmly 'NOTE—no cheques to be cashed or credit given'![92] But having laid this ground rule the club stuck to its decision throughout the war. On several occasions the members nearly faltered. In October 1941, for instance, a skeleton committee of seven secured a four to three majority in favour of a resolution that 'on account of the shortage at present of refreshments & cigarettes that the Rule regarding Officers of H. M. Forces be rescinded'. However, the dissidents managed to rally enough support to get the decision reversed six to five against only a week later, although it was agreed that 'no further written invitation be sent to any troops coming into the Town'.[93] And that is how the situation remained for the rest of the war. Indeed, in August 1945 the committee decided 'that the privileges this club has given to officers of HM Forces since the outbreak of the War, be extended till the 31st December'.[94]

The most notable feature of the war from the WLYC's point of view was its sheer drudgery and monotony. With little or no sailing activity to attract younger members in the 1930s, the club largely consisted of those who had started yachting before or just after the First World War. Whereas the WLYC had produced a 'Roll of Honour' listing twenty-four members in its 1915 Yearbook as 'O.H.M.S.', there was clearly a less direct involvement during the Second World War. The vast majority of members were over the age for enlistment or in key reserved occupations such as medicine. They faced shortages of fuel, materials, whisky and cigarettes along with the rest of the population on the 'home front'. Most were involved in some aspect of the war effort and the committee members had to adapt as best they could by holding meetings less frequently and with fewer attending. Added to the austerity, were the ever present demands of the 'black-out', which always seems to have been in need of improvement. Then there was the fire watching together, of course, with a permanent fear of an air raid. Being so near to Liverpool, bombing was seen as a real threat in Southport and one can only wonder at the thinking behind the committee's plans in the event of a warning:

> Air Raid Warning … in case of an Air Raid the Steward may use his own discretion about vacating the Premises—should he do so he will fasten a notice on the street door saying the premises are closed & will be reopened when the 'All Clear' is given. He will close the Bar but in the event of any Members being present not wishing to leave—he may leave the Bar open should any member of the Committee be present.[95]

There is no record of this procedure ever having been put to the test! Indeed, the most exciting event occurred on 'VJ night + 1 … with the disappearance of the Union Jack and buntings' from the front of the club headquarters.[96] The guilty revellers were never caught and the club's insurance company actually agreed to the bill of £12 for replacements, with the proviso 'that this did not create a precedent as the property stolen was not inside the Club & was therefore not covered by the policies held by the club'.[97] Having paid very high wartime rates of insurance on its stock and other property throughout the war, without a single claim, the committee clearly regarded the club's position as justified and took the £12.

Looking back over the twenty years from 1926 to the end of the Second World War, it was fortunate that the WLYC had strengthened its social activities by opening the new headquarters. The building became a focal point for members who might well have left in the 1930s. It ensured that the WLYC retained a loyal core of about 160 to 180 members who continued to support the club when, in terms of sailing, there was no longer any logical reason for them to do so. Admittedly, they became more concerned with its social atmosphere than any immediate connections with sailing, but it remained above all a yacht club and it did act as a focal point for those who retained a strong interest in yachting. Many of the photographs and mementos which survive in the modern clubhouse were presented as gifts for the promenade headquarters during the inter-war years. And it is clear that the generosity of many older members, including some of the 1894 founders, was channelled into this direction. Their interest and support included interest free loans in the form of WLYC bonds redeemable at face value when funds allowed. Few, in fact, were redeemed because it became something of a custom in the next ten to fifteen years for members to hand them over to the club for nothing. Sums of £20 or £30 cleared in this way were a further, generally unpublicised, gesture which helped the WLYC to survive until better times arrived.

Before that could happen, though, wartime pressures inevitably brought some decline in membership as people moved away on various forms of government service and were obviously not expected to maintain their subscriptions unless they wished to do so. Others, like Dr Charlick and Rory Moore, both founder members, died during the war.[98] Meanwhile, as might be expected, there was very little recruitment of new members so that the club was left with less than 120 on its books by 1945. That, however, was enough to ensure the WLYC's survival into the post-war years. Support built up again fairly rapidly to around 180 in 1950 after the club began sailing on the Marine Lake again. Then it slowly gained ground over the next ten years so that there were exactly 200 members on the books for the start of the 1960 season.

Chapter 7

New Faces and Old

1. The Great War

A T LEAST THIRTY MEMBERS joined the club's 'roll of honour' as members of the armed forces during the First World War. Perhaps because there was a desire to forget the horrors of the 'War to end War', the WLYC never prepared an honours board after 1918, an error of omission repeated in 1945, and during both conflicts there were undoubtedly some members who were killed in action and simply disappeared from the club records without any acknowledgement. Even so, of nearly thirty who are known to have done some form of military service between 1914 and 1918, it is heartening to find that only three failed to reappear in the 1919 'Victory' members' yearbook.

Beyond that, we know something about the diversity of wartime service undertaken by these people. They included, for instance, Maudie Hall—the daughter of the commodore William Lawton Hall—who went overseas as an auxiliary nurse until the end of hostilities.[1] Among others, Henry Newton became a Lieutenant in the Royal Naval Volunteer Reserve (RNVR), while the club's first honorary secretary, Major J. J. Bailey, had joined the National Reserve in 1914, at the age of fifty-three, served in the army on various duties, including that of adjutant at a prisoner of war camp on the Isle of Man.[2] Nearer home, Major A. J. Pease took over as the Officer Commanding the Southport Battalion of the National Reserve. In the meantime, one of his sons was dangerously wounded in 1918 during service as a Lieutenant in the Durham Light Infantry.[3] Furthermore, the Armistice did not end the trials of war for all members. In January 1922, for instance, the WLYC 'Members learnt with much regret of the death of Mr T. W. Faithwaite caused through a wound received during the war—the Hon. Sec. reported having sent a wreath from the members & also a letter to the family'.[4]

The sheer diversity of these contributions indicates how the Great War reached most homes in Britain in one way or another. Yet there remained individual acts of heroism which stood out above the rest. The yacht clubs belonging to the YRA were justifiably proud of their members who received an impressive number of awards for gallantry; including no less than twenty-four DSCs, seven DSOs, two Albert Medals and, most notable of all, three VCs.[5] The presence of Lieutenant Commander Percy Dean VC in this distinguished group struck an immediate chord with many yachtsmen. Percy Dean was among the numerous yacht club members across the country who had joined the Royal Naval Volunteer Reserve during the war and he was the first officer in this branch of the armed services to gain the Victoria Cross. Inevitably, the fact that he learnt to sail at the turn of the century as a member of the WLYC did not go unnoticed at Southport! In a sense, Percy Dean was from the same mould as Dudley Coddington. Born in 1877, he came from a very wealthy Lancashire family which owned cotton mills in and around Blackburn. His grandfather, John Dean had been a Tory mayor for Blackburn, while his father—John Dean junior—had expanded the family business by purchasing slate quarries at Port Dinorwic. After attending the prestigious King Edward's School at Bromsgrove, Percy Dean joined the family firm in the early 1890s.[6]

Wealthy, well-educated, confident and a good sportsman; he was readily accepted into the tight-knit social circle of yacht clubs around the North West. His yachting began when he joined the WLYC in 1899, after which he bought the Seabird half-rater Seamew from Herbert Baggs in July 1902, while the following month he shipped her over to the Belfast Regattas for the one-design racing between West Lancs' Seabirds and the Donaghadee Sailing Club's Cariads.[7] By then he had become actively involved in the club and he even allowed the members to choose him as honorary secretary at the AGM in December 1902, which indicates that he was still young and keen if not naive![8] He must have got on well with Walter Scott Hayward to even consider taking on this not exactly sought after duty. When Scott Hayward resigned as commodore a year later, however, Percy Dean was one of the three committee members who gave up their responsibilties at the same time.[9] For all that, he remained in the club and regularly took part in racing. He actually won a crew's race for the 0.75-rater class the following season, although he never did very well in Seamew which, for example, was still finishing near the back of the Seabird fleet in 1906 and never appeared in the WLYC prize lists.[10] By 1914 he is listed in the club Yearbook as owning the 11-ton auxilliary cutter Iere which, in fact, Herbert Baggs purchased from him during the war. Meanwhile, though, Percy Dean had joined several other clubs in the North West as his sailing interests switched towards the Wirral. These included the West Kirby Sailing Club, from 1907, followed by election into the Royal Mersey Yacht Club and the Hoylake SC a year later. Early signs of his political interests were also emerging. In 1911 he became chairman of the Young Unionist league at Blackburn, while he went on to win one of the local wards from the Labour Party at the municipal elections two years later.

Away from the view of friends and business connections, though, Percy Dean's private life was following a somewhat turbulent course. John Millar has lucidly described this side of the public hero in his book about the West Kirby Sailing Club. In 1907, Percy Dean's first wife died only a year after their marriage leaving him with a son. There followed a brief romance with a young trainee typist who lived on the Wirral and a secret marriage at a Croydon Registry Office in October 1908, after she had become pregnant. For some twelve years, Percy kept this marriage a secret from his family—including his first son—by living what can only have been a bizarre double life. Financially, this was well within his means and by all accounts he fully accepted the need to support his wife and second son. But he began by promising his second wife, Jeanne, that he was only waiting 'until a more opportune time came to make the announcement'.[11] That time never arrived and, of course, the chances of it doing so diminished the longer he waited.

Meanwhile, business took him to various places in the North West. On one visit to Blackpool in 1913, he was severely injured when he tried washing his feet in a hand basin and it broke leaving a sharp edge which cut a tendon in his leg. By now he was 35 and, through this chance incident, he became unfit for service in the army; as he discovered the following year when he tried to join-up and was rejected on medical grounds. Doubtless many people would have quietly counted this as fortunate, especially after the first months of war began to expose the true horrors of life at the front. In fact, Dean was selected as the temporary chairman of the Blackburn Conservative Party in October 1916—his predecessor became the mayor—but he also persisted with his efforts to enlist and by the end of that year he had been accepted for a commission in the RNVR. As Millar explains, he 'impressed the interviewing officer with the fact that he had done quite a bit of sailing at Southport, on the Mersey and the Dee'.[12] He was immediately posted to the Dover Patrol which made use of fast, well armed, launches to attack German warships in the Channel. Lieutenant Dean's ten-man crew on his fast motor motor launch ML 282 were completely untrained and largely inexperienced with boats. All thoughts of his double life in the North West must have faded as he became totally absorbed in the task of getting ML 282 and its crew ready for action. By April 1917, they were in the Straits of Dover attacking German warships.

Throughout the next year ML 282 continued with its high speed attacks on the enemy in the Straits of Dover. During 1917, however, the German U-Boat fleet was threatening Britain's Atlantic supply routes by sinking merchant shipping at an alarming rate. In fact, those commanders in the Royal Navy who favoured the use of the convoy system to protect shipping were winning the day. Support came from the Americans, who had just joined the war and throughout 1916 there was an increase in the rate of U-Boat sinkings. But the Royal Navy wanted more than this. One of the main bases for the U-Boats lay at the inland port of Bruges, from which they reached the sea through canals to either Ostend or Zeebrugge. Both outlets were very heavily defended, but the Royal Navy planned to close them by sinking block ships, five old concrete filled cruisers and a submarine, at the mouth of each canal. Such an operation required extremely careful planning. Even then, the risks were enormous.

Lieutenant Dean was one of four motor launch commanders chosen, from sixty volunteers, to take part in the operation. His task was to follow the three cruisers into the canal entrance at Zeebrugge and pick up the crews as the ships were scuttled. On the night of the attack, 22 to 23 April 1918, a support landing by Royal Marines, together with the use of a smoke screen and an intense naval bombardment, could only do so much to cover the operation. With extreme coolness and skill, Percy Dean took ML 282 to its pick-up point to find that there were far more men to take on board than he had expected. Dangerously overloaded, and with rudders jammed by debris, he turned and headed for the sea by steering with the throttles of its twin engines. Three of his steersmen were killed by enemy fire and on each occasion he took over himself, bringing ML 282 close into the mole which protected the harbour entrance. Near to the wall he was safe from the huge German guns, but faced a intense machine gun and small arms fire. The crew returned fire, with Dean using revolvers which he had stowed in a rack on the bridge, until they got clear of the harbour entrance. He then had to resist suggestions from other, more senior, officers on board that they head for neutral Holland—and internment—rather than risk being swamped at sea. Fortunately, they were saved by the fleet which found ML 282 and took the wounded and dead on to a destroyer, while the remaining crews of the sunken cruisers were transferred to the larger flagship.

ML 282 then reached Deal Harbour safely, with Percy Dean having been on the bridge for 21 hours during which he had displayed magnificent courage and seamanship. In purely miltary terms, the operation was neither necessary nor a success. The attack on Ostend had failed because the Germans had moved the canal entrance marker buoys and the two blockships were sunk in the wrong place. Even at Zeebrugge, the effects were short-lived. The Germans soon managed to clear a route out for their U-Boats. For all that, the sheer audacity of the raid at a time when the Germans were on the offensive—albeit unsuccessfully—on the Western Front did much to raise civilian morale in Britain. In A. J. P. Taylor's words, it was a 'romantic venture' which 'brought a gleam of light during the days of gloom'.[13]

Official recognition of Percy Dean's bravery followed three months later when the London Gazette announced that he had been awarded the Victoria Cross. But fame had its price as he soon discovered. John Millar makes the point only too clearly when he writes that 'Poor Percy's ordeal was just beginning for when he arrived home everybody wanted him'.[14] To be fair, though, he was probably not surprised by the response. He must have realised that he was the first member of the RNVR ever to gain a VC and that was something of particular significance to yachtsmen who were prominent among the wartime volunteers in this branch of the Royal Navy. But it was not only yachtsmen and yacht clubs who showed an interest. His 'home' town of Blackburn also sought him. The combination of his family's reputation as conservative party leaders in the town and his newly awarded VC must have been irresistible. In the so-called 'coupon election' of December 1918, he stood for the manifesto of Lloyd George's Liberal–Conservative coalition and defeated Philip Snowden, the Labour candidate who had opposed the war, to gain one of the two parliamentary seats for Blackburn.

The campaign against Snowden and other Labour candidates did the coalition little credit and reflects the near hysteria against 'pacifists', however sincere their views, which was one of the less creditable features of British politics in the immediate post-war years.[15] Certainly, Percy Dean was no politician. He got away with it immediately after the war when, at his maiden speech; 'the House was charmed to note that the gallant VC was suffering from a nervousness which he never displayed on the sea'.[16] Nevertheless, he did not stand as a candidate at the next general election in 1922 when Sir Sydney Henn won for the Conservatives at Blackburn, although he was chosen as the leader of the local party in 1930 when Sir Russell Hornby retired and he held that responsibility for three years.[17]

Politics apart, the WLYC was among those yacht clubs which were justifiably proud of Percy Dean's wartime achievements. Within weeks of the Zeebrugge raid, the committee sent a letter 'congratulating him on the successful services he rendered the country whilst in charge of a motor launch in the recent naval blockade of Zeebrugge'.[18] Following the award of his VC he was elected as an 'Honorary Life Member of the Club in recognition of the gallant services rendered to his King and Country'.[19] He was then invited to attend a dinner in his honour at the Queen's Hotel—still the club's shore base at the time—on 21 December 1918.[20] The event revived the atmosphere of pre-war dinners, with guests attending from all the most prominent clubs in the North West, including the Royal Mersey, the West Kirby and Hoylake SC, as well as W. J. Bibby who was by then vice-president of the British Motor Boat Association. Now a Lieutenant Commander, Percy Dean clearly enjoyed the occasion and towards the end of the evening George Simpson presented him with an appropriately inscribed gold cigarette case as well as a silver cigarette box and matchbox.[21]

Private troubles almost swamped this public recognition. His second wife had allowed him to keep their marriage secret, but she became less amenable after the Zeebrugge raid when he returned home to announce that he wanted to leave her and asked for a Deed of Separation. He might have got away with it in pre-war days, but times were changing and Mrs Dean said no! He left her and four years of legal wrangling culminated in divorce proceedings in which he tried to ensure that he only paid a level of maintenance appropriate to her social status as a trainee typist before they were married in 1908. Fortunately, the judge took a different view and, although Dean got his divorce, he had to pay his former wife £1,500 a year while he was also 'awarded'—as they say—the costs of the case. It might not have been what he was hoping for, but the decision did ensure a measure of justice for his wife who stood by him in a way that was, commented the judge, 'impeccable and beyond reproach' for over ten years. Wealth and personal resilience ensured that Percy Dean survived. He actually married for a third time in 1927 and lived in London until he died in March 1939.

Although he maintained close links with Blackburn, Percy Dean appears to have had little contact with his old yacht clubs in the North West from the 1920s and his death passed without comment in the WLYC minutes. However, he did become a member of the Royal Thames Yacht Club, where he maintained his life-long interest in sailing, and he remained a member of the YRA. Furthermore, he kept in touch with many old friends from wartime days. He was, for instance, a member of the RNVR Auxiliary Patrol Club, while Harry Spurrier—commodore when he was at the WLYC—was among the large congregation at the public memorial service held in his honour at Blackburn in 1939. Percy Dean's bravery and skill in war had been truly exceptional and this was never forgotten despite a turbulent personal life which must have played some part in his decision not to seek re-election as an MP in 1922.

2. Changing faces

The commodores who served before the First World War effectively stayed in post for as long as they saw fit. There appears to have been no precedent for removal or determining a fixed term of duty. William Lawton Hall and Harry Spurrier both stood down of their own accord, the latter undoubtedly because his business interests in the motor industry left little spare time. Prior to the war he had been elected as a member of the Royal Mersey Yacht Club, with Dudley Coddigton proposing him in 1910 and J. F. Jellico acting as seconder.[22] His 133-ton auxilliary engined sloop Ranger had been better known on the Mersey rather than in the confines of the Bog Hole, but he was clearly a prominent local yacht owner with a strong interest in the WLYC. During the war, though, the motor industry had expanded at an enormous pace. As a managing director involved with motor vehicle production at Leyland, Spurrier played a key part in these changes. He then had a spell in Berkshire in 1919, which forced him to give up as commodore, although when he returned to the Leyland Motor Works in 1920, he agreed to become the club's second president.[23] Eventually, he could find little time for even this less demanding duty and he wrote to the WLYC committee in September 1923

> intimating that as he was now resident in the South & had little prospect of ever being at Southport & taking any active interest in the Club he wished to resign his Office.

The committee's response indicates that they were still unsure about what they expected of a club president, following the years under 'Sir George'. They hesitated and

> resolved that a letter be sent in reply to Mr Spurrier giving him the best thanks of the members for his very generous help & support in the past & that he be asked to reconsider it.[24]

Harry Spurrier meant what he said, however, and he left the committee with no choice but to make a decision! Did they choose Aristides Bersi, as the former commodore who had succeeded Harry Spurrier and then handed over to John Heyes at the end of 1922, or should they opt for another figurehead? It would have been logical to elect Bersi. Nevertheless, even the measured tone of the club minutes reveal signs of his being out of favour with other members of the committee at this stage. As mentioned in the last chapter, the negotiations with the Southport Corinthians had just ended in disarray with Bersi as commodore and he can hardly be said to have taken a firm line on the matter. He was a former Southport Corinthian member, in the same way that Dudley Coddington and Leo Garge belonged to both clubs. Furthermore, at the AGM in January 1922, the 'Hon. Sec. reported having received a wire from the Commodore (Mr A. Bersi) regretting his inability to be present'[25] and his attendance at meetings remained patchy throughout the following summer. Rory Moore—later to become President from 1936 to 1940—actually resigned from the committee and the club in June 1922. Then a committee meeting chaired by Bersi included several members who 'expressed their regret' at this decision and secured a decision that they; 'absolutely refuse to accept his resignation as a member—he being far too old and valuable a member to lose'.[26] This persuaded Rory Moore to withdraw his resignation and the next committee—this time in Bersi's absence—'unanimously' elected him to the vacant post of rear-commodore.[27] Bersi reappeared at an October committee meeting and one in December, but he was away on 9 January 1923 when, with Rory Moore now in the chair, the

> Question of Flag Officers for 1923 was discussed & several members expressed the opinion that it was an opportune time for a change of Commodore in the interest of the Club.[28]

It fell to George Simpson to let his commodore know! A scribbled draft of his letter the following day has survived, which effectively repeats the above and ends with the cryptic postscript:

> I hope you are having a very enjoyable time, at any rate I know you are away from the awful wrath here.[29]

Bersi did not attend the AGM a fortnight later! The meeting chose him as a vice-president out of courtesy, but he was not elected as president the following year when Spurrier resigned. Instead, now with John Heyes as commodore, they chose a wealthy outsider from Liverpool, W. R. Davies, whose only obvious qualification for the position seems to have been his ownership of the 81-ton auxilliary yawl Vanderdecken. Certainly, he was new to the club. George Simpson did not even know his initials when he wrote up the AGM minutes and they were pencilled in afterwards![30]

Aristides Bersi—Commodore of the WLYC 1919–22, President 1926–35.

It seems reasonable, then, to regard the new president as a compromise choice. The election of Aristides Bersi as president two years later, when things had settled down again, seems to confirm that. Moreover, with the exception of W. Paulden, all other WLYC presidents since the 1920s have previously served as flag officers and this has now become an accepted convention within the club. W. Paulden took over from Harold Hall who had filled in as a stop-gap following Rory Moore's death in January 1940. Hall was then also the club captain. The committee was always having trouble forming a quorum during the war, so that much of the responsibility fell upon Harold Hall, especially after George Simpson's eyesight deteriorated in 1941. The committee was therefore grateful for Paulden's help. He was the Mayor of Southport when he took over as president and undoubtedy brought the club valuable local support during the war. It is a reflection of the members respect for him that he stayed on for ten years before handing the responsibility back to Harold Hall, who became president for a second time in 1951 after a valuable five years' service as commodore.

Harold Hall was also one of what the WLYC still liked to refer to as the 'Manchester contingent' throughout the inter-war years.[31] As earlier chapters have explained, the Manchester connection went back to the foundation of the club and persisted through the First World War. The Manchester Cruising Association was formed in 1914 by yachtsmen in the city who belonged to various clubs in the North West and wanted to meet regularly during the week.[32] At least six WLYC members had joined by 1918, including John Heyes—a wealthy 'jam salesman' and Royal Mersey member—who had succeeded Aritides Bersi as commodore in 1923.[33] Strong Manchester links arose also through the likes of Herbert Baggs, the electrical engineer who had designed the Seabird with Scott Hayward. As might be expected, though, cotton textile interests predominated and—perhaps more surprisingly—were still a factor to be reckoned with after the Second World War. For example, the aniline dye manufacturer John Houston joined in the 1890s and was the WLYC rear commodore when he died in the closing months of the First World War.[34] An early fellow-member, William Shaw (Rory) Moore was a Manchester character who served as a constant reminder of the 'old days'. He raced a 12-footer in the 1890s, followed by the Seabird Puffin which he shared with Raymond Hall in the 1920s and then sold to Raymond's brother Harold. Rory Moore was a manufacturer's agent at Manchester and lived in Southport where, like many other WLYC members, he was also a keen golfer, playing with the Hesketh Club.[35]

Harold and Raymond Hall were influential members with a wide range of business and leisure interests. Both were connected with the cotton trade around Manchester and Oldham during the 1920s. They were both members of the Southport and Ainsdale Golf Clubs, with Harold also joining the Royal Birkdale later on. When Raymond died in 1935 at only forty-eight years of age, he was already the WLYC commodore and vice-chairman of Southport Football Club. He was, reported the *Southport Visiter*, 'a good pal' to many in the town and he had certainly done much to support the club during the inter-war years.[36] His brother served briefly as president when Rory Moore died in 1940 and then handed over this position the following year to concentrate on the work of the club committee in the absence of younger members during the war. In the meantime, his business interests diversified as he became a director of several cinemas in Lancashire, while his election as commodore from 1947 to 1951 and then president for another six years proved crucial for the WLYC's post-war recovery. He was the main instigator of the resumption of sailing on the Marine Lake in 1949 and he still took part as the keen owner and helm of a Flying Ten.[37]

Basil Monkhouse never became a commodore of the club, but he was a key member who was always ready to back new ideas and encourage changes which he often supported with generous gifts to the club. A former cotton broker, he joined the WLYC in 1926 and was never really out of the limelight for the next thirty years. In 1932, for instance, he shared the cost of a new radio for the club with Raymond Hall, while he was then to be found eighteen years later, this time with Harry Leigh, urging a reluctant committee to buy a television set! They gave in after a year, agreeing to buy one 'in the region of £60-£70'.[38] His personal generosity is remembered today through the Monkhouse Cup. In 1951, he gave the then substantial sum of £100 for the club to buy its own 'sailing dinghy for the use of

Members to learn & practice sailing'.[39] A grateful committee decided to respond by purchasing a 'Cup to be called the "Monkhouse" Challenge Cup to be competed for annually by all Club Boat owners'.[40] The event is still held at the end of every season, with the winner being chosen on a very flexible handicap system for individual helms which bears little resemblance to the usual Portsmouth Yardstick ratings! Six years later, Basil Monkhouse was elected a life member in recognition of his long and valuable service to the club, an honour which he shared with Harry Leigh.[41]

Leo Garge—Commodore of the WLYC 1936–46.

As commodore from 1936 to 1946, Lionel—or 'Leo'—Garge was responsible for coaxing members through, perhaps, the worst years of doubt in the club's history. Originally a cotton manufacturer, he was another early WLYC member, joining in 1909, who had also been in the Southport Corinthians. Nonetheless, he had little time for the wrangling which occurred in the early 1920s and he is to be found as a regular WLYC committee member by 1924. Ever the optimist, he had the knack of making the late 1930s annual dinners cheerful occasions even though the sailing on the Bog Hole had stopped, and during the war years he never gave up on the long term aim of the club reviving at some point in the future. His two sons, Tom and Dennis, shared their father's interest as keen Seabird sailors. Tom, the eldest, who became president of the Seabird Association in 1938, sailed Penguin while Leo Garge had Whaup throughout the seasons that the WLYC raced on the Bog Hole between the wars.[42]

By contrast to these figures, Harry Leigh was perhaps the first 'modern' WLYC commodore. He had little time for the old ways and he built on Harold Hall's efforts to bring about significant changes of attitude between 1951 and 1956. In business, he was a local butcher with a successful family firm in Birkdale and he adopted a refreshingly new approach as a WLYC flag officer. He appears as a supporter of just about every proposal for reform in the post-war years with, for instance, the lady members eventually gaining access to the clubhouse because he agreed to it. Harry Leigh certainly had little time for the old fashioned outlook which some members took towards Cyril Davies, the club steward. As vice-commodore in 1950 he became so fed up with the committee's reluctance to employ a stand-in each week—so that Cyril Davies could have a night off—that he 'withdrew from the discussion but wished it to be recorded in the Minutes his great dissatisfaction and considered it a most short sighted outlook'.[43]

Once Harry Leigh was commodore, the 'Steward's night off' became a regular agenda item. A rota was established and, for example, the 'Commodore & Dr Roberts kindly offered to take on this duty' for one evening in September.[44] Indeed, it became the regular practice for two committee members to attend to the bar on Cyril Davies' nights off.[45] Harry Leigh was equally cutting about the attitude of some members towards sailing and his report to the AGM in 1952 can have left nobody in any doubt as to the way things were going.

'the Members were always being thought of, from the point of view of their comfort, installation of two gas fires, a television set etc.', and he thanked the committee for this. But on the 'Sailing side. He did not think that it was being supported as it should be and he requested all Members to try and come down to the lake more often when races were on. He stressed the point to all present, that after all, the primary object of this club was SAILING !!'[46]

Harry Leigh—Commodore of the WLYC 1951-7, President 1957-9.

That view, more than any other, formed the basis for club policy in the 1950s and 1960s. Another key change began in 1957. Dr Angus Robertson had taken over as commodore at the AGM but he died only six months later. He had only joined the WLYC in 1942. However, he was a keen supporter of the sailing revival and bought one of the first Flying Tens in the club. Beyond sailing, his chief contribution stemmed from the fact that he was a well known local figure held in great respect throughout Southport. At a time when the club was fighting to protect its position on the Marine Lake, such influence was invaluable. Born in Glasgow in 1898 he had qualified in medicine at St Andrews University before volunteering for military service in 1914. He had been severely wounded as an officer in the Seaforth Highlanders and it was during his convalescence at Blackpool that he took a liking for Southport—apparently because of its golf links!—and he settled in the town as a general practitioner. Beyond medicine and his golf, he was a member of the Southport Caledonian Club and regularly attended the local Presbyterian Church with his family.[47]

Gerald Pearce immediately stepped in as acting commodore until he was elected by the next AGM which was held in December

Dr Angus Robertson—Commodore of the WLYC 1957.

1957, rather than in March as previously.[48] During this interim period, there was considerable discussion with the Corporation and within the club about the dinghy park and launching slip on the promenade side of the Marine Lake. Meanwhile, the 'vexed question' of the Lady members was still an issue and Gerald Pearce clearly did well to keep things going. Even so, the fact that he was only 'acting' commodore seems to have led to his leadership being resented by the old guard. Somehow, this got on to the AGM agenda and his supporters decided to speak up for him. Three members, including a younger member named Bill Collins 'expressed their appreciation of the way in which the chairman & committee had run the club & gave their assurance that the chairman did have the backing of the club members if he would accept nomination as Commodore.' More significantly, Charles Oliver added 'that it was particularly disappointing not to receive the expected support of older members'![49]

Gerald Pearce was, in fact, then elected as commodore and Charles Oliver followed him two years later. They had clearly settled for a new convention. The role of commodore was certainly becoming more 'political' and called for an increasing amount of time and effort. Any hope of regular sailing had to go by the board for much of the season and that must now have been a very real sacrifice as the club's activities on the water were increasing rapidly. Logic, then, more than any hard and fast rule established the current practice of electing commodores for a maximum of two years. It means that the 'list' of commodores for the past thirty years is nearly twice as long as that for the first seventy! Nonetheless, it has also ensured a regular influx of new faces and new ideas. Equally, those who have taken on the responsibility have not been totally worn out by the growing demands faced by all WLYC commodores since the late 1950s.

3. The Lady Members

Male attitudes towards yachtswomen in late Victorian society appears to the modern reader as extremely patronising. At times, though, women demonstrated such a high level of skill as helms that their talents could not be ignored. In one sense, the customary end-of-season ladies' race—which persists in many clubs today—did not help matters. Men could watch the sailing, even admire the skilful handling, and yet avoid the risk of a direct comparison with themselves. That, in turn, fitted in with the role which most women have always taken as crews, especially in small yachts and dinghies where there was much less use of paid hands than on larger boats. On a growing number of occasions, though, this meant that women were also beginning to make their presence felt in the equally frequent crews' races. When they won, praise was duly given, although not—it should be added—without a strong suggestion that much of the success was down to the guiding presence of a male crew!

There is nothing exceptional about the history of the WLYC in this respect. The club put itself ahead of many with 'Lady' members involved from the early days in the 1890s. Walter Scott Hayward's support for his daughter Gladys emphasised the point, and the WLYC held its first ladies race in June 1899, using 12-foot centreboarders on the sea.[50] By the mid-1900s this had become a regular event, with women sailing the Seabirds very effectively. The 1905 WLYC Ladies' Race actually drew praise from the *Yachting World* as 'undoubtedly one of the best of the season, the way in which the fair skippers worked the boats to windward showing a marked improvement on previous races'. Six boats took part and it was, by all accounts, small yacht racing of a high standard.[51]

Such guarded compliments were probably the best which any women could hope for, not only before 1914 but also for many years afterwards. If anything, the prospects for yachtswomen were better than for their counterparts in sports like tennis, golf and the 'man's world of rowing'.[52] In these, and others like them, physical strength ensures that the male-female divide remains at most levels in sport even today. That does not need to be the case in yachting where skill can be the determining factor if an appropriate design of boat is used in races. In practice, however, yachting at all levels continues to be dominated by men and the reasons for this lie as much in the development of the social side of the sport as in the handling of boats. By ensuring that women continued to play a subordinate role in most clubs—if membership was permitted—yachtsmen managed to keep the sailing skills of their wives, sisters and girlfriends safely under control.

At the WLYC, for instance, lady members were kept out of the main clubrooms for almost seventy years. Meanwhile, they were also denied the right to attend the AGM and the annual dinner, which in effect meant that they had no formal say in decision making. Irritation, perhaps rather resentment, about this situation emerged on more than one occasion after the First World War, which in itself did much to throw the position of all women in British society open to far more debate. Many middle-class women in particular—and they were the norm within yacht club membership—had gained new confidence and a sense of status from the war which had shown that they could secure economic independence in a way which had been denied them in Edwarian society.[53] They proved increasingly less passive when faced with illogical club rules. At the WLYC, for instance, their most effective sanction immediately after the war was simply to leave the club. In 1920, there were thirty-one Lady members, virtually all of whom were either the wives or daughters of male members. By the 1930s their number had dropped to a loyal eight who continued to allow themselves to be 'coopted' on to the occasional sub-committee, to organise the annual dinner-dance for instance, even though they were excluded from the main club rooms. Once the sailing had stopped, any worthwhile connection with the club must have seemed at an end for these women. None remained by the end of the Second World War, and they only started to come back when sailing revived in the 1950s. Indeed, women alone account for the modest rise in total membership during the next ten years, with nearly fifty Lady members in the club by 1959.

The experiences of the formidable Maudie Hall, 'one of Southport's most distinguished yachtswomen', provide just one example of why women simply became fed up with the club during the inter-war years. She returned from wartime 'nursing service abroad' in 1919 and continued to prove herself a match for the club's helmsmen whenever she got the chance to do so.[54] She also crewed regularly for Harold Hall in the Seabird Puffin and appeared as a regular winner of the WLYC's prize in the crews' race. Simply one example is needed to show what problems could arise from her success. At the 1934 annual dinner, the announcement that Miss Hall had won the crew's prize in Puffin was greeted with loud applause, but she was not able to be there to receive it. Almost incredibly, though, Leo Garge the vice-commodore then presented 'two pieces of silver plate in cases to Mr Moore and Mr Bailey, who he said, had no doubt given excellent service to Miss Hall when she won her race'. Rory Moore found this 'all very unexpected': Miss Hall's views were not reported![55]

Meanwhile, the WLYC committee remained unshaken by the election of Miss Christiana Hartley as Southport's first lady mayor in November 1921.[56] Their customary practice since the 1890s had been to invite the mayor to the annual dinner, which always included the main prize-giving. Apparently without a moments thought they simply invited Colonel Dalrymple

White—MP for Southport and a WLYC vice-president—to become guest of honour instead.[57] There is certainly no suggestion of discourtesy in this decision. Club activities, including the bar, snooker and billiards, and events like dinners and 'smokers' were still accepted by men and women alike as male preserves. Even so, the practice of using the exclusive reserve of club-life as an arena for all decision making was increasingly resented by women. Of course, most male members had other 'club' interests, including golf, motoring, the conservative party and strong masonic links, which were the norm for middle-class British men in this period. To that extent, the WLYC lived up to what they expected of a 'club' and it was regarded as a point of principle that they had a right to maintain this status quo.

Obviously, these differences of opinion could not continue indefinitely. Common sense told even the most intransigent that the club could not have lady members and ignore them! At its most blatant, the rise in wages for workers in 'service' and for people who might have worked as paid hands before the war, put a premium on the possible contribution from wives and girlfriends as sandwich cutters and jib trimmers! It was even accepted that they might be able to help with organising the annual dance, and they were drawn into a 'sub-commit-tee'—in this case called a 'Dance Committee'—as early as 1919.[58] They even shared in a 'hearty vote of thanks' in 1920 after the dance made a profit of £25![59] Throughout the 1920s the Ladies' Dance Committee did much to organise what were, by all accounts, very successful social events, including a fancy dress ball at the Victoria Hotel in 1922 and a more formal do at the Palais de Danse in 1925.[60]

Out on the pier, the ladies were also taken for granted. It seems that their ladies' room on the pier had become a combined creche and dropping-in point for male members looking for a cup of tea or Bovril. By 1928, the rightful occupants were clearly fed up with this, and the WLYC committee found itself forced to accept certain ground rules for the ladies' room. The rules were of admirable simplicity; i.e. 'no guests or children allowed in the Ladies Room on Race Days'; and, for the members, 'Gentlemen are only to be allowed in the Ladies Room by invitation and subject to consent of any Ladies present at the time'.[61] To their credit, the WLYC committee 'adopted' these requests without demur. However, they seem to have missed the general point because three years later the club committee decided that it would draft some bye-laws for the ladies' room. To their surprise, seven women imme-diately held a 'meeting of the Lady Members of the WLYC' at the Victoria Hotel in April 1931. They resolved

> not to do any General Catering, but the Ladies would be prepared to cater for any special event if requested by the Committee. It was also suggetsed by Mrs Garge & unanimously agreed that no hard and fast rule should be made for the Ladies room & the arrangements be left to the Lady members themselves.
> Yours sincerely, Elizabeth Hatch.[62]

A comparison of this and some other surnames—Mrs Garge, Mrs Simpson and Mrs Harold Hall—with the list of club commodores suggests that there were at least a few silent drawing rooms in Southport that week! Anyway, the ladies immediately got all that they demanded. In the event, the loss of the pierhead premises soon afterwards and the end of sailing effectively denied them any role in the club. By 1939, there were only eight lady members, compared to thirty-one just after the war, and it is fair to say the the WLYC had become an all-male club. That situation only altered with the revival of sailing and associated growth in social activities during the 1950s, when the club moved in entirely new and more promising directions.

Indeed, the Second War diminished the remaining foundations for the assumptions which allowed the members to run their club as an exclusive male preserve. Experiences gained during the war had in themselves led a great number of people from all social backgrounds to question what they had taken for granted in 1939. Concrete changes, of course, took far longer. But as the WLYC revived its sailing programme, the 'younger element' appears as a term in the club minutes which seems to have been regarded by the committee with a strange mixture of apprehension and relief. Young members were a threat to existing habits but they also pointed to survival and growth in the future. In fact, concessions on the presence of women in the clubhouse had to be made by the mid-1950s, not least because the young men supported them! Gradually, the obstacles to a fairer representation for women who joined the club were reduced. By the early 1950s, in fact, the old guard were clearly losing ground. In 1952, after a 'long discussion' the committee decided that ladies under twenty-one years of age should be allowed in as 'cadet' members—giving them the same status as boys of the same age.[63]

But that was clearly the limit for some members. They became alarmed at the 1953 AGM, for instance, when Bill Collins 'brought up the vexed question of inviting ladies into the Club on special occasions'.[64] Bill was a relatively new inport member, elected in 1947, and he had already started to make his mark on the sailing committee. In 1949, he had argued strongly for the introduction of Fireflys to the club, and he clearly had a knowledge of the modern racing scene beyond Southport.[65] But this obviously carried little weight with many members. Bill Collins supported a very mild amendment to the rule 'governing Lady members', which would have added:

> the Committee may at their discretion, allow Lady Members the amenities of the shore premises up to 9.00 p.m. on the occasion of the Annual Invitation race.[66]

Bill might well have been bewildered by the apparent vehemence with which other members 'ventilated their opinions' against the amendment. But the vote of twenty-six to four defeating it left no doubt as to the strength of that opinion amongst those at the AGM. By this stage, however, this inner core—out of a total membership of some 180—was out of tune with the times. Admittedly, the committee actually discussed the possibility of inviting the lady mayor to the 1954 annual dinner at the Royal Hotel. But they resolved four to three that 'she should not be asked'.[67]

Their resistance to ladies coming into the clubhouse was also increasingly looking simply ridiculous. After the next big open invitation race in September 1954, 140 male visitors and members had a supper of 'Pies, Sandwiches, Cheese & Biscuits' at the headquarters. Meanwhile, it was arranged for 'Approximately 45 Ladies ... to have tea at the Royal Hotel', about fifty yards along the promenade.[68] Perhaps the ladies from different clubs talked to one another over tea? If so, it might not have gone unnoticed that the male members of the West Kirby Sailing Club—and doubtless others—were trying to come to terms with a similar threat. A proposal to let women into the West Kirby SC clubhouse on one evening a week until 10.00 p.m. had been rejected in 1953 as 'extremely dangerous just before the building of the new clubhouse, because it might be difficult to exclude them from the 'men only' room when the new clubhouse was built'.[69] At the West Kirby Sailing Club, in fact, the opening of the new clubhouse in 1955 marked the beginning of the end for male privilege, which now confines men to seclusion in the relatively small billiard room on weekdays.[70]

In the end, it took the building of a new clubhouse across the Marine Lake to shake the remaining diehards at the WLYC in 1967. Meanwhile, their determination could never be underestimated. A special general meeting was called in February 1955 to revise the membership rules and the only contentious issue, again, concerned a proposal to allow ladies into the club 'at the discretion of the Committee'. It led one irate member to protest that this term 'meant nothing and stated that this Club should remain a mans' Club. He also considered it was the thin end of the wedge'.[71] On that point, at least, he was right. Harry Leigh, then commodore, gave his full support to this proposal. His characteristically blunt report to the AGM a month later focussed upon the 'apparent apathy of a number of Members and suggested that the Club wanted an influx of new members'. Rather than face another debate about the rules, however, the AGM opted for a 'Gentlemans' agreement ... without altering the Rules. Whereby Ladies on very special occasions could be invited by the Committee to the Shore Premises'.[72]

That was as far as the committee were prepared to go against the opposition in the clubhouse on the promenade. The rise in the number of lady members from twenty in 1954 to forty-seven by 1959 suggests that the concession suited most needs at the time. Obviously, with more young men joining the club to sail rather than sit at the bar, the social side altered for the better and this, in the long run, must have further weakened any resistance to women using the club's facilities to the full. The next major rule changes concerning lady members were made after the club had moved across to its new premises on Marine Drive in 1967. The WLYC has actually retained a class known as a 'Lady Member' who can only attend the club 'on such conditions as the Club Committee shall from time to time determine'. Such members only have one vote at general meetings compared with inport members who have two. However, any lady over eighteen who wishes to become an inport member may apply to do so if she is prepared to pay the considerably higher annual subscription.

A glance at the current club handbook for 1993 will confirm that the vast majority of lady members do not consider the extra cost worthwhile. At the same time, women now play a far greater role on the WLYC sub-committees. In 1975, for instance, only the Junior Committee showed a fair balance, with five boys and four girls. Beyond that, except for the Ladies Committee, Louise Halliwell was the only woman member, serving on the Publicity Committee. Today, there has been some improvement. Anne Harper has been coopted onto the main Club Committee, because she chairs the 24-Hour Race Executive, and just over a quarter of approximately seventy sub-committee places—excluding the Ladies Committee—are occupied by women. Judging by the experiences of the previous eighty-five years, that is probably all that could be hoped for in the last fifteen.

4. Income and outgoings

One reason why sailing in small yachts and dinghies has become increasingly accessible during the past hundred years is that most of the clubs involved place a very heavy reliance upon voluntary effort. Even the briefest of glances at any yacht club minute book will show that the ubiquitous 'hon. sec.' and 'hon. treas.' represent but part of the story. There has always been a large number of members who contribute towards their club's organisation on a voluntary basis. It is equally important to emphasise that, although yacht clubs are run as a leisure activity, they do have many of the characteristics of a business firm. They can only exist if they succeed in generating a good level of income and, in turn, holding down costs. Like the minutes of any other yacht club, those for the WLYC demonstrate this basic point. The essence of committee work was to tailor the sailing programme to what was affordable or, if the club was more ambitious, finding ways of generating more income.

Everything previously written in this book has focussed on the pleasures and hazards of sailing, together with the diverse social activities of club life. It is not oversimplifying to say that all of these have survived for a century at the WLYC because, whatever the setbacks, successive generations of flag officers and their committees have kept a close eye on the 'books'. In part, yacht clubs were like many others enjoying middle-class support. Their minute books and financial procedures would have done credit to any bank, insurance company, small firm or solicitor's office. And that, of course, is to be expected; a good many of the members were drawn from these occupations and were simply bringing their professional knowledge into their leisure interests. Until 1926, the WLYC even managed without professional auditors. The entire process of keeping revenue and expenditure accounts and producing regular balances fell to a succession of members, most of whom, fortunately, seem to have known what they were doing.

Even so, the opening of the new club headquarters, on a seven-year lease—at £100 per annum for the first three years and £125 after that—made the WLYC's accounts far more complex than they had been previously.[73] For a start, the club now employed two stewards throughout the year. They, in turn, had to run the bar and receive members' payments for the use of the new billiards and snooker table. A summary of the club's annual accounts, which have for the most part survived since 1926, shows the importance of these new revenue sources (see table, Appendix 1, p. 151). Meanwhile the additional costs of the two stewards' wages also had to be taken into the account. After only the briefest of hesitations, the committee realised that the time had come to appoint professional auditors. They chose the Southport firm of Messrs Davies & Crane, with the resolution: 'it now being essential to have qualified Accountants', giving only the barest of hints as to their concern about the cost of the new club headquarters.[74] The choice was clearly a good one, because Davies & Crane have remained as the WLYC auditors ever since.

Until 1927 subscription income was the WLYC's largest form of revenue and it had been declining steadily as the number of people resigning exceeded new applicants. As anticipated, the opening of the clubhouse attracted new members and the total therefore recovered. Apart from the £2 2s. annual subscription for male inport members over twenty-one, there was also an 'entrance fee' of £1 11s. 6d. to pay, which is why subscription revenue rose faster than the rate of growth in membership for a few years after 1926. Even then, the long term significance of bar and billiard receipts immediately became obvious, because the opening of the headquarters added at least £300 to the club's annual income. In fact the overall effect was to more than double annual income within a year, from £376 to £874, and initially to create a profit for the club as well.

At the same time, the wages bill had also risen with the two stewards joining the club boatmen as employees. Wages therefore remained by far the largest single cost for the club during the period to 1959 shown in the table. Until 1927, the boatmen had been the only people who were paid directly by the WLYC and the committee had long since laid down clear rules about how members should use them. By contrast, the club had no direct experience of employing stewards and running what soon became an attractive source of income. The rules on behaviour in the bar, for members and stewards, of dress, times, stock-taking, and so on, emerged as the committee gradually found its feet. The contrast between these two forms of club employment is striking. While boatmen and stewards worked for the same employer, their experiences were poles apart and they shared little in common other than their source of pay and the committee's need to control the costs of both forms of employment, particularly when revenue was tight and there was some concern about the future of the club.

A photograph from the early 1930s showing a club boatman—probably 'Smiler'—with the boat used to ferry members to their moorings.

When sailing ended in 1937, the reduction in the wages bill was easily swallowed up by the gradual loss of members. Even after the Second World War, the club's finances did little more than stagger along until the committee managed to convince the members that an increased subscription would help. They agreed to £3 3s. in 1949 and then £4 4s. in 1957, coupling the latter with concessions on the entrance fee aimed at encouraging new members generally and those under twenty-one in particular.[75] The result was that the total membership at last started to make a significant recovery. Total income was actually rising faster than inflation and the club's finances were moving on to the more ambitious footing needed to take it in new directions. Before considering that optimistic theme, however, the rest of this chapter examines the central part played by the WLYC's employees up to the 1960s.

5. Working for the WLYC

'Clubmen' were paid summer wages from April to October inclusive. On the relatively few times when members asked them to crew as a paid hand, the payment seems to have been made to the club, not the boatman. According to the early WLYC Yearbooks, this also applied for routine sail drying, boat bailing and cleaning. Furthermore, the boats needed to be hauled out and stored for the winter in the WLYC's own shed at Crossens Sluice. Whether sailed to Crossens or towed, the clubmen did much of the work involved in getting the boats out of the water and then returning them to moorings for the new season. That is why their wages were paid from the last week in April to the end of October, which included not only the racing from May to September but also ensured their availablity to bring boats in from moorings and return them the following spring. In theory at least, each boatman

Three photographs taken in the early 1920s
of Seabirds being sculled up Crossens Sluice
by WLYC boatmen and then hauled into
the boatshed.

(Photographs courtesy of Mrs Davies.)

received his instructions from a member via a slip which was to be placed 'in the Box provided for the purpose at the Canteen' on the pier.[76] Apart from ferrying members to and from their moorings, such work might consist of bringing out or collecting heavy gear and any number of minor tasks which have a habit of cropping up on a busy mooring. That apart, if the clubmen were 'available', they could be hired as paid hands at 1s. 6d. per hour from 9 a.m. to 6 p.m. or 2s. at other times.

In fact, the Crossens boat shed figures prominently in the history of the club during the inter-war years. Members had designed and built it for about £200 in 1920 after the local boatbuilder Peter Wright had ended their tenancy on the club's pre-war storage shed at Crossens.[77] The new shed had impressively large doors opening directly on to a slipway into Crossens Sluice.[78] As soon as it was available, in October 1920, the committee introduced storage charges of £4 a year. Boats could either be sailed around, a gradually increasing problem as the silting continued, or members could hire the use of a 'truckle' for 10s. to tow their boat to or from Crossens.[79] Presumably, horses could be used for this 'truckle' in the early 1920s, although enough members had motor cars to make their use possible, say, for a Seabird. Certainly, when a member of the Pilkington family gave the club a new 'trailer' in 1936, it was made available to members for towing Seabirds with motor cars at 30s. hire each way to Menai, 20s. for Mersey and the Wirral and, still, 10s. for the 'Shed'.[80] Regrettably, it was sold off with everything else at Crossens the following year, after the committee had decided to end sailing from the pierhead moorings.[81]

Boat handling was also labour intensive and therefore relatively costly. The two photographs of Seabirds on the Crossens slipway—one being the Batten family's Fleetwing—give an idea of the amount of physical work which hauling out and launching created for the clubmen in the early 1920s when there were still some twenty boats of this class alone off the pierhead. Furthermore, the wages paid to the senior clubman—although far from generous—were higher

A photograph taken in the early 1930s of three WLYC boatmen on the pier. Left to right,
'Wee' William Sutton, Tom Sutton ('Smiler'), and 'Long John'.

during the season than, say, a skilled craftsman would receive. In 1919, for instance, James Lord was still senior clubman from pre-war days, and he received £3 a week during the sailing season.[82] Moreover, this wage rate had increased with prices by the following year, to £3 10s., and the second clubman received £3.[83] Others were also employed on what seems to have been a casual basis and these included Thomas Sutton until June 1920, when he took over as the Senior Clubman at £4.[84] Tom Sutton, known to everyone as Smiler, remained as Senior Clubman until his retirement in 1936, just before the club gave up sailing on the sea.

Smiler's reputation as a boatman had spread well beyond the WLYC by then. As explained in chapter 2, he had been with the club for just over twenty-one years when he retired and during that time he had carried out many a rescue of yachtsmen and others out on the Bog Hole, quite apart from his continued interests in fishing. On the face of it, his wages hardly did justice to his immense value to the club. With prices falling from their post-war peak, the committee 'reluctantly' reduced Smiler's pay for the 1926 season to £3 in 1926 and kept them there until 1933 when, like the club's head steward, Smiler 'voluntarily' took a 5s. cut to £2. 15s.[85] These trends mirror exctly what was happening to wages for skilled men nationally. Comparisons are very difficult, but the wage rates for, say, a skilled bricklayer fell from an average of £3. 13s. to £3..9s. between 1924 and 1936 across the country as a whole.[86] However, the point is that prices also fell more rapidly during this period and the spending power of employees like Smiler and the club stewards had gradually increased. Again, the national figures fairly reflect their own position, with the spending power of their wages at Smiler's retirement being at least 10 percent higher than when the stewards were first employed in 1926.[87]

Another point is that both jobs offered a degree of security not to be found in much of Lancashire's industry of even in sectors like retailing. Besides, there were additional sources of income and benefits for stewards and boatmen which escape these statistics. Neither, for instance had to pay for their work clothing or uniforms, which were purchased as part of the club's regular outgoings—sometimes at more than several weeks' wages—throughout the inter-war years.[88] It took the rigours of wartime clothing coupons to end what was a decided benefit in 1944, when the stewards were allowed a maximum of £2 10s. apiece to buy new trousers 'instead of the Club providing them, and this would enable them to get a full outfit—the waistcoat & coat being at their own outlay'. Hard times indeed![89] Smiler and the other boatmen had retired long before that. But when they were still employed, there was further income to be earned from November to mid-April. Throughout the winter months, for instance, Smiler was paid a 'retaining fee' of £1 a week with the far from onerous 'conditional that he is impowered & willing to contract on his own behalf to do the members boats up during the winter, and that he agrees to act as Clubman next season'.[90]

Of course, the work was hard and the hours were long. Apart from this repair and maintenance work, Smiler regularly joined the other shrimp 'putters' for a day's work in the Ribble Estuary when he was not at the pier with the club. A later article about Smiler described this part of his work as 'a killer—particularly if shrimps were plentiful and they found themselves with their baskets full towards the end of the day'.[91] He was clearly an exceptional boatmen and craftsman, and enjoyed a wide respect for his ability. To that extent, then, although the boatmen were not exactly well paid there were the compensations of perks, a measure of security and considerable respect. Lowerson, in a study of inter-war golfing has referred to the degree of 'social blindness' with which well-to-do amateur golfers treated paid professionals when out on the course and he likens it to the relationship between Scotties 'gillies' and the wealthy anglers who needed their knowledge to catch salmon.[92] And the sea was certainly a great leveller in this sense. Men like Tom Sutton, knew the Ribble Estuary extremely well and were physically better able to stand the rigours of handling boats than most club members. The wise member realised this and offered a kind of mutual respect through which many a newcomer to sailing, as they later generously acknowledged, learnt a lot and could count on help from the clubman whenever it was needed. It does not take too much imagination to picture the reverse situation if an 'unpleasant' member suddenly needed help, for whatever reason!

Compared with life on the water, the steward's lot was safer but potentially more stressful. Members could easily maintain a clear social distance from club employees in the bar and, indeed, the whole structure of rules for the new headquarters seems to have had that aim in mind. Much emphasis was placed upon rules of dress—the stewards wore a 'uniform' style of trousers and waistcoat—as well as on time-keeping and maintaining an appropriately polite attitude towards members. It was clearly a task for a particular type. And with its stewards, as with the clubmen, the WLYC has had a very fortunate record. Those who were approved of and who, in turn, liked the club, stayed. Those who didn't left, mostly of their own accord and always within a short space of time! Typically for their generation, the WLYC's inter-war stewards appear as the remote figures, J. Thompson and J. Grant, with very few indicators about who they were and where they came from. Mr Thompson served as the club's senior steward for over twenty years from 1926 until he retired due to ill health in 1949. From the start he was paid the same rate as Tom Sutton and the changes, including the 'voluntary' reduction of 5s. per week, remained identical. Later on, after Smiler had retired, Thompson received increases which were in line with inflation and had brought his wage to £3 5s. by 1937, while the second steward,

Mr Grant, was paid £1 13s. by this time.[93] Apart from their wages, though, both stewards took the largest share of a customary 'gratuities' collection which the committee introduced as 'Xmas gifts' from 1926 onwards. Members were invited to subscribe a modest amount to this account and donations were actually paid over the bar to one of the stewards who then recorded them in a book.[94] The committee established a system of sharing out this benefit in 1927 and it held good with incredible consistency for thirty years. In 1927, for instance, £22 was collected and this had risen to £35 10s. for 1938. The war led to a slight reduction to 1943, then the practice ceased until 1947 when £44 was collected, rising to £66 by 1950.[95] In the years before 1937, it had been the custom to give Tom Sutton £6 10s. from the total, then everything apart from a small token gift to the 'Charlady'—always under £1—went to the stewards. Indeed, with Tom Sutton's retirement, the payments became almost a steward's right by custom and practice. And the addition of between £15 and £20 to the Senior Steward's wage, at £3 5s. a week in the late 1930s, was obviously a valuable boost to his income.

However, the Second World War changed attitudes gradually and by the 1950s the formality of these payments was clearly viewed as outdated. Indeed, their distribution led to 'lengthy discussions and arguments' as new faces on the club committee questioned the established convention for this as in other things.[96] Sailing arrangements had become the key issue, once again, and committee members of the 1950s gradually avoided the somewhat dated practice of dividing up these 'gratuities'. The House Committee had taken over responsibility for them by 1956 when it decided once and for all to simply leave the matter 'in the hands of the treasurer'.[97]

The Second World War had certainly initiated a change in the relationship between the members and their handful of employees. On the one hand, the committee needed to comply with the terms of the 1943 Wages Act which, among its numerous clauses for club stewards, laid down a strict sliding scale linking wage rates to hours attended.[98] This altered the whole basis for employing stewards after the war, with much tighter statutory rules about their maximum hours of work and holiday entitlements. From 1939 to 1945, however, the sense of crisis appears to have overshadowed the finer points of this legislation. The committee knew that good stewards were hard to find—due to enlistment—and they acted as generously as any club, while always bearing in mind the need for 'reducing expenditure in the present crisis'.[99] For instance, from 1941, the head steward got a 5s. a week rise in wages 'owing to increased cost of living',[100] while the club also introduced a system of fines upon the growing number of members who were arriving late in the bar and wanted it kept open. Of course, the war effort required all civilians to work longer hours. Nevertheless, the committee decided that it was fair to levy a fine on those who kept the bar open after midnight and they had to pay 1s. apiece for every extra hour. The spoils of this informal tax were then shared with the steward, who got seventy-five percent of the total as a reward for his own extra work.[101]

No record exists of how much was collected. However, it is fair to say that in this, as in other instances, the committee backed the club's staff when it was clear that support was needed. Certainly, it was not uncommon for the committee to receive members' allegations of 'incivility' by the staff, or of a lack of punctuality, and so on. These were invariably treated with caution by the committee members who, rather than giving a formal reprimand, much preferred the quiet assurance that a flag officer had 'spoken to' a steward.[102] At the same time, the stewards were expected to report any member who had broken the club's rules to the committee. The consequences of not doing so became evident in 1936. The club's honorary treasurer had decided to pay the substantial bar receipts into the bank less

John Sutton with Jim Morgan's restored Seabird 'Seasnipe' in the early 1970s. The boat is on the hard-standing on the promenade side of the North Marine Lane. The 'islands' can be seen in the background.

(Photograph by courtesy of John Sutton.)

frequently than required. He was forced to resign, although he retained his membership because there had been no question of dishonesty. Meanwhile, the committee decided that Thompson ought to have reported the treasurer's inefficiency to them. He was called in and 'severely reprimanded' in front of the whole committee, the only recorded action of its kind towards staff in the minutes.[103] This must have made Thompson more vigilant, because the following year he reported two members for 'unseemly behaviour' after the annual dinner.[104] They were reprimanded, and one who was actually a valuable committee member had to resign from this position, although he was re-elected several years later.

The terms of service for WLYC stewards gradually changed in the post-war years, especially after Thompson's retirement in 1947. Furthermore, from 1950, the club started to employ boatmen again and faces still familiar to members today appeared on the scene.[105] They have included John Sutton—not related to Smiler—who is justifiably renowned for his craftsmanship as indicated in the photograph of him standing beside Jim Morgan's Seabird named Seasnipe which John had just restored. The recent death of Peter Larkin, in June 1993, will remind many members of another modern boatman who did a great deal for the club in its recent years of change and growth on the sea and at the new clubhouse beside the Marine Lake. Meanwhile, after a false start with a new steward who only stayed for a few months, the committee employed Cyril Davies from September 1950.[106] Cyril was a local man who had been educated at Holy Trinity School and then joined the Royal Air

Cyril and Marjorie Davies at the bar in the old WLYC headquarters on the promenade.
(Photograph courtesy of Mrs Davies.)

Force. After completing his twelve-year engagement, which included war service in India, the Middle East and Italy, he joined the staff of the Royal Birkdale Golf Club in 1949. Fortunately, he decided to move to the WLYC when they were looking for a new steward and he proved an immediate success. Within a month of Cyril's arrival the committee recorded that 'The Commodore was then asked if he would convey the Committee's thanks for his good work during his first month with us'.[107]

'Davies', as he was always known to adult members, retained the committee's full support throughout his long service of twenty-five years with the WLYC. A minute in 1952 thanked him for his 'good work and loyalty throughout the year'[108] and that could just as well have been written of him at any stage when he was with the club. He was certainly a traditionalist when it came to standards of behaviour in the bar and yet he also proved himself to be the ideal person for the club's move into its new premises. There was a phase during the move between 1965 and 1967 when the club had to run two premises and Cyril together with his wife, Marjorie, ensured that everything ran smoothly on both sides of the lake. Their contribution was greatly appreciated by the committee, at a time when some members were far from happy about the changes taking place at all! Cyril Davies further helped matters by ensuring that the new clubhouse retained many of the traditions of the old. It was largely due to him that the WLYC managed to keep some of the atmosphere of its old 'headquarters', with the snooker table, and various mementos which still play a central part in the life of the club today.

Cyril Davies with WLYC members at an October 1966 Fun Race, just before the new clubhouse was built at this location in 1967. John Dennis, the Finn helmsman, can be seen in the background.

As the photographs of Cyril in the 1960s suggest, he bridged the gap between the young and older members of the club. Cyril Davies could be very formal when the need arose and his 'presence' in the club house was all that any traditionalist could asked for, with his efficiency and incredible memory for the names of members and regular guests from other yacht clubs. Meanwhile, he also showed a keen interest in the activities of the 'younger element'. Many members who joined as juniors benefited from the advice and support of 'Mr Davies' during their early years in the club. As Kirk Wilson—commodore 1964–5—writes, 'although a disciplinarian, he established a rapport with them and earned their respect'. Indeed, Cyril Davies was justifiably respected by all those members who knew him and the WLYC greatly regretted the need to accept his resignation in 1975 due to an extended period of ill health.

This chapter has focussed upon the WLYC during a long period of some difficulty in its hundred-year history. The point is that even in such years of doubt, the processes of change and improvement were at least being planned if not initiated. For all the possible criticisms of the WLYC's apparent lethargy in the 1930s and its somewhat crusty image in the next ten years or so, there is no doubting that changes for the better had taken place. Some were simply responses to national pressures within the world of yachting or in society as a whole. Others, however, owed their origin to those members who continued to believe in the club's long term future, not at Wigan or off Ainsdale Beach, but in Southport. The final chapter summarises the changes which arose largely because at least some of the key figures who had been members before and during the war actively supported the new ideas and proposals coming forward in the 1950s and 1960s.

Chapter 8

New Directions

1. A World of Changes

THE WLYC'S EARLY SUCCESS with one-designs drew well deserved praise from the yachting press during the years before 1914. By the 1970s the club could justifiably claim to have more than recovered this early reputation for progressiveness. Total membership had passed 600 and there were over 120 sailing dinghies in the club, quite apart from another thirty or so 'offshore' boats following the revival of sailing off the pier in 1962. The latter has once more declined, with further problems in the Southport Channel. However, the WLYC has retained a strong offshore interest with over thirty boats moored at various locations in the North West. Furthermore, the WLYC holds regular 'offshore nights' at the clubhouse and Bob Willetts—the offshore captain— has organised a highly successful commodore's cruise off the West Coast of Scotland for the past two years.

Even so, the Marine Lake has provided the main focus for the club's impressive growth since the early 1950s. The increase in size of the lake in 1962 and then a move to the new clubhouse on Marine Drive five years later provided the foundations for future growth and development. Plans were still being made for the 'return to the sea' and these certainly ensured a continuity with the past. In the event, though, local 'offshore' sailing has only been possible because the lake attracted a growing number of boat owners who were then prepared to sail on the tide when conditions were safe to do so. Meanwhile, the Marine Lake served as the venue for the vast majority of series and handicap races, training sessions and open meetings.

The WLYC's achievements from the 1950s have taken place in a sport which has itself grown and changed at an unprecedented pace, with new materials, new designs and many more people taking part. Arguably, there were times in the 1950s, at least, when the WLYC could still have been overwhelmed by the sheer pressure and pace of developments else-where. It was due to the combined efforts of flag officers like Harold Hall and Harry Leigh and the newly arrived 'younger element', that fresh ideas were eventually pushed through in time to secure a future for the club. To outsiders, the WLYC had a certain old-world charm about it in the early 1950s and there is no doubt that the sailing members enjoyed themselves immensely from them onwards. Behind the scenes, though, there were some pretty turbulent AGMs and Special General Meetings which serve as a reminder that successive flag officers and their committees had to work very hard to achieve changes. Some idea of the strength of feelings among a vocal minority at the time can be seen from the reaction of one, clearly shocked, member who had just attended a General Meeting about the proposed move to a new clubhouse in 1965. 'During the course of my life', he wrote, 'I have sat through many meetings, but have never witnessed such a sorry exhibition as this from so called intelligent people'. The transition to a modern club was certainly not smooth and peaceful! But then why should it be so? Whatever the content of such discussions, they were certainly preferable to apathy.

The point is that from the late 1940s onwards the WLYC committee members obviously wanted to move in new directions. The priorities were to boost the membership and restart sailing. The questions and disputes concerned such matters as the types of boats to use, where to sail and the future composition of the membership. The all-important discussions about the rights of Lady members have been dealt with in the last chapter. Suffice to emphasise here that women now play a key role in the sailing as well as the social life of the club. Meanwhile, the other two questions have given rise to contrasting responses in the years since 1945. It is fair to say that the discussions concerning the types of boats to be sailed and the organisation of racing were generally rational and increasingly well informed. So too, was the related decision to revive sailing on the sea. By contrast, as just indicated, the move over to the Marine Parade site in 1967 took place in the face of bitter opposition from some members, although the change proved an almost immediate success with everyone as soon as the new premises were open. Certainly, there would have been no 24-Hour race without the new clubhouse and, since it began in 1967, that particular event has done more than any other to give the WLYC a prominent place in the dinghy racing scene throughout Britain.

It is equally important to emphasise the genuine obstacles facing even those members who wanted changes to occur. The club minutes show clearly that old fashioned ideas were fast losing ground by the 1950s, but things still took time to happen. That is why WLYC commodores of the 1950s made a habit of re-emphasising in their AGM reports that 'Rule II states, "The primary object of the Club shall be the encouragement of Amateur Yacht and Boat sailing"'. They got the message through in the end. But it is fair to recognise the difficulty of translating a club resolution, say, to adopt a particular class of boat into action. The outcome also depended on the state of the economy, including the costs of raw materials and the general level of confidence among consumers. These factors carried just as much weight with most potential boat owners as the technical advantages of one design over another or the state of local sailing waters.

In the long term, during the 1950s and 1960s, the growth of white-collar employment, the increase in leisure time and the introduction of new materials reducing real costs, encouraged a boom in dinghy sailing which indicates the existence of a long-felt desire to participate. The number of clubs recognised by the RYA, for instance, rose from 250 to 831 between 1945 and 1958, to be followed by another surge to 1400 by the early 1980s, while sailing also diversified with inland venues and all-the-year-round-sailing becoming popular.[1] Fortunately, the types of new dinghy appearing in the 1950s and 1960s were, if anything, more suitable for the Marine Lake at Southport than for the sea and that was another factor working in the WLYC's favour. Just after the war, though, conditions were still tight for most people and they thought twice before spending money on something like a new boat which even the relatively well-off still viewed as something of a luxury.

Other essentially middle-class activities remained under similar constraints at this time when, for instance, golf 'came slowly out of Crippsian austerity' and did not really begin to recover until the 1960s. Only then did golf clubs start attracting the newer house and car owners of the 'property owning democracy'[2] who were also the most likely recruits for sailing club membership. It is notable, for instance, that the early success of the *Yachting World* Heron class reflected this change, until it was ousted by the even cheaper Mirror in the early 1960s. Designed by Jack Holt in 1951, this 11 feet 3 inches gunter-rigged dinghy was aimed at 'the family who like to store their boat at home and who do not wish to incur the expense of a trailer for taking her to the water'. One, perhaps optimistic, writer added in the 1960s that the 'Heron can easily be stowed on the roof of an average 10-h.p. car resting on rubber chocks or rollers'.[3] Be that as it may, the Heron certainly appealed to a growing number of WLYC members after its first appearance on the Marine Lake in 1955 and the class was to figure prominently in the club's series races of the 1960s.

More recent developments in sailing have ensured that there remains a need to weigh up costs carefully despite rising prosperity. Just under thirty years ago, one popular book about the sport assured readers that the costs of 'clothes are a negligible item since dinghy sailing is an admirable way of wearing out old pieces that would otherwise be on scare-crow duty'.[4] With one or two notable exceptions, such clothing has long since disappeared as today's club members zip into their wet or dry-suits, flashy boots and other 'gear'! It is clear that, along with rising real incomes, new elements of cost have to be reckoned with. Indeed, Tom Vaughan's recent analysis of more than fifty attendances at the national championships of various dinghy classes in 1992 dispels any doubts concerning the powerful impact of economic factors. Referring to the returns for the season, he concludes that 'the near universal fall in support does suggest that it is the current recession that is the single reason for this year's fall off as people have to reconsider their financial priorities'.[5] It is worth remembering this obvious point when discussing the progress of the WLYC since 1945. There was an immense difference between what many members wanted to do and what could be afforded. The club was effectively starting from scratch so far as sailing was concerned and in terms of resources as well as experience this soon became evident.

2. The Revival of Racing

When the WLYC committee met in October 1947,

> The Commodore informed the Meeting that subject to the Committee's approval he, & the Hon. Sec. had withdrawn the Club's Sailing Cups from Wm Deacons Bank, where they had been for Ten years. Taken them to be cleaned & laquered & proposed to display them at the Annual Dinner & afterwards to keep them on the Club premises.[6]

With that, Harold Hall began to revive interest in sailing on the Marine Lake. But progress on the sailing plans still seemed to move at snail's pace because the committee also faced other post-war problems, not least those of timber and other material shortages. Besides, the war had also postponed plans for the extension of the North Lake and there was little mention of starting that project immediately, although the Corporation did carry out a major dredging operation in 1948 and its longer term commitment to further improvements undoubtedly helped to keep things going.

Discussions about sailing continued throughout 1948, while the WLYC also revived its popular social activities. Even during the war, the annual billiards and snooker handicap competitions had kept interest in the club going and these were continued with growing support. The committee also started the traditional annual dinners again and held its first dinner dance since the war in 1948. Meanwhile, by January 1949, the ground had been prepared for a 'Special Sailing Meeting' at which Harold Hall as: 'The Commodore reminded the meeting that the Marine Lake had been dredged, & there were now ... excellent opportunities for getting some good sailing in'. He went on to explain the terms which had been agreed with the Southport Boating Company. Above all, the company was now willing to allow the club sole use for racing on two nights a week after 7.30 p.m. throughout the season, and every Sunday morning of the year until 1.00 p.m., with the

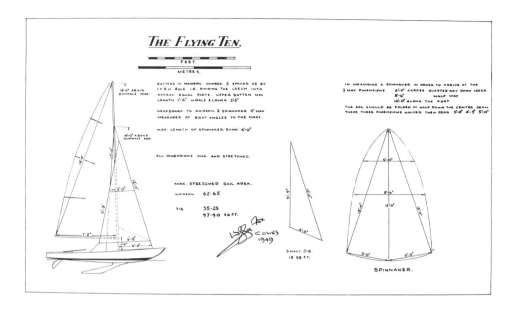

An original plan of the Flying Ten, signed by Uffa Fox.

understandable exceptions of July and August. Even better, the company had agreed to 'provide facilities to store a number of boats on the North Landing Stage'.[7]

Admittedly, the North Lake was still fairly small. But it was better than nothing and the dredging had apparently improved things to the point that it now had an even depth of 4 feet throughout. Even so, ten to fifteen years off the water had left the average member out of touch with what was going on in sailing generally. Harold Hall clearly appreciated this because he invited Sid Cross, the commodore of the West Kirby Sailing Club, to advise the meeting and his extensive knowledge of recent developments proved a great help. The need for such advice soon became obvious when one member admitted, without any protest from the others present, that 'as a social club our activities are second to none:– As a sailing club, through force of circumstances we are, I am afraid, somewhat behind the times'.[8]

Fortunately, the whole tone of the meeting remained friendly and constructive. In a well-informed and realistic discussion, it was accepted that membership would not grow overnight because 'it would be some time before the present generation, now in its early twenties could be coaxed away from other activities'.[9] As an interim measure, the meeting agreed that the WLYC would adopt the Uffa Fox designed Flying Ten keel boat as a class for racing on the Marine Lake. There was some pressure on the members to reach a decision quickly because the club had been offered a five percent discount on the price of £160 per boat if they ordered at least six Flying Tens from the builders, Woodnut & Co. Ltd. Furthermore, the inclusion of Harold Hall, Harry Leigh and Angus Robertson on a list of members willing to 'take delivery' undoubtedly did much to get the ball rolling.[10]

Of course, the choice of the Flying Ten might simply have been taken in response to the wishes of one member who 'thought the older members of the Club who had kept it in being should have a comfortable boat to sail in'![11] More seriously, though, there was much to be said for this decision. The Flying Ten was a relatively modern design which looked very attractive on the water. The boat was also stable, while reasonably small—at some 14 feet l.w.l.—and manoeuvrable. Other advantages were that it could take three people, while the fixed keel draft of only eighteen inches allowed plenty of clearance across the entire lake. Even so, at 310 lbs, the Flying Ten was fairly heavy when compared to the more modern centreboard designs coming along by 1949, including the Firefly and the latest National Twelves. At first it was thought that the Flying Tens would have to be permanently moored in the lake, but that was never agreed to by the Boating Company and the owners had to use a derrick to lift the boats from their cradles into the water each time they sailed. By all

Flying Tens moored beside the slipway on the Marine Lake before the start of a race.

accounts, the system was very efficient, but it obviously took longer than launching a dinghy from a trolley. Besides, with their fixed keels, the Flying Tens could never be used on the Bog Hole, where the moorings now dried out at most low tides. Finally, they were costly boats to maintain. Their eventual demise as a club class in 1963, undoubtedly stemmed from a combination of these factors despite the fact that those who owned them had enjoyed some excellent sailing throughout the 1950s.

The choice of the Flying Ten is therefore best seen as a sensible compromise between the traditional and the new at this stage. The 1949 Special Sailing Meeting considered several other options carefully and gave logical reasons for turning them down. Despite the sturdiness and proven reliability of the lug-rigged BRA 12-footers, for instance, the meeting accepted that they would probably 'soon become antiquated'.[12] On the other hand, the attitude towards the new Firefly allowed for the rustiness of the average member's sailing skills so far as 'livelier' dinghies were concerned. Little progress had been made in this direction even two years later in April 1951 when the club received a tempting offer from the Hollingworth Lake SC. The latter was hosting the North West of England Firefly Challenge Cup in June 1951 and they asked the WLYC to provide a 'Sailing and Protest Committee'. The committee declined with disarming honesty: 'It was felt that no one had the up-to-date knowledge of Firefly racing and rules to do this job efficiently, much to our regret.'[13]

Other clubs in the North West had started to use the Firefly by this stage, but they have only ever appeared on the Marine Lake in limited numbers and never as an adopted class boat. Initially, the WLYC seems to have been all but persuaded of their merits. Members were told that the Firefly was livelier to handle than the BRA 12-foot dinghy which had been considered. It was, however, a new design with a future which cost little more than the BRA 12-footer, at about £125 compared with £100. In fact, Sid Cross tried his best.

> If you want to keep up with the times & race, you cannot beat Fireflys. They could be obtained fairly easily & would stand a lot of knocking about, though he admitted it was no use to take any one out in for pleasure.[14]

After that, several members said that they would guarantee to buy one if the class was accepted and Bill Collins was certainly keen to do so. The point was also made that 'sister' clubs 'at West Kirby, Heswall & so on were running them & inter-club races could be arranged'.[15] Much emphasis was also given to the fact that the Royal Mersey Yacht Club had recently invested in six Fireflys and recruited students from Liverpool University to sail them who had, in turn, then been considerd for the recent Olympic trials.[16] It was certainly a 'modern' and attractive boat, designed by Uffa Fox and constructed from laminated moulded veneers by using techniques which had been developed for building aircraft during the war. Furthermore, the choice of the Firefly as the single-hander class in the 1948 Olympics at Torquay had done much to boost its reputation.

Eventually, in 1966, the University of Liverpool became associated with the WLYC so that eight LUSC Firefly dinghies were at the new club site in the late 1960s.[17] They held their own regular series on Wednesday afternoons and their team actually played a key part in the early 24-Hour races from 1967 onwards. At first, though, there was some hesitation. Despite evidence to the contrary from many coastal venues, Harold Hall argued that 'in any good breeze the sea would be too much for them at the end of the Pier'.[18] There were other cautionary warnings; 'we are trying to encourage those who have not been in a boat at all—it takes years to pick up all the experience required for racing—most members were very inexperienced helmsmen—if they were to interest the older people they should have something less sporty than Fireflys'—and so on. There was still much to do in 1949! Even so, merely taking the decision to start sailing again was enough to break the near-deadlock which threatened the club's future. The early 1950s saw regular racing in the Flying Tens, with a maximum of nine boats in the fleet, and considerable progress was made in either reviving old skills or learning to sail.

However, conditions in the Marine Lake were far from reassuring because it had started to fill in with sand and silt again. By the summer of 1955 the WLYC was getting seriously worried about the shallow water. Better news came at the end of 1955 when the Corporation announced a revival of its plan to extend the Marine Lake. Ministerial approval for a massive commitment of £97,000 was being promised in the local press by December 1955 and this did more than anything else to encourage WLYC members to believe that their club really did have a future at Southport. Apart from the promise of funds, new techniques had been developed when building the dykes for the Zuider Zee—where bitumen was mixed with sand—and it was clear that the project at Southport would at last go ahead.[19] The Corporation obviously stood to gain because the lake was one of its major attractions. Furthermore, it had at last come to regard the WLYC's well handled yachts as an attraction. Quite apart from the series races, the club was also making good progress with its open invitation event for the Coddington Cup. The first in 1954, it will be recalled from the last chapter, brought in over two hundred visitors.

Perhaps the insistence on keeping the ladies out of the clubhouse after the races for the 1954 Coddington Cup was unwise—it did not happen again—but the event was equally notable for its excellent organisation. Sixteen clubs took part in 1954, with two heats,

The Heron and GP14 fleets on the Marine Lake in the early 1960s.

whereas twenty-four turned up the following year and the event was extended into three heats to select the finalists. Ella Coddington actually presented the cup to the 1955 winners in the promenade headquarters and there was a clearly a feeling at the time that another landmark had been reached in the club's history.[20] Furthermore, the Coddington Cup invitation races remained as a highpoint in the WLYC's calendar throughout the 1950s. Indeed, the Corporation realised its potential as an attraction and in 1957 they laid on loudspeakers so that Gerald Pearce—then vice-commodore—could give the public a running commentary! He was obviously good at it because he starred again the following year when he was commodore.[21]

Membership was picking up as well by then and the WLYC had adopted several dinghy classes which put it on the threshold of a rapid expansion in the 1960s. In broad terms, the total number of members had risen to just over 200 by 1960—which was viewed with some satisfaction—but it then increased to more than 600 during the next ten years.[22] By the 1970s, in fact, the 'West Lancs' enjoyed a national reputation, with its diverse activities and achievements bearing very little resemblance to the almost bucolic days of sailing on the lake in the early 1950s.[23] Part of that success lay in the popularity of the new classes. By 1957, GP14s and Herons had their own series races and—with the addition of an Enterprise fleet by 1961—this laid the basis for the WLYC's racing programme in the 1960s. Initially, the Herons did very well, with the fleet reaching a peak of some twenty-five boats in 1962. They had first appeared on the Marine Lake in 1955 when the Ribble Cruising Club brought some of their Herons to the club for a friendly race against the Flying Tens.[24] After that the Heron fleet grew steadily as the boat proved highly suited to the lake while, from 1962, it also performed well on the sea. The subsequent decline to only four Herons by 1971 was largely due to the attractions of the much faster Enterprises and GP14s. In 1971, for instance, the club's GP14 fleet already consisted of fifty-three boats and this had risen to sixty-three only four years later. Meanwhile, the Enterprise did almost as well, with forty-eight boats by 1971. However, that total included six from the Liverpool University Sailing Club and their departure by 1975 partially accounts for the fleet's more modest total of thirty-two boats at this stage.[25]

The presence of large Heron, GP and Enterprise fleets enabled the WLYC to produce a good turnout each week for the series racing; and this allowed the club's younger helms to gain the experience needed for competition at higher levels. By the 1960s, sailors from the 'West Lancs' were making their mark in open meetings throughout the North West and the club produced some of the best helms in the country. John Dennis, for instance, began in GPs and then moved over to the Finn. By 1962, he was taking his Finn—Dolphin—to the World Championships at Tonsberg in Norway, while the following year he did extremely well at an internatioanl event in Holland where he was placed ninth out of seventy-nine boats. John's achievements led to his selection as a reserve for the British Olympic team, but he also ensured that his experience was passed on to other club members. As the WLYC Captain in 1963, he was responsible for the Finn being adopted as a club class and it was launched

Jack Whiteley and Brian Randall sailing their International Finn class dinghies off the pier in the early 1960s.

in style at the start of the season with a champagne reception attended by 100 people, including the mayor.[26] After that, the Finns enjoyed a brief spell of popularity, with seven in the club at one stage, but they then declined. Some of the single-handed sailors joined the other dinghy or offshore fleets, while a few tried Solos in the late 1960s. However, the arrival of Lasers at the club during the next few years met the needs of most members who preferred single-handed dinghies. And this enthusiasm has continued so that—with thirty-three boats—the WLYC currently has one of the largest Laser fleets in northern England.

Andrew Read (right) and Justin Felice, his crew, holding the 1971 GP14 World Championship trophy. His boat 'Dreuid' is standing in front of the new WLYC clubhouse. Dick Atkinson—Commodore 1970–1—is also in front of Dreuid. Other WLYC members in the group include Martin and Reg Sayer, Vic and Julie Basil, Brian and Beryl Randall, Roger and Winnie Whittam, Teddy and Bill Read, Bob Willets, Bob Little, Ian Hirsch, Roy and Margaret Gambie, Herbert Lea, Tom Stout, Charles Wingrove, Bill Aspin, Keith Blackshaw, Tom Finlay, Nick Aubrey, Stan Whittaker, Ralph Pickering and, among the children seated at the front, David Porter on the far right.

Meanwhile, the GP14 fleet results were showing wins for another helm who was to achieve international success. Andrew Read joined the club as a junior in 1961 and he was already making his mark four years later when, at only nineteen, he won the Southport Town Cup and was then the youngest person ever to become the North West Area GP champion when the event was sailed on the sea at Southport.[27] Andrew continued to do well in various championships, and was a member of the winning West Lancs team at the first 24-Hour race in 1967. When he won the North West Area championship for a second time in June 1971, with Justin Felice as crew, it was clear that his boat Dreuid was going very well. Six weeks later, Andrew and Felice took Dreuid to the GP14 World Championships at Thorpe Bay Yacht Club in Essex. With 64 entries, including boats from Ireland and Australia, Andrew put in a remarkably consistent performance in which he counted a 2nd, two 3rds and a 4th place to, as the *Daily Telegraph* put it, 'clinch' the title.[28] Quite apart from their personal achievement, this success by Read and Felice meant that the WLYC gained their first world champions, and it undoubtedly did much to enhance the club's reputation well beyond the North West during the 1970s.

The contributions of individuals like Andrew Read and John Dennis were one aspect of the WLYC's increasing success during the 1960s and 1970s. At the same time, the long term value of training young members began in the early 1960s and has continued to be fully appreciated in recent years. In May 1964, for instance, the WLYC and Liverpool University Sailing Club very successfully hosted the British Universities Sailing Championships, using Fireflys on the Marine Lake. This was the first time that the event had ever been held outside of the London area and it certainly put Southport on the map so far as younger dinghy sailors were concerned. It also led to the LUSC becoming affiliated with the club.[29] Indeed, some three years later, it was a student member of the WLYC, representing the LUSC, who triggered off the idea of a duration race which, as soon as the sailing committee took it up, got a bit out of hand and became the 24-Hour Race.[30]

The WLYC sub-committee structure also evolved in a way which reflected the new priorities. In 1963, the Junior Members were allowed to elect their own committee for the first time and Tony Halliwell—commodore from 1991-2—became their sailing captain. Tony actually went on to win the Oxford University Yacht Club Class 'A' Cup, for experienced helms, in 1965 and 1966 while he remained a member of the

Dreuid.

Sailed & Owned by Andrew Read

8118

Ist. G.P. 14. World Championship. 1971.

Line drawing of Andrew Read's GP14 Dreuid, by P. J. Chester.

WLYC.[31] Furthermore, these junior members eventually provided the core of the WLYC team which won the first 24-Hour Race in 1967. Since the 1960s, in fact, the need to encourage younger members has always remained a priority and another significant step was taken, with the support of a Sports Council Grant in 1987, when the club purchased a fleet of six fibreglass Optimist dinghies built by Moores of Wroxham. That has already proved

The future. Young Optimist sailors and their parents at the WLYC 'Oppie Camp' held beside Lake Coniston in June 1993.

to be a far sighted decision. Above all, it is ensuring that a constant stream of new young members are learning to handle a boat well at a very early age, with the help of experienced 'parent-sailors' like Andrew Berry, Tony and Louise Halliwell, Dave Taylor, Anne Hivey and Nick Miller. This 'pump priming' approach has also encouraged many parents to buy boats for their children and the WLYC now has a thriving fleet of twenty-seven Optimists, which take part in numerous open events as well as a regular club series of races, while two Optimist sailors—David Hivey and Nigel Hunt—have spent time training as part of the National Squad at Torbay.

Although class racing has always been given priority, the club has also made provision for members who want to race dinghies other than Lasers, GPs and Enterprises. There is, in fact, a Mirror fleet of seventeen boats, a few of which take part in handicap races, while these boats are also popular for cruising. Fireflys, Merlin Rockets, International 14s, Toppers, Wayfarers and Laser 2s have also figured among the WLYC dinghy fleet at various times during the past twenty years, to add some diversity and prevent too narrow a focus upon class racing. Another change has been the recent growth in popularity of sailboards. Large numbers have appeared on the Marine Lake in recent years and some of them are owned by WLYC members. It is now possible to race then in club events, although they are used mostly when there is no racing going on and they are particularly spectacular during high winds, when some members clearly prefer the brief inconvenience of falling off a board to righting their dinghy.

Meanwhile, the development of successful racing and training programmes has required sound foundations within the club. The growth of WLYC dinghy and offshore fleets during the 1960s took place against a hectic round of administrative activity. Some of it was simply hard work but apparently good fun, if you happen to like wallowing in mud when helping to set moorings in the Bog Hole. Other duties were more tiresome. Above all, the WLYC flag officers and other committee members soon realised that, quite apart from any remaining objections within the club, they were going to need considerable diplomacy and tact when dealing with Corporation officials, as well as a new Lake licensee and the recently formed Southport Sailing Club.

3. Old Problems, New Faces

Any older member who had welcomed the signs of recovery in the late 1950s could have been forgiven for becoming somewhat gloomy, if not relapsing into despair, by the end of the decade. It would be fair to say that the problems began in 1960 when the Southport Boating Company lost its licence to Tommy Mann who, as immediately became clear, was intent upon injecting a healthy entrepreneurial spirit into the management of the Marine Lake. Until then, the Corporation had allowed the WLYC to use the lake and boat park facilities without charge because, firstly, officials regarded the yachting as a tourist attraction and, secondly, they were realistic enough to realise that the club was in no position to pay a great deal in the immediate post-war years. Tommy Mann took a less charitable view! He required a Lake user's rent and a dinghy park fee for each boat. By March 1960, Charles Oliver—commodore 1960 to 1961—had secured his committee's agreement to accept an offer by Tommy Mann for the WLYC to rent space on the town side of the Marine Lake as a boat park at the considerable rate of 10s. a month for each boat owner.[32] Responsibility for payment rested with the club, which invoiced individual members to recover the fees.[33] With the recently formed Southport Sailing Club (SSC) clearly demonstrating that the WLYC was still failing to provide for a genuine and growing local interest in the sport, the time had clearly arrived for another change in club policy. Rather than simply exhorting existing members to sail, the WLYC needed to open its doors to more people.

Successive WLYC committees, and their membership sub-committees, have struggled with a dilemma since then. On the one hand, they were keen to retain a high standard of sporting and social behaviour while, on the other, they wanted to lose what even sympathetic press reporters viewed as the 'snobby' image of older clubs like the WLYC. Membership figures for the period since 1960 are solid evidence of the success of these committees. It is equally fair to comment that potential competition from the SSC served as a powerful motivator for this change of attitude. As early as June 1960, the WLYC committee was offering to consider applications for membership from 'suitable boatowning members of the Southport Sailing Club'. They were even offered the right to transfer any boat licence fees paid through the SSC for that season, while the WLYC would also allow half of its annual subscription to count as payment for the remaining racing and landing fees due.[34] This very 'modern' offer met with at best a lukewarm response, as the SSC's membership figures and sailing fleets grew more rapidly than those for the WLYC during the 1960s.

Fortunately, the WLYC had the wisdom to realise that the SSC was here to stay and there was a gradual improvement in the relations between the two clubs which, on balance, has probably been beneficial to both. Certainly, each knew that the other was always on the lookout for new ideas and this competitive spirit did much to encourage change. A good start was made in this direction at the end of 1960. Until then, the WLYC had been opposing the SSC's application for RYA recognition on the grounds that they were based in Tommy

Mann's bar at the side of the Marine Lake and, it was argued, he had an undue commercial influence upon their 'amateur' activities.

Lengthy meetings with the Corporation Publicity and Attractions Committee, Tommy Mann and the SSC [35] led to an encouraging reassurance from the latter that 'Mr Mann was no longer associated with the affairs of the SSC'.[36] That was enough for the WLYC committee members who immediately withdrew their objections to the SSC's application for RYA recognition. Another long term benefit, whose timing was too close to be coincidental, was that the WLYC immediately resolved to initiate plans for 'making the club into mixed membership'.[37] With the more obvious barriers to Lady members already being reduced, this alteration to the membership rule—Rule VII—would put both clubs on an equal footing so far as voting rights of members were concerned. The WLYC therefore began the necessary modernisation of its membership rules. At the same time, as if to emphasise its traditional values, the club introduced the now familiar *Golden Lion* newsletter in 1963 and, the following year, the first pre-season annual church service was held at St Andrews Church, in Southport, on 5 April. Both of these innovations received a strong welcome from all members and they have continued ever since. The WLYC committee must have been relieved to find that it could do some things without cost or controversy which were also approved of!

4. On the Sea Again

At first, in fact, the sea actually came to the club in 1958. An unusually high tide in September 1958 flooded over the outer wall of the Marine Lake leaving parked cars stranded with the club's dinghies sailing past them for a brief excursion on to the sea.[38] Less than a year earlier, members at the annual dinner had applauded a proposal to restart sailing on the sea and it is clear that this was one outstanding 'agenda' item which many in the club were determined to see through.[39]

Then, in 1961, while the lake racing was going from strength to strength, Geoff Atherton arrived off the pier in his Hilbre and proved that it was possible to sail in the vicinity for some 2½ hours on either side of high water. The boat also moored safely in a remaining patch of deeper water on the north side of the pier. This early success was soon followed by the massive work on the extension of the Marine Lake which began during the winter of 1961-2.[40] After decades of pessimism, then, the signs for sailing as a whole at Southport were very encouraging. Both clubs clearly benefited from the publicity given to the new Marine Lake project as potentially the largest 'inland' sailing venue in the North and even the Channel was looking more promising again.

Permission had to be obtained from the Corporation before the WLYC could either start organised racing or lay down moorings off the pier. A little persuasion was needed at first, but it is fair to say that local officials were generally very supportive. By November 1961, for instance, the Publicity and Attractions Committee had drafted conditions for the club to use the pier again as a base for off-shore sailing. None of the requirements could be described as unreasonable. The WLYC, for instance, had to guarantee that only club members would use the facilities, while they were quite understandably not allowed to sail 'in the vicinity of bathers', and so on.[41] Having accepted the rules in principle, the club spent the winter planning for its long anticipated revival of sailing offshore. Early signs of interest by dinghy sailors appeared when WLYC members took their boats across to the sea during a high tide in July 1962.[42] This proved that centreboard dinghies could do just as well on

The Seabird Whaup returns to Southport in September 1961, sailed by Jim Morgan and Geoff Binks.

Enterprise class 13 feet 3 inches one-design dinghies sailing off the pierhead in the early 1960s.

the sea at Southport as anywhere else and, in fact, the WLYC went on to host the North West Area GP14 Championships on the Southport Channel in 1965,[43] while the club also organised a very successful Lytham race the following year.[44]

In the meantime, attempts were being made to establish a permanent offshore fleet with moorings in the old Bog Hole. Jim Morgan, then the WLYC Captain, had already got things moving in that direction in July 1961 when he purchased the Seabird Whaup from two members of Wallasey Yacht Club. Whaup had a reputation for being the fastest Seabird on the Mersey, while the fact that she had originally belonged to Leo Garge added to the historic significance of his return trip, with Geoff Binks as his crew, when he sailed her past the pierhead in September 1961.[45] Over the next two seasons Whaup took part in all of the Seabird events in the Mersey regattas, while Jim also bought a second Seabird—Seasnipe— with Martin Clucas, another WLYC member. They picked the boat up from Hoylake and after a hair-raising crossing in force 6 to 7 winds—which included a spell on Formby beach!—Seasnipe also joined the WLYC fleet. Unfortunately, the Southport moorings soon lived up to their reputation for rough conditions and Whaup was sunk during a storm at the end of the 1963 season. She is still laying buried in the sand today, a total loss except for her spars and decking, which came away, and were salvaged. Even so, four other Seabirds had been purchased by WLYC members by the 1965 season and the fleet began to do well in various Mersey regattas, with Andrew Read winning the coveted Gibson trophy in the Seabird inter-station race in 1966, which was the first time that it had been in the club since 1934.[46]

Four of the small Vivacity class cruisers had also appeared on the moorings to strengthen the WLYC offshore fleet which had increased to a total of 28 boats by the early 1970s. By then, however, the larger yachts were moored elsewhere, on the Ribble or in the Mersey and even the Seabirds had been moved away again by the end of the decade. Attempts to revive local offshore activities have had limited success since then, with two Liverpool Bay Falcons moored off the pierhead as a lone reminders of past hopes. There is, however, a keen offshore dinghy fleet which races regularly on the sea with the Falcons when the tide is right. Furthermore, this handicap series of 'tidal' races is open to members of SSC who, in turn, welcome WLYC boats at their winter racing on the Marine Lake.

5. The New Premises

Once the Corporation had gained ministerial approval for the lake extension scheme, it was clear that the WLYC's future lay in this direction rather than on the sea. Funding of some £75,000 was organised and contractors began the process of digging out the new lake area, building sea walls and creating the now familiar 'islands'. There was some concern about the size of the islands which, for instance, the WLYC regarded as too large and likely to restrict racing. In practice, both clubs have adjusted to them very well. The widening of the Marine Lake also created the prospect of a new clubhouse site becoming available on the seaward side. In the early 1960s, the WLYC was already worrying about the future tenure of its promenade headquarters because the Corporation had plans for an improvement to the baths which threatened the position of the club. They had, therefore, started to negotiate for the purchase of a large house on the promenade. However, Charles Oliver and then Ken Colley made progress on the negotiations for the new site, so the promenade plans were dropped in 1962.[47] The negotiations with the Corporation took several years. As the Mayor readily admitted when he attended the WLYC annual dinner in 1964, the 'wheels of local government turn slowly', and it had by then taken nearly two years to confirm all the lease arrangements with the Corporation.[48]

However, this delay had its advantages. Some four years earlier, Charles Oliver had emphasised that they would probably have to move and 'with this in mind it was necessary to conserve & build up club finances'.[49] It was fortunate that the WLYC took this line from the start. While the lease negotiations were absorbing time, the club also set about obtaining estimates and plans. Outline sketches were available by May 1962 [50] and this led to a series of committee meetings to arrange costings for the design and materials. By June 1964, there was a growing network of sub-committees all having a go at various sections of the problem. Fortunately, Lloyd Hayes suggested that it was time to create a special committee to coordinate all 'matters relating to the New Premises'.[51] Kirk Wilson, as commodore, took the chair for these meetings. After his two-year term as commodore, Kirk then remained as Chairman of the Development Committee until the entire project was completed in 1974. George Hayward—commodore 1968-9—was another key member of this committee and he was largely responsible for the financial planning of the second phase of the project after the initial expense of building and moving in to the new premises had been completed.

The creation of a Development Committee chaired by Kirk Wilson enabled successive commodores to maintain the progress of the development with consistency. At the start, however, it took a considerable time to even get reliable estimates. In all twenty-nine contractors had been approached by December 1964 and only three replied.[52] Nonetheless, their ideas

Formal opening of the first phase of the new clubhouse in April 1967. Jack Whiteley is on the left with Kirk Wilson standing immediately next to him. Others present include Harry Leigh, Ben Hepton, Jim Morgan and Charles Oliver. Cyril Davies is at the new bar.
Vic Basil included the half-section of a Flying Ten into the design of the bar and it remains in place today.
(Photograph courtesy of Mrs Davies.)

were apparently acceptable, and the committee had also agreed to purchase some plans for a 'package deal Clubhouse' from Taylor & Woodrow in August 1964, so its members did have enough reliable information to be getting on with.[53] Besides, some progress had also been made with the Corporation on the question of the lease. Kirk Wilson, therefore decided that it was time to seek the views of the members. By December 1964, an informal 'poll' was indicating strong support for the move. Out of sixty-four replies, forty-one wanted the whole scheme, eight a limited version and only nine were against leaving the existing clubhouse. He therefore proposed holding an extraordinary meeting in September to vote on the plans, which were presented in a very informative pamphlet entitled 'Project 65'.[54] Approval was gained at this stage, but the AGM in December 1965 was less peaceful. The funding for the scheme relied very heavily on a Department of Education and Science Grant which amounted to fifty percent of the total costs. By then, with estimates running at around £18,700 for completion, the government's support was obviously vital.[55] But the grant had been frozen and the members at the AGM were understandably worried about proceeding until the position had been clarified. That was fair enough, but by all accounts a few members who were opposed to the move took the opportunity to revive old quarrels and the meeting was far from pleasant. Such fears as the risk that there would be a loss in bar profits because nobody would go over to the new clubhouse in winter were given another airing. Indeed, someone was worried that the sand from the dunes would blast the paint off members' cars at the new site if there was a strong wind!

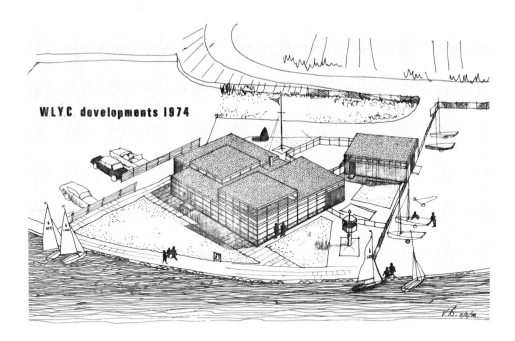

WLY.C developments 1974

A sketch by Vic Basil showing the new clubhouse after the 1974 extension.

Perhaps it is worth emphasising, that a large majority at the meeting actually supported the members of the Development Committee who were 'empowered to proceed with the Project as funds are available at their discretion'.[56] That was enough for the time being. The grant, plus other financial support, came through eventually and the committee returned to the task of planning. Yet again, though, they met with serious problems in 1966 because the original design included brick walls and it seems that their weight would have made the building sink! Vic Basil—a WLYC member—then took over as the project architect in May 1966 and produced an amended plan within a few months. His design relied upon using a pre-fabricated construction with materials which were both lighter and less costly than those envisaged in Project 65.[57] This last minute intervention saved the project from further delays. Meanwhile, Vic Basil had also designed a novel form of control tower. Originally, the idea had been to have the starting box on the clubhouse roof, but his new building could not take the weight. Instead, the commodore—Jack Whiteley—had the idea of producing an enclosed hexagonal shaped metal structure, with all-round windows, which would be supported upon a steel pillar. As Jack was the managing director of a Liverpool engineering firm, he knew that the idea could work and he offered to make the tower free of charge at his factory if Vic Basil could design it. The end result, still a centrepiece of the club today, won a design award both for originality and its aesthetic appeal.

With the committee pressing on, and the new plans viable, the Marine Parade premises were ready for a formal opening by Jack Whiteley in April 1967. Few of the thousands of visitors milling around the clubhouse and starting tower at the first 24-Hour Race only five months later probably noticed either, let alone appreciating how much time and trouble the original project had taken. For all that, the success of this race and of the many open meetings which have followed is in itself a tribute to the effort of those who organised the move from the old clubhouse. Furthermore, a second phase of the project began in December 1973, when the members approved an extension of the existing ground floor. Again, plans for a second storey were wisely dropped and the club has kept to the original principle of relying upon a lightweight structure which is fairly easily maintained, light and airy, but also offers a substantial floor space.

The 1967 clubhouse had been fitted out with a snooker room which was lined with the original oak panelling from the old headquarters. It had large double doors which opened out on to a paved area. The new extension covered all of this former patio, to provide a 32 feet by 32 feet floor space for dances and other social events. It meant that the club no longer needed to rely upon local hotels for its larger social functions and that has, in the long term, brought an additional saving. In 1992, the clubhouse was given a major 'face-lift'. But the structure completed by Project '65 and its follow up in 1974 still forms the basis for the premises as they stand today. They have proved capable of meeting the needs of the widening interests of a growing membership. The 'traditional' snooker and billiard room with its wood panelling remains intact. But there is also a general bar, a separate kitchen with galley for serving food, plus a large floor space for anything approved of by the house committee, including—believe it or not—a pool table and, just once, a karaoke machine. Times have changed!

6. The 24-Hour Race

No other single event in the WLYC calendar attracts as much time, effort and public interest as the 24-Hour Race. Its significance today is reflected in the existence of a permanent 24 hour Race Executive which is currently chaired by Anne Harper. Beyond that, there is the obvious point that virtually every member has at some time or other been directly involved with the event, either as a competitor or in one of the many 'voluntary' duties which have always provided the foundation for its success. The original idea for the race came from the Liverpool University Sailing Club representative on the WLYC sailing committee in 1966. At the time, the WLYC was considering putting on an event to mark the centenary of the Borough of Southport in 1967. Apparently by coincidence, the LUSC wanted to hold an invitation twelve-hour race for university sailing clubs in the September of that year. September was chosen because students were most likely to be free just before the start of their new academic year, while the LUSC thought that something 'unusual' would attract entries. The success of the British Universities championships on the Marine Lake in 1965 provided firm grounds for expecting a good response. Nevertheless, there is barely enough time, if starting and finishing are included, to fit such an event into the daylight hours in September. So the sailing committee, chaired by Jack Whiteley, took a logical decision to run it for 24 hours! The basic idea, which has been retained, is for each team's boat to sail around the Marine Lake for twenty four hours, and the one which goes the farthest wins. Perhaps even more surprising, the WLYC committee agreed to the event. By the early months of 1967—before the new club premises had been completed—the planning for the first 24-Hour Race had started.[58] The committee decided to invite Fireflys, Enterprises and GP14s, and the early races timed each class on the basis of their Portsmouth Yardstick Handicap. No limit was placed upon the number of crew changes or the total size of a club's 'team', while the shallow waters of the Lake have contributed towards the event's excellent safety record. However, there have always been strict rules concerning the change-overs in the docking area which, in fact, becomes a focal point of interest in high winds when the vast majority of those in the 'audience' seem to be on the lookout for a spectacular mishap, but not for their club's boat of course!

An early 24-Hour Race start in peaceful conditions. The award-winning Tower is on the left.

Simply because so many people have always been involved, it is virtually impossible to do justice to their individual efforts in a general history of the club such as this. Suffice to say that the planning for the twenty-eighth of these annual events is already well under way and the race has probably done more than anything else to keep the WLYC to the fore in British dinghy sailing over the past quarter of a century. Certainly, the sheer scale of the organisation was appreciated from the start. Changing technology has brought computerised result sheets and more sophisticated monitoring. However, many of the principles established by members in 1967 still hold good today. It was immediately appreciated, for instance, that any mistakes in the scoring would have near fatal consequences for the WLYC's reputation. Even in the fairly relaxed atmosphere of the first race, the progress of each team was studied with immense interest by all competitors and RYA officials as well as reporters from the yachting and local press.

It was therefore essential to get everything right and a system of delegated planning was established in 1967 which would still be recognisable by those who hold responsiblities for the race today. Very broadly, the sailing committee had to prepare everything under three main categories; the organisation of race entries; the creation of special rules acceptable to the RYA and clearly defined in the race instructions; and, finally, the basic racing and social needs of the visiting teams had to be provided for. In starting from scratch, the first committee was surprised at the immediate interest in the event. Letters had been sent to every club in the North West and to all British universities with sailing clubs. Nearly sixty teams entered and fifty actually took part.[59]

But the 24-Hour Race could also be lively!

It was also clear that the start would be the crucial time when any unforeseen problems would emerge in front of several thousand spectators, most of whom would almost certainly understand what was going on. Meanwhile, it was essential to know what was happening on the course, and the committee used two mark boats at either end of the lake in the early races with the one at the southern point connected to the scoring section on shore by a submarine telephone cable. Furthermore, the course was sailed as a simple triangle, always clockwise around the islands, and volunteers on the mark boats certainly found that life could be exciting in high winds, especially if they were 'in' the gybe-mark, which is why their launches were always very well clad with protective tyres!

In the early years, scoring was done with a paper-based system while Jack Whiteley's company produced a set of three drums fitted with rolls of paper and driven by differential gears. There was a drum for each of the three classes then in the race, with gearing set according to their respective Portsmouth Yardstick Handicap numbers. This enabled a scorer's assistant to write in a running log on the respective paper rolls as incidents occurred and the end result was three 30-metre-long wallpaper-like rolls of information which could be used to confirm any disputes at a later stage. Of course, it was also essential to have the results out within an hour or so of the finish; and getting everything ready in time for the massive prize-giving so quickly was something else which called for intricate planning and then hectic last minute activity. Computerisation has inevitably altered the task in more recent 24-Hour races. It is an open question as to whether it has made things easier or simply

Life in the docking area is always hectic whatever the weather.

Part of the WLYC winning team of the first 24-Hour Race in 1967. This photograph includes Peter Chester, Tony Halliwell, Martin Holman, Andrew Read, Louise Thompson, John Thorougood and John Warren.

more complex. However, some form of paper back-up is still maintained and everyone involved still seems to be worked off their feet. Many other club members have volunteered year-in-year-out for the apparently thankless tasks of 'security', no alsations yet!, car parking, refreshments and bar and, the most dedicated, keeping the mobile toilets clean throughout the two day period. Without their efforts, the race could never work and involvement in some way or other has become something which most members appear to look forward to despite the fact that it takes about a week, at least, to sleep off the after effects.

On the water, the Fireflys were withdrawn after five years and the event has since been confined to Enterprises and GP14s which now race on a par with one another. In practice, it is believed that the GPs have an advantage in heavy weather, while the Enterprises tend to come into their own in lighter winds. But there have been many exceptions and the 24-Hour Race remains a remarkably open event, with the outcome often decided in the closing laps. Overall, teams in GP14s have won sixteen times while ten first places have gone to the Enterprises. More significantly, no less than sixteen clubs have appeared among the winners in the past twenty-six years, with only Bolton Sailing Club's impressive eight victories threatening to reduce the spread of honours. The 24-Hour Race trophies are another measure of the spirit underlying this event. It was originally raced for the magnificent Southport Centenary Cup which went to the winning team. From the start, though, there were other prizes and these have grown in number over the years as interest widened. By 1971, for instance, there were already seven prizes including the Kicking Strap Trophy presented by the 1969 WLYC Sailing Committee. It is awarded for the best position by a team which has not won any other prize and is based over 100 miles from Southport, with the aim of encouraging participation by smaller clubs throughout the country.

The transfer of the Coddington Cup from a separate invitation event on to the 24-Hour list of prizes in the early 1970s added an element of historical interest. It means that a trophy in memory of Dudley Coddington, donated by his wife Ella, now goes to the Enterprise or G.P. crew which achieves the fastest lap after 9.00 a.m. on the Sunday morning of the race, when their boat has been going for some nineteen hours. That is a far cry from its original use at relatively sedate invitation events but the change is, for all that, a fitting tribute to one of the club's earliest flag officers. Meanwhile, the presence of three trophies specifically for university sailing club teams is a reminder of the original idea behind the 24-Hour race. The open nature of the race is also indicated by the fact that the twenty-four trophies currently awarded are held by crews from fifteen different clubs. Bassenthwaite SC—as the overall 1992 winner—received four trophies and Bolton SC holds three, but there is no other club having more than two of them. It is equally notable that 'local knowledge' does not count for much because the WLYC and SSC have each only won the Southport Centenary Cup on two occasions.

It is appropriate to end a history of the WLYC with the remarkable successes of the 24-Hour Race. The changing fortunes of the club over the past hundred years have reflected the influence of national as well as local economic, geographical and social pressures. At times, the WLYC faced the risk of disappearing as many clubs have done since the emergence of yachting as a popular sport in the late nineteenth century. Of course, like most other long-established clubs, the 'West Lancs' has preserved an element of continuity through the insistence of an influential majority that 'traditions' should be maintained. And it is true that the attitude of a tiny diehard element has inevitably led to friction on occasions. For all that, I hope that this book has shown that there have always been progressives— young and old—who appreciated when the time was ripe for change. Certainly, those in charge as flag officers and committee members have never lost sight of an ultimate aim which has been retained in every set of rules, including the current Handbook, as

> The primary object of the Club shall be the encouragement of Amateur Yacht and Boat Sailing.

It is equally important to emphasise that, with the tragic exception of the accident in 1913, the club has maintained an impressive safety record not only in its 'home waters' on the Marine Lake and the Southport Channel, but also at other venues where boats have sailed under the 'golden lion' burgee. Indeed the 'West Lancs' has much to celebrate in its centenary year, with a successful record in racing as well as in social events and—above all—in the club spirit and the enthusiasm for sailing which has survived throughout the hundred years since its foundation in 1894.

Notes to Chapter 1. *Southport Yachting—Origins and Background*

1. P. Bailey, *Leisure and Class in Victorian England. Rational recreation and the contest for control* (Methuen, 1987), p. 53.

2. See Chapter 2.

3. P. Bailey, op. cit., pp. 12, 21–2, 24–5, 69, 130, 188.

4. J. K. Walton, *The English Seaside Resort. A Social History 1750–1914* (Leicester University Press, 1983), p. 71.

5. J. K. Walton (1983), op. cit., pp. 13, 70–1, 112–13.

6. P. Bailey, op. cit., pp. 161–4. J. Liddle, 'Estate Management and land reform politics: the Hesketh and Scarisbrick Families and the making of Southport, 1842 to 1914', in D. Cannadine (ed.), *Patricians, Power and Politics in nineteenth-century towns* (Leicester University Press, 1982), 133–74, pp. 136–7.

7. J. Liddle, op. cit., 138–9.

8. J. K. Walton (1983), op. cit., pp. 161–4, 171.

9. *Southport Visiter* (SV) 12/7/1883, p. 5.

10. F. A. Bailey, *A History of Southport* (Southport, 1955), pp. 100–3.

11. J. K. Walton (1983), op. cit., p. 71.

12. Annual lists of clubs were given in the Lloyds Register of Ycahts which began in 1878. Accurate summaries of growth in the period appear in *The Yachtsman* (YM). 23/5/1891, p. 92 and *Yachting World* (YW). 10/10/1907, p. 269.

13. J. D. Hayward, *A Short History of the Royal Mersey Yacht Club 1844–1907* (Liverpool, 1907), pp. 19–29.

14. J. D. Hayward, op. cit., p. 30.

15. G. Fairley, *Minute by Minute. The Story of the Royal Yachting Association 1875–1982* (Royal Yachting Association, 1983), pp. 1–3.

16. YW 10/10/1907, p. 269.

17. G. Fairley, op. cit., pp. 3, 21–2.

18. B. Heckstall-Smith (ed.), *Dixon Kemp's Manual of Yacht and Boat Sailing* (10th edition London, 1904), p. 598.

19. P. Bailey, op. cit., pp. 140, 143. J. Crump, 'Tennis' in T. Mason (ed.), *Sport in Britain. A Social History* (Cambridge University Press, 1988), pp. 44–77, pp. 49–51. J. Lowerson, 'Angling', in T. Mason (ed.), pp. 15–16. J. Williams, 'Cricket', in T. Mason (ed.), pp. 116–45, 138–9.

20. P. Bailey, op. cit., pp. 139–40. C. Dodd, 'Rowing', in Mason (ed.), 276–309, pp. 279–80, 282, 285.

21. P. Bailey, op. cit., pp. 72–3, 83–5, 136, 139, 144. C. Dodd, op. cit., p. 285. J. Lowerson, in Mason (ed.) pp. 17, 188–9.

22. R. Simper, *Victorian and Edwardian Yachting from old photographs* (Batsford, 1978), pp. 1–3. YW 18/5/1911 pp. 349–50.

23. G. Fairley, op. cit., pp. 11–15, 44–5.

24. J. Lowerson, *Sport and the English Middle Classes* (Manchester University Press, 1993), p. 53

25. J. Lowerson, in T. Mason (ed.), p. 189. H. Walker, 'Tennis', in T. Mason (ed.), pp. 245–75, pp. 249–56.

26. Examples taken from Lloyds Register of Yachts, 1885, 1895.

27. Royal Mersey Yacht Club (RMYC), Register of Members.

28. YW 20/1/1899 p. 174.

29. O. M. Westall, 'The Retreat to Arcadia: Windermere as a Select Residential Resort in the Late Nineteenth Century', in O. M. Westall (ed.), *Windermere in the Nineteenth Century* (University of Lancaster, 1991), pp. 38, 42.

30. G. Fairley, op. cit. p. 44.

31. RMYC, Register of Members; J. Lowerson (1993), op. cit., p. 50 on Royal Welsh Yacht Club.

32. G. Fairley, op. cit. pp. 11–12, 44–5.

33. YW 4/3/1909 p. 106.

34. Ibid.

35. P. Barnes, *The Norfolk Broads Yacht Club. A Short History* (Norwich, 1982) p. 3.

36. YM 22/6/1899, p. 362.

37. YM 4/5/1893 pp. 43–4.

38. J. Lowerson (1993), op. cit., p. 50.

39. YW 15/6/1911, p. 448.

40. J. Lowerson (1993), op. cit., pp. 50–1.

41. YW 10/10/1907, p. 269. YW 4/2/1909 pp. 49–50.

42. J. Crump, in T. Mason (ed.), 48–50. C. Dodd, in T. Mason (ed.), 277–9. G. Williams, 'Rugby Union', in T. Mason (ed.), pp. 312–14.

43. G. Fairley, op. cit., pp. 64–9.

44. P. Aughton, *North Meols and Southport. A History* (Carnegie, 1988) pp. 131–2, F. A. Bailey, op. cit., pp. 152–9.

45. J. Liddle, in D. Cannadine (ed.), op. cit., pp. 149–57.

46. F. A. Bailey, op. cit., p. 205.

47. P. Aughton, op. cit., p. 132.

48. F. A. Bailey, op. cit., pp. 102–3, 210, 216. J. K. Walton, op. cit., pp. 147, 174.

49. On seaside resort 'zoning' of social activities generally, see J. K. Walton, op. cit., p. 225. See also, O. M. Westall, 'The Retreat to Arcadia: Windermere as a Select Residential Resort in the Late Nineteenth Century', in O. M. Westall (ed.).

50. SV 18/6/1903, p. 10.

51. *Southport Guardian* (SG). 2/6/94, p. 5.

52. SV 17/7/83, p. 5.

53. PCMB, No. 3, 7/3/1883.

54. SV 12/2/84, p. 3.

55. PCMB, No. 3, p. 133, 9/6/1884; p. 178, 16/7/87, on 5gns prizes. *Hunt's Yachting Magazine* (HYM), xxxv (1886), p. 458, 17/7/1886 reported prize by Pier Company. PCMB, No. 3, 9/2/1883; No. 4, 12/6/1894 on £30 p. a.

56. N. Wrigglesworth, 'A History of Rowing in the North West of England', *British Journal of Sports History*, vol. 3, no. 2, 1986, 145–57, p. 155.

57. SV 4/9/1883, p. 5.

58. SV 12/2/1884, p. 3. PCMB, No. 3, 26/4/1884, Pier Manager's report to directors.

59. HYM, xxxiii (1884), p. 486, first report, race on 14/6/1884, regular item thereafter.

60. SV 12/2/1884, p. 3.

61. HYM, xx (1871), p. 237, May 1871 'club report' on the Temple Yacht Club. Anon., *British Yachts and Yachtsmen. A Complete History of British Yachting from the Middle of the Sixteenth Century to the Present Day* (The Yachtsman Publishing Company, 1907), pp. 519–20 give a brief history of the Temple, founded 1857, which became the Royal Temple Y. C. in 1897.

62. YM 16/5/1891, p. 76.

63. Ibid.

64. See, for example, YM 6/6/1891, p. 135. The SCYC 'mosquito' fleet events were regularly reported in the YM.

65. YM 9/3/1893, p. 293.

66. SV 11/6/1929, p. 3. obit. Also, Royal Geographical Society, Certificate of Candidate for Election, elected FRGS. 13/11/1922.

67. See Chapter 3.

68. YW 8/6/1894, p. 146, see also Chapter 3.

69. HYM, xxxvi (1887), last volume's frontispiece 'address' thanking patrons and contributors, but 'regret that we have not received the support our long service in the cause of Yachting entitled us to expect'.

70. G. Fairley, op. cit., pp. 20–2.

71. Ibid.

72. B. Heckstall-Smith, op. cit., 598, 600. YM 23/5/1891, pp. 91–2, article on 'Yacht Club Seniority'. See O. M. Westall, op. cit., p. 42, on the social significance of the Royal Warrant granted to the wealthy Windermere Y. C. in 1887. It had been founded as the Windermere Sailing Club in 1860.

73. Many texts deal with the development of rating with varying degrees of accuracy and detail. G. Fairley, op. cit., passim, discusses the administrative aspects so far as the YRA was concerned: B. Heckstall-Smith, op. cit., pp. 634–42, gives Dixon-Kemp's summary of rating development up to 1896, with this edition adding developments to 1901. J. Irving, *The King's Britannia. The Story of a Great Ship* (Seeley Service & Co, London, c. 1937), Chapter 1, gives a sound outline of the rating system: A. Viner *A History of Rating Rules for Yachts 1854–1931* (Maritime Monographs and Reports No. 41, National Maritime Museum, 1979), gives a very clear account of the development of rating systems.

74. B. Heckstall-Smith, op. cit., p. 639.

75. A. Viner, op. cit., pp. 3–4.

76. J. Irving, op. cit., p. 25.

77. B. Heckstall-Smith, op. cit., pp. 639–41.

78. A. Viner, op. cit., p. 7.

79. Ibid., G. Fairley, op. cit., pp. 2, 6–8.

80. A common theme in the contemporary journals. See, for example, YW 1/2/1895, p. 703, 'The Yacht Designers and Their Present Rating Rule'.

81. A. Viner, op. cit., p. 7.

82. B. Heckstall-Smith, op. cit., p. 597.

83. A. Viner, op. cit., p. 6.

84. A. Viner, op. cit., p. 11.

85. A. Viner, op. cit., p. 12.

86. YW August 1898 'Cowes Supplement', p. 4.

87. My thanks to Jim Morgan, WLYC member and owner of a surviving 0.75-rater, for emphasising this point which is borne out by the evidence from reports in YM and YW.

88. SV 6/12/1894, p. 7. SG 8/12/1894, p. 7.

89. PCMB Vol. 4, 12/6/1894, SG 1/8/1894, p. 6.

90. YW 23/10/1902, p. 242.

Notes to Chapter 2. *Sailing Waters 1894 to 1937*

1. Anon., *British Yachts and Yachtsmen* (London, 1907) pp. 519–20.

2. P. Barnes, *The Norfolk Broads Yacht Club* (Norwich, 1982), p. 3.

3. See Chapters 3 & 6 below.

4. See Chapter 4.

5. YM 16/5/1891 p. 68 on Blundellsands SC.

6. See, for example, P. Aughton, *North Meols and Southport: A History* (Carnegie, 1988), pp. 35, 162–3.

7. YM 2/3/1893 p. 279; YM 9/3/1893 p. 293; YM 16/3/1893 p. 307.

8. YW 16/11/1894 p. 573.

9. YW 26/10/1894 p. 540.

10. See Chapter 3.

11. YW 9/1/1907 p. 21.

12. YW 3/11/1904 p. 293.

13. YM 16/3/1893 p. 307.

14. J. K. Walton, *The English Seaside Resort. A Social History 1750–1914* (Leicester University Press, 1983), p. 212.

15. Walton (1983), op. cit., p. 148.

16. YW 8/10/1908 p. 261.

17. YW 2/4/1908 p. 196.

18. Walton (1983), op. cit., p. 143; Aughton, op. cit., pp. 160–1.

19. SV 30/6/1894 p. 3.

20. Ibid.

21. PCMB No. 5, 24/9/1897.

22. Walton (1983), op. cit., p. 143; Aughton, op. cit., pp. 160–1.

23. PCMB No. 4, 15/12/1894; 19/12/1894.

24. PCMB No. 4, 21/2/1895.

25. See Chapters 3 & 6 below.

26. J. Barron, *A History of the Ribble Navigation. From Preston to the Sea* (Preston, 1938), pp. 40–1.

27. Barron, op. cit., pp. 100–7, 121–2; Southport Library, 'Pier Box', Item 10. George Hacking, Proof, House of Lords Session 1896, Preston Corporation, Ribble Navigation, Draft Case for Southport.

28. Barron, op. cit., pp. 170–1.

29. Barron, op. cit., pp. 40–4, 450–2.

30. F. A. Bailey, *A History of Southport*, (Southport, 1955), p. 210; see also Chapter 5 below.

31. L. F. Vernon-Harcourt, *Report on the Extension of the Navigable Channel of the Ribble to the Sea, to the Corporation of Southport* (Southport, 1891), pp. 7–9.

32. F. W. Jarrad, *Ribble Navigation. Report on the Silting in the South (Bog Hole) Channel* (London, 1907), p. 11.

33. Jarrod, op. cit., p. 3.

34. Barron, op. cit., pp. 42–3; Jarrod, op. cit., pp. 4–6.

35. Bailey, op. cit., pp. 100–1.

36. Bailey, op. cit., pp. 101, 204; C. Bainbridge, *Pavilions on the Sea. A History of the Seaside Pleasure Pier* (London, 1986), pp. 52, 60.

37. Bainbridge, op. cit., p. 60.

38. Ibid.

39. Bailey, op. cit., p. 102; PCMB passim.

40. PCMB No. 3, 21/7/1883.

41. PCMB No. 5, 25/2/1897; 5/3/1897; 25/3/1897; YW 26/2/1897.

42. YW 16/4/1897 p. 9.

43. PCMB No. 8, 19/4/1923.

44. Bainbridge, op. cit., pp. 156–7; *Post Magazine and Insurance Monitor*, Vol XCIV, No. 47, 25/11/1933, pp. 2007–11.

45. PCMB No. 3, 26/4/1884.

46. PCMB No. 5, 18/9/1897.

47. PCMB No. 5, 13/1/1898.

48. *Post Magazine and Insurance Monitor*, Vol XCIV, No. 47, 25/11/1933, pp. 2007–11.

49. Southport Library, 'Pier Box', Item 30, 'Case for the Opinion of Counsel', Town Clerk, 12/7/1934.

50. Ibid.

51. Bainbridge, op. cit., p. 154.

52. SV 25/7/1933 p. 5.

53. Vernon-Harcourt, op. cit., 20 pages with chart.

54. Barron, op. cit., pp. 100–7; J. Dakres, *The Last Tide. A History of the Port of Preston, 1835–1981* (Carnegie, 1986), pp. 101–6.

55. Walton (1983), op. cit., p. 117; Dakres, op. cit., p. 115.

56. Barron, op. cit., p. 133; Dakres, op. cit., pp. 149–166.

57. Barron, op. cit., pp. 163–4.

58. Barron, op. cit., p. 174.

59. Barron, op. cit., p. 149.

60. Barron, op. cit., pp. 155, 238.

61. Barron, op. cit., p. 171.

62. Dakres, op. cit., pp. 190–3.

63. YW 15/5/1896 p. 98.

64. YW 15/6/1905, p. 369.

65. YW 14/9/1905, p. 249.

66. Barron, op. cit., pp. 173–6, 257.

67. Southport Library, 'Pier Box', 'Ribble Navigation Bill, 1896. Notes for Opening Speech on Behalf of Southport'; Dakres, op. cit., pp. 202–5.

68. PCMB No. 8, 25/7/1918; 24/7/1919; 16/6/1924; Dakres, op. cit., p. 204.

69. See Chapter 3, and below pp. 18–9.

70. Barron, op. cit., pp. 241–4, 257.

71. Bailey, op. cit., p. 189.

72. Jarrad, op. cit., pp. 6–7.

73. See Chapter 3 below.

74. WLYC MB B, 8/7/1926, with correspondence from Simpson to J. Ernest Jarratt, Town Clerk, 9/7/1926.

75. WLYC MB C, correspondence, from Egan, 26/5/1936; Corporation, 10/6/1926.

76. WLYC *Southport Visiter*, November 1935 press cutting, p. 10, 'Interesting Presentation'.

77. Information provided by Mr William Sutton, Smiler's son, in June 1992.

78. WLYC MB B 7/9/1926.

79. WLYC MB B 13/4/1928.

80. WLYC *Southport Visiter*, November 1935 press cutting, p. 10.
81. WLYC MB C 16/7/1936, correspondence from Tom Sutton to Hon. Sec. 16/7/1936.

82. WLYC MB C 23/3/1937; 17/6/1937; 25/11/1937.

Notes to Chapter 3. *Early Days—'This Young but Certainly Go Ahead Club'*

1. YW 25/5/1894 p. 122.
2. RMYC, 'Minute Book of the Secretary of the Royal Mersey Yacht Club', from 1862 onwards. Records details, with occupations in many cases, of those proposed for election to the club.
3. YM 14/4/1892, p. 1052.
4. See Chapter 1, p. 10.
5. SV 6/12/1894 p. 7; SG 8/12/1894 p. 7.
6. See Chapter 5.
7. Ibid.
8. YW 20/1/1899 p. 174, 'Yachting Celebrities— Mr W. Scott Hayward. Commodore, West Lancashire Yacht Club'.
9. YM 12/4/1894 p. 338.
10. Southport Library, 'Pier Box', 'Ribble Navigation Bill, 1896, p. 2; YW 15/5/1896, p. 98.
11. YM 8/3/1894 p. 259.
12. YW 12/4/1894 p. 338.
13. YM 8/3/1894 p. 259.
14. YM 24/1/1895 p. 252.
15. YM 25/4/1897 p. 42, and similar report in YM 10/3/1898 p. 120.
16. SV 6/12/1894 p. 7; SG 8/12/1894 p. 7.
17. YW 10/5/1895 p. 60.
18. PCMB No. 4, 12/6/1895 pp. 205–6.
19. YM 15/12/1910 p. 346.
20. WLYC MB 'D' 22/11/1941; 28/3/1942.
21. SV 11/6/1929 p. 3, obit.
22. YW 6/7/1894 p. 230.
23. YW 22/6/1894 p. 188.
24. SV 11/6/1929 p. 3, obit.
25. YW 20/7/1894 p. 271, and cartoon below p. 8.
26. PCMB No. 4, 12/6/1894; 19/7/1894; 28/3/1895.
27. See Chapter 2 above.
28. SG 1/8/1894 p. 6.
29. Ibid.
30. See Chapter 2.
31. SG 1/8/1894 p. 6.
32. Ibid.
33. PCMB No. 6, 28/5/1900, for an example of a dispute with an SCYC member.
34. PCMB No. 4, 10/9/1894; and see Chapter 2.
35. YW 20/7/1894 p. 270.
36. SV 19/6/1894 p. 5.
37. P. Aughton, *North Meols and Southport. A History*, (Carnegie, 1988), pp. 161–2.
38. PCMB No. 4, 31/7/1895.
39. PCMB No. 8, 22/12/1921.

40. YW 8/3/1895, p. 795; YW 5/4/1895, p. 860.
41. YW 24/1/1896 p. 236.
42. WLYC MB B, 7/9/1926.
43. J. Lowerson, 'Golf' in T. Mason (ed.), *Sport in Britain. A Social History*, (CUP, 1989), pp. 187–214, pp. 191–5.
44. Ibid.
45. YW 9/12/1898 p. 105.
46. SG 8/12/1894 p. 7.
47. YW 30/11/1894 p. 597.
48. Ibid.
49. SG 8/12/1894 p. 7; YW 11/1/1895 p. 676.
50. YM 29/11/1894 p. v.
51. YM 17/1/1895 p. 235 on Latta's football career; YM 10/5/1895 p. 61.
52. YW 25/5/1895 p. 93.
53. Ibid.
54. YW 6/9/1895 p. vi; YW 13/9/1895 p. v.
55. RMYC Register of Members.
56. YW/8/3/1895 p. 795.
57. YW 12/10/1894 p. 512.
58. H. C. Folkard, op. cit., pp. 267–8; also, YW 21/1/1895, p. 168; YW 27/8/1897 p. 330: YW 30/11/1894 p. 604.
59. YW 22/11/1895 p. 90; 29/11/1895 p. 104; 6/12/1895 p. 119.
60. YW 13/12/1895 p. 131.
61. See, for example, WLYC MBA 7/1/1918, £1. 1s. armorial bearings tax.
62. See section 6, Corinthian Tensions, below.
63. For example see *Yachting World* 'Southport' reports in YW 15/3/1895; 17/5/1895; 14/6/1895; 26/7/1895.
64. YW 14/6/1895 p. 160.
65. YW 21/6/1895 p. 172.
66. YRA Council Minutes, 17/6/1895.
67. YW 28/6/1895 p. 208.
68. YW 7/6/1895 pp. 147–8.
69. YW 13/9/1895 p. v.
70. YW 13/9/1895 p. 423.
71. YW 20/9/1895 p. vi.
72. YW 30/4/1897 p. 31.
73. YW 20/9/1895 p. vi.
74. YW 8/11/1895 p. v.
75. YW 11/5/1891 p. 332.
76. YW 24/1/1896 p. 236.
77. YW 31/1/1896 p. 247.
78. See Chapter 5; and, for example, YW 25/10/1906 p. 292, report on SCYC annual dinner.

79. YW 10/12/1903 p. 410.
80. YW 8/12/1894 p. 355.
81. WLYC MB A 9/9/1918.
82. YW 10/12/1903 p. 410.

83. YW 3/12/1908 p. 354; YW 6/5/1909 p. 232.
84. See Chapters 2 & 6.
85. WLYC MB A correspondence 14/12/1920, hon. sec SCYC to hon. sec. WLYC.

Notes to Chapter 4. *'Principally Sailing Members': Club Life before 1914*

1. YW 3/3/1904 p. 107; YW 8/12/1904 p. 354.
2. SV 3/12/1901 p. 8, Hayward's speech; SV 4/12/1900 p. 5, Baggs the previous year.
3. See Chapter 4 (iii). below.
4. SV 3/12/1901 p. 8; WLYC 'Season 1914' Club Handbook.
5. J. Lowerson (1993), op. cit., p. 53.
6. SV 3/12/1901 p. 8.
7. YW 9/10/1896 p. 488.
8. SV 27/3/1934 p. 5.
9. YW 27/12/1900 p. 667.
10. YW 3/1/1901 pp. 34–5.
11. YW 31/1/1901 pp. 57–8.
12. Yachting and Boating Weekly, 21/4/1966, p. 11.
13. H. C. Folkard, op. cit., pp. 261–5.
14. N. Lee and P. C. Stubbs, *The History of Dorman Smith 1878–1972*, (London, 1972), p. 81.
15. Lee and Stubbs, op. cit., p. 82.
16. YW 23/9/1898 p. 131.
17. F. Bailey, op. cit., pp. 211–2; Lee and Stubbs, op. cit., p. 56.
18. Lee and Stubbs, op. cit., p. 82; YW 7/3/1901 p. 117, retiring hon. sec. ; YW 21/3/1901 p. 141, YW 4/4/1901 p. 161, on lecture.
19. YW 10/7/1902 p. 34.
20. RMYC Register of Members.
21. YW 11/5/1905 p. 279, 8 ton cutter on Bog Hole; WLYC 'Season ...', Year Books for 1914 to 1924.
22. YW 9/12/1898 p. 105.
23. YM 15/12/1898 p. 341.
24. YW 31/10/1907 p. 316.
25. 'The Seabird Half-Raters', pp. 83–6, in a 'Classic Boat' article, a copy of which is held in the MMMRC 'Seabird' file.
26. YW 24/3/1939 p. 292.
27. 1990, Seabird Association Handbook.
28. YW 12/10/1894 p. 512; YW 20/12/1895 p. 148; YW 10/1/1896 p. 207, on various builders.
29. YW 30/4/1897 p. 31; H. C. Folkard, op. cit., p. 262.
30. YW 8/10/1903 p. 301.
31. YW 3/8/1905 p. 106.
32. YW 15/5/1902 p. 211; YW 29/5/1902 p. 233.
33. YW 29/8/1907 p. 177.
34. YW 24/1/1907 p. 47.
35. YW 29/8/1907 p. 177.
36. YW 28/11/1907 p. 360.

37. YW 19/12/1907 p. 400; YW 9/1/1908 pp. 23–4.
38. Lancs. R. O. DDX 734 1/1, Blackpool & Fylde Y. C. Committee Minutes, 5/10/1908, 23/10/1908.
39. SV 11/10/1910 p. 8.
40. SV 13/8/1910 p. 8.
41. YW 27/5/1898 p. 80; YW 17/6/1898 p. 120.
42. YW 9/9/1898 p. 297; YW 18/4/1901 p. 189.
43. YM 1/9/1898 p. 150.
44. HYM Vol. XXVI 1877, pp. 301–3, 417, 629, 672; Anon. *British Yachts and Yachtsmen*, (London, 1907), pp. 186–91.
45. HYM Vol. XXVI, 1877, pp. 302–3.
46. See Chapter 1 on rating.
47. Anon. *British Yachts and Yachtsmen*, (London, 1907), p. 188.
48. YM 1/6/1893 p. 96.
49. SV 15/12/1896 p. 4.
50. YW 17/8/1905 p. 151; see also reports in YW 27/7/1905 p. 81; YW 10/8/1905 p. 125.
51. YW 11/3/1909 p. 119.
52. YW 11/6/1908 p. 347.
53. Percival, *From Zulu to Zulu Chief*, unpublished typescript, 1990, pp. 3 and 18.
54. YW 18/6/1908 p. 381.
55. YW 3/12/1908 p. 354.
56. YM 2/2/1911 p. 75.
57. Percival, op. cit., pp. 7–11.
58. Percival, op. cit., p. 3.
59. YW 5/12/1907 p. 372.
60. YW 29/7/1909 p. 66.
61. YW 6/5/1909 p. 232; YW 5/5/1910 p. 181.
62. YW 17/9/1908 p. 220; YW 27/7/1911 p. 81.
63. YW 21/4/1910 p. 160.
64. The following account is based upon the very long and detailed reports of the disaster and subsequent inquest and funerals which appeared in; SV 22/7/1913 p. 7; SG 23/7/1913 pp. 7–8; SV 24/7/1913 p. 7.
65. YW 17/10/1907.
66. YW 2/11/1911 p. 377.
67. YW 9/11/1911 p. 393.
68. YW 28/9/1911 p. 296.
69. YW 4/6/1908 p. 337.
70. SV 24/7/1913 p. 7.
71. SG 22/7/1913 p. 7.
72. SV 22/7/1913 p. 7.
73. SV 9/12/1913 p. 4.

Notes to Chapter 5. *'Figureheads' and Leaders before the First World War.*

1. J. K. Walton, *Lancashire. A Social History 1558–1939*, (Manchester University Press, 1987), pp. 223–5.
2. YW 29/12/1898 p. 388.
3. YW 25/10/1906 p. 292, an apology for absence.
4. Anon. *British Yachts and Yachtsmen*, (London, 1907), p. 477.
5. YW 14/9/1905 p. 249; YW 25/10/1906 p. 292; see also, J. Liddle, op. cit., pp. 161–3 on Hesketh's noted absenteeism from council meetings as Mayor of Southport 1905–6.
6. J. Dakres, op. cit., p. 115.
7. SG 4/12/1895 p. 7.
8. RMYC Secretary's Minutes, 3/4/1884, 4/12/1884.
9. YM 1/6/1893 p. 96.
10. SV 15/12/1896 p. 4.
11. SV 29/1/1916, obituary; see also Southport Library file on Sir George Pilkington.
12. J. K. Walton (1987), op. cit., p. 228.
13. J. Liddle, op. cit., p. 163.
14. YM 1/9/1898 p. 147.
15. YM 3/3/1898 p. 108; YM 31/3/1898 p. 156.
16. YW 25/10/1900 p. 556.
17. J. K. Walton (1987), op. cit., pp. 228–9.
18. F. Bailey, op. cit., p. 210; J. Liddle, op. cit., p. 158; J. K. Walton (1987), op. cit., pp. 233–4.
19. F. Bailey, op. cit., p. 210.
20. SG 21/12/1895 p. 5.
21. YW 15/5/1902 p. 211.
22. MMMRC, Seabird Box, Anon. list compiled from B. Heckstall Smith's *Yacht Racing Calendar and Review*, (1902, 1903, 1904).
23. YW 23/9/1898 p. 131.
24. SV 3/12/1901 p. 8.
25. On amateurs and corinthians, see P. Bailey *Leisure and Class in Victorian England*, (Methuen, 1987), pp. 139–44; G. Fairley, op. cit., pp. 42–3, 131–2; B. Heckstall-Smith, op. cit., p. 551, on the term 'corinthian, in yachting 'synonymous with amateur'; I. Wrigglesworth, op. cit. pp. 146–53.
26. HYM, Vol. 20, May 1871, p. 237; & Vol. 21, Nov. 1872, p. 598.
27. HYM Vol. 20, May 1871, p. 237.
28. Anon. *British Yachts and Yachtsmen*, (London, 1907), p. 402; also, biographies in reports and obituaries published in, Belfast Newsletter, 20/8/1913 & 24/8/1911, copies courtesy of Ulster Folk & Transport Museum; YW 25/8/1910 p. 152; YM 25/8/1910 pp. 92–3; SG 24/8/1910, p. 5; SV 20/8/1910, p. 7. ; also details in YW 20/1/1899 p. 174 'Yachting Celebrities'.
29. YW 19/8/1898 p. 258, explains significance of the qualification.
30. RMYC MB of Secretary, 1/2/1883.
31. Anon. *British Yachts and Yachtsmen*, (London, 1907), p. 402.
32. YW 14/9/1894 p. 431.
33. Anon. *British Yachts and Yachtsmen*, (London, 1907), p. 402.
34. YM 27/9/1900 p. 248; YW 27/9/1900 p. 509; Anon. *British Yachts and Yachtsmen*, (London, 1907), p. 438.
35. YW 23/10/1902 p. 242.
36. Anon. *British Yachts and Yachtsmen*, (London, 1907), p. 402; YW 21/9/1905 p. 240; YW 18/11/1906 p. 43; YW 12/12/1907 p. 385; YW 23/1/1908 p. 39; SG 24/8/1910 p. 10.
37. YW 1/1/1897 p. 165.
38. YW 17/8/1905 p. 161.
39. YW 31/1/1907, p. 54; YW 10/9/1908 p. 205; YW 17/9/1908 pp. 214, 217, 219.
40. YW 3/12/1908 p. 355.
41. YW 9/3/1911 p. 132.
42. The following account includes evidence in family obituaries and probate reports in; SV 19/12/1903 p. 5; SV 22/12/1903 pp. 2 & 4; SG 13/6/1928 p. 3; SV 14/6/1928 p. 3; SV 13/10/1928 p. 8.
43. YW 6/7/1894 p. 230; YW 20/5/1898 p. 68; YW 11/6/1897 p. 123; YW 23/8/1900 p. 155; YW 22/5/1902 p. 224; SV 22/12/1903 p. 4.
44. SV 19/12/1903 p. 5.
45. RMYC MB of Secretary 2/9/1897.
46. SV 19/12/1903 p. 5.
47. SV 13/10/1928 p. 8 local will.
48. YW 3/3/1904 p. 107.
49. YW 7/12/1905 p. 408.
50. SG 13/6/1928 p. 3.
51. SV 13/8/1910 p. 8.
52. Ibid.
53. J. K. Walton (1987), op. cit., p. 237.

Notes to Chapter 6. *Years of Doubt*

1. J. K. Walton (1987), op. cit. pp. 329–40.
2. WLYCMB B 1/11/1926; 6/12/1926, with corres.
3. WLYCMB B 20/5/1926 to 15/11/1926.
4. SG 4/12/1926 p. 7.
5. G. Fairley, op. cit., p. 53.
6. PCMB No. 8, 5/2/1915.
7. C. Bainbridge, op. cit., p. p. 165.
8. WLYCMB A 4/2/1918.
9. PCMB No. 8, 15/4/1918.
10. PCMB No. 8, 13/5/1918.
11. PCMB No. 8, 4/9/1921.
12. PCMB No. 8, 17/10/1921.
13. PCMB No. 8, 19/12/1921; 22/12/1921.
14. WLYCMB A 12/12/1921.
15. PCMB No. 8, 18/10/1920.
16. PCMB No. 8, 22/12/1921.
17. PCMB No. 8, 14/8/1922.
18. WLYCMB A 4/6/1923.
19. See Chapter 7 (iv).
20. WLYCMB A 14/12/1920; corres. from SCYC.
21. See Chapter 1 (iv); WLYCMB A 29/11/1920; 10/1/1921.
22. WLYCMB A 29/11/1920.
23. WLYCMB A 5/1/1922.
24. WLYCMB A 13/3/1922.
25. WLYCMB A 19/4/1922.
26. WLYCMB A 5/2/1923.
27. WLYCMB A 18/9/1924, corres.
28. SG 4/12/1896 p. 6. ; SV 4/12/1896 p. 5.
29. G. Fairley, op. cit., p. 79.
30. YW 22/11/1924, p. 1050; R. Knox Johnston, op. cit., pp. 84–92.
31. J. Fisher, *Sailing Dinghies*, (Adlard Coles, 1961 ed.), p. 24.
32. G. Fairley, op. cit., p. 55.
33. RMYC Minute Book of the Secretary, 3/5/1883; YW 21/7/1899, p. 50.
34. See Chapter 4; WLYC Yearbooks 1919–24; RMYC Minute Book of the Secretary & Membership Book, passim.
35. G. Fairley, op. cit., p. 64.
36. WLYCMB A 2/10/1922.
37. WLYCMB A 4/12/1922.
38. Based on figures in; SV 4/12/1926, p. 6, motor vehicles; F. Bailey, op. cit., p. 208, Southport population; W. J. B. Hunt, 'Compulsory Third Party Motor Insurance', *Journal of the Chartered Insurance Institute*, 1927, Vol. XXX, pp. 126–7, for national figures of vehicle ownership. Even allowing for anomalies in licence administration, the Southport figures were well above the national average.
39. F. Bailey, op. cit., p. 173.
40. Southport Library, Sp. 796. 37 BIR R. H. K. Browning, *The Birkdale Golf Club*, (undated pamphlet), p. 8.
41. F. Bailey, op. cit., p. 173.
42. J. Lowerson, 'Golf', in Mason Ed., op. cit., pp. 192–5.
43. WLYCMB E 25/5/1951; and see Chapter 7 (iii).
44. J. Lowerson, 'Golf', in Mason (ed.), op. cit., p. 202.
45. F. Bailey, op. cit., p. 171; J. Lowerson, 'Golf', in Mason ed, op. cit., p. 204; H. Walker, 'Tennis', in Mason Ed., op. cit., p. 251.
46. SV 27/11/1934 p. 9.
47. J. K. Walton (1987), op. cit., pp. 341–51.
48. P. Thane, 'Social History 1860–1914', in R. C. Floud & D. N. McCloskey, eds., *the Economic History of Britain Since 1700: 2. 1860 to the 1970s*, (CUP, 1981), p. 199; J. K. Walton, (1987), op. cit., pp. 336–7.
49. F. Bailey, op. cit., p. 209.
50. Southport Town Council Minutes; 17/1/1927, p. 169, item 480; 14/2/1927, p. 254, items 681, 682; SV 3/12/1939, p. 3.
51. SV 4/12/1926 p. 5; P. Aughton, op. cit., p. 81.
52. G. Fairley, op. cit., p. 68.
53. G. Fairley, op. cit., p. 82.
54. J. Fisher, op. cit., pp. 31–2.
55. WLYCMB A 10/3/1919; 4/4/1921.
56. WLYCMB A 4/4/1921.
57. WLYCMB A 2/2/1920.
58. WLYCMB A 3/6/1918.
59. The details in this section are based on details provided by John Batten.
60. WLYC 'Victory Season', 1919, Yearbook: score sheet for Stars has been completed.
61. WLYCMB A 4/4/1921.
62. WLYCMB A 14/6/1921; 4/7/1921.
63. John Millar, op. cit., pp. 103–10; WLYCMB A 1/5/1922; 24/5/1922; 24/5/1922.
64. WLYCMB A 14/7/1920, authorised captain to buy the 'Star Class Boat "Iris" for a sum not exceeding £30', for the club.
65. See Chapter 7, section (iv).
66. WLYCMB A 1/5/1922.
67. WLYC Yearbooks 1919–24.
68. WLYCMB A 21/12/1920, corres.
69. Anon., *Star Class. West Kirby Sailing Club*, 12 pp. pamphlet, c. 1986; also information from John Batten.
70. Ibid. ; J. Millar, op. cit., pp. 103–8; West Kirby SC, *The Achievers*, 1991, includes the 'West Kirby Star Class, 1922–1991'.
71. J. Millar, op. cit., p. 109.
72. J. Millar, op. cit., pp. 101–2, 146.

73. WLYCMB D 30/10/1947.
74. MMMRC, Seabird Box, WLYC Yearbook 1936; see also, e.g., SV 27/11/1934, p. 9, Annual Dinner & Prize Giving.
75. Anon. WLYC Typescript, 'Tell Me Maxwell', no date, pp. 25–6.
76. Ibid. ; WLYCMB C 10/7/1934; 17/7/1934.
77. SV 31/7/1934 p. 7.
78. WLYCMB C 16/5/1941, corres.
79. WLYCMB E 28/4/1953; F 16/12/1966.
80. Anon., 'Tell Me Maxwell', p. 6; and conversation with Bill Sutton who is Smiler's son.
81. Script provided by Jim Morgan.
82. WLYCMB C 19/1/1939.
83. WLYCMB B 28/7/1927.

84. SV 6/12/1938 p. 3.
85. Millar, op. cit., pp. 80–4.
86. G. Fairley, op. cit., pp. 64–9; 88–90.
87. SV 6/12/1938 p. 3.
88. Ibid.
89. Ibid.
90. WLYCMB C 20/7/1939.
91. WLYCMB C 18/5/1939.
92. WLYCMB C 21/9/1939.
93. WLYCMB C 10/7/1941; 17/7/1941.
94. WLYCMB D 23/8/1945.
95. WLYCMB C 17/10/1940.
96. WLYCMB C 23/8/1945.
97. WLYCMB D 18/10/1945.
98. SV 13/10/1940, p. 15; SV 20/6/1940, p. 3.

Notes to Chapter 7. *New Faces and Old*

1. SV 2/10/1919, p. 7.
2. SV 11/6/1929, p. 3.
3. SV 24/12/1915, p. 8; WLYCMB A 6/5/1918.
4. WLYCMB A 18/1/1922.
5. G. Fairley, op. cit., p. 55.
6. Millar, op. cit., pp. 89–100, gives a detailed account; *Blackburn Times* 24/3/1939, a full page obit. ; G. C. Miller *Blackburn Worthies*, (1959), pp. 90–1, on Dean. Other sources annotated below.
7. see Chapter 4 (ii); YW 10/7/1902, p. 34.
8. YW 18/12/1902, p. 337.
9. YW 31/12/1903 p. 440.
10. YW 10/12/1903, p. 410; 31/5/1906, p. 306.
11. Millar, op. cit., p. 90.
12. Millar, op. cit., p. 91.
13. A. J. P. Taylor, *English History 1914–1945*, (OUP, 1975), p. 103.
14. Millar, op. cit., p. 97.
15. C. L. Mowat, *Britain Between the Wars 1918–1940*, (Methuen, 1955), p. 5.
16. *Blackburn Times*, 24/3/1939.
17. G. C. Miller, op. cit., pp. 90–1.
18. WLYCMB A 6/5/1918.
19. WLYCMB A 9/9/1918.
20. WLYCMB A 19/9/1918; 3/2/1919.
21. *Liverpool Courier*, 21/12/1918; *Liverpool Post and Echo*, 21/12/1918.
22. RMYC Register of Members.
23. WLYCMB A 20/12/1920.
24. WLYCMB A 3/9/1923.
25. WLYCMB A 30/1/1922.
26. WLYCMB A 12/6/1922.
27. WLYCMB A 17/7/1922.
28. WLYCMB A 9/1/1923.
29. Ibid.
30. WLYCMB A 29/1/1924.
31. SV 6/12/1938, p. 3.

32. Manchester Cruising Association (MCA) *Season 1918*, contains 53 pp. of information about MCA members and activities. Information from John Batten.
33. RMYC Register of Members, elected 21/6/1917.
34. SV 15/6/1918, p. 3.
35. SV 13/1/1940, p. 15.
36. SV 3/9/1935, p. 5.
37. WLYC Press Cuttings 1954–1969, SV 7/8/1956; 9/8/1956.
38. WLYCMB B 12/10/1926; 10/2/1932; E 28/6/1950; 24/10/1951.
39. WLYCMB E 4/7/1951.
40. Ibid.
41. WLYCMB E 14/3/1957.
42. See tribute, WLYCMB F 21/12/1967; also, WLYCMB C 15/12/1938; MMMRC, 1936, WLYC Yearbook.
43. WLYCMB E 25/10/1950.
44. WLYCMB E 22/8/1951.
45. See, e.g., WLYCMB E 20/3/1952.
46. WLYCMB E 12/3/1952.
47. WLYCMB D 16/4/1942; WLYC Press Cuttings 1954–1969, SV 3/8/1957.
48. WLYCMB E 10/12/1957.
49. Ibid.
50. YW 16/6/1899, p. 459.
51. YW 13/7/1905, p. 41.
52. See, Mason, (ed.), op. cit., the following articles; C. Dodd, 'Rowing', p. 298; J. Lowerson, 'Golf', pp. 204–8; H. Walker, 'Lawn Tennis', op. cit., pp. 260–3, 271–2.
53. A. Marwick, *The Deluge*, (Macmillan, 1965), pp. 93–4.
54. SV 2/10/1919, p. 7.
55. SV 31/7/1934, p. 7.
56. SV 10/11/1921, pp. 5–6.
57. SV 20/12/1921, p. 7.

58. WLYCMB A 3/11/1919.
59. WLYCMB A 20/1/1920.
60. WLYCMB A 18/1/1922; 5/11/1925; 14/1/1926.
61. WLYCMB B 23/5/1928.
62. WLYCMB C 4/5/1931, corres. 20/4/1931.
63. WLYCMB E 25/6/1952.
64. WLYCMB E 24/2/1952.
65. WLYCMB D 13/2/1949; 22/4/1949.
66. WLYCMB E 12/3/1953.
67. WLYCMB E 27/11/1954.
68. WLYCMB E 28/9/1954.
69. Millar, op. cit., p. 475.
70. Millar, op. cit., p. 477.
71. WLYCMB E 11/2/1955.
72. WLYCMB E 8/3/1955.
73. WLYCMB B 20/5/1926.
74. WLYCMB B 12/1/1927.
75. WLYCMB D 16/3/1949; E 19/4/1956.
76. WLYC Yearbook 1914.
77. WLYCMB A 2/9/1919; 19/4/1920; 23/8/1920; 4/10/1920.
78. SV 26/5/1934 p. 12, an 8 x 6 inches photograph taken through the doors on to the sluice and titled 'Up Stream at Crossens. The West Lancashire Yacht Club's winter quarters'.
79. WLYCMB A 4/10/1920.
80. WLYCMB C 1/10/1936.
81. WLYCMB C 25/11/1937: see also Chapter 2.
82. WLYCMB A 7/4/1919.
83. WLYCMB A 12/4/1920.
84. WLYCMB A 7/6/1920.
85. WLYCMB A 4/3/1924; B 11/4/1926; C 3/4/1933.

86. S. Pollard, *The Development of the British Economy—1914–1967*, (Arnold, 2nd. ed. 1969), pp. 142–3.
87. S. Pollard, op. cit., p. 290.
88. WLYCMB A 2/9/1919, and then WLYC Annual Accounts 1926–59.
89. WLYCMB E 21/9/1944.
90. WLYCMB B 1/9/1925.
91. *Fishing News* 27/11/1959 p. 7.
92. J. Lowerson, Mason ed. op. cit., p. 196.
93. WLYCMB D 25/11/1937.
94. WLYCMB B 6/12/1926.
95. This was a regular item at every WLYC committee meeting in Jnauary or February, e.g., WLYCMB D 20/1/1938; E 16/1/1947; 25/1/1950.
96. WLYCMB E 25/1/1950.
97. WLYC House Committee Minutes, 24/2/1956.
98. WLYCMB D 23/3/1949, specifically calculated wage rates according to the 'Catering & Wages Act 1943 L. N. R. 13, "club stewards" ' for J. Thompson's replacement.
99. WLYCMB D 20/6/1940.
100. WLYCMB D 19/1/1941.
101. WLYCMB D 21/11/1940.
102. for example, see, WLYCMB C 20/10/1938.
103. WLYCMB C 13/3/1936.
104. WLYCMB C 16/12/1937.
105. WLYCMB D 28/12/1949.
106. WLYCMB E 30/8/1950.
107. WLYCMB E 27/9/1950.
108. WLYCMB E 12/3/1952.

Notes to Chapter 8. *New Directions*

1. Fairley, op. cit., pp. 125, 131; Fisher, op. cit., p. 7.
2. Lowerson, 'Golf', Mason ed., op. cit., pp. 208–9.
3. Fisher, op. cit., pp. 37–8.
4. Fisher, op. cit., p. 7.
5. Yachts & Yachting 4/12/1992 p. 20.
6. WLYCMB D 30/10/1947.
7. WLYCMB D 27/1/1949.
8. Millar, op. cit., pp. 299–301, on Sid Cross: WLYCMB D 27/1/1949 Special Sailing Committee Report (SSCR), p. 2.
9. SSCR p. 7.
10. SSCR passim.
11. SSCR p. 13.
12. SSCR p. 5.
13. WLYCMB E 25/4/1951.
14. SSCR p. 8.
15. SSCR p. 7.
16. SSCR p. 9.
17. WLYCMB F 8/2/1966; 17/11/1966.

18. SSCR p. 10.
19. WLYC Press Cuttings 1954–1969; SG 12/2/1955; SV 12/2/1955.
20. WLYC Press Cuttings 1954–1969; SV 5/10/1954; SV 24/9/1955; SV 4/10/1955; SG 6/10/1955.
21. WLYC Press Cuttings 1954–1969; SV 'Sept' 1957; SV 4/10/1958.
22. WLYC Yearbooks 1971. 1975.
23. See, e.g., profile of the WLYC in Lancashire Life, October 1959, pp. 52–3.
24. WLYC Press Cuttings 1954–1969; SV 13/9/1955.
25. Information from Yearbooks provided by John Batten.
26. WLYC Press Cuttings 1954–1969; SV 14/7/1962; 22/3/1963; 20/4/1963; 27/4/1963; and information from Brian Randall.

27. WLYC Press Cuttings 1954–1969; SV 2/5/1965; 18/9/1965.
28. *Daily Telegraph* reports on 'G.P. World Championship Yachting', 21/7/1971 to 25/7/1971.
29. WLYCMB F 11/12/1964, Commodore's Report.
30. See section (v), below.
31. WLYC Press Cuttings 1954–1969; SV 4/5/1963; J. Atkins, *A Hundred Years of Sailing at Oxford University—1884–1984*, pp. 44, 120.
32. WLYCMB F 29/3/1960.
33. WLYCMB F 27/6/1960.
34. Ibid.
35. WLYCMB F 19/10/1960; 25/10/1960.
36. WLYCMB F 29/11/1960.
37. WLYCMB F 25/10/1960.
38. WLYC Press Cuttings 1954–1969; SV 20/9/1958.
39. WLYC Press Cuttings 1954–1969; SV 23/11/1957.
40. WLYC Press Cuttings 1954–1969; SV 10/2/1962.
41. WLYC Correspondence; H. R. Morton to R. Kirk Wilson, Hon. Sailing Sec. 1/11/1961.
42. WLYC Press Cuttings 1954–69, SV 14/7/1962.
43. WLYC Press Cuttings 1954–69, SV 18/9/1965.
44. WLYCMB F 16/12/1966.
45. WLYC Press Cuttings 1954–69, SV 5/9/1961.
46. WLYCMB F 6/12/1966; and details provoded by Jim Morgan.
47. WLYCMB F 3/5/1962.
48. WLYCMB F 11/12/1964.
49. WLYCMB F 19/12/1960.
50. WLYCMB F 1/5/1962.
51. WLYCMB F 5/6/1964.
52. WLYCMB F 11/12/1964.
53. WLYCMB F 21/8/1964.
54. WLYCMB F 3/9/1965.
55. e.g. WLYCMB F 16/12/1965.
56. WLYCMB F 16/12/1966.
57. WLYCMB F 6/5/1966.
58. WLYCMB F 8/2/1967; this section is very largely based upon a detailed typescript prepared by Jack Whiteley.
59. WLYC 'Southport Centenary Invitation Dinghy Race, 16/17 September 1967. An Analysis of Results.'

Bibliography

Primary Sources

I have referred to the following documents or journals myself. Other advice by correspondence is acknowledged in the text. The sources are listed in order of most frequent reference.

West Lancashire Yacht Club

1. Club Committee Minute Books have survievd from 1917. Those up to 1967 have been available for this study as follows:
   WLYCMB A 15/12/1917 to 20/1/1925
   WLYCMB B 30/1/1925 to 6/1/1930
   WLYCMB C 30/1/1930 to 18/9/1941
   WLYCMB D 15/10/1941 to 15/3/1950
   WLYCMB E 26/4/1950 to 29/12/1959
   WLYCMB F 19/1/1960 to 21/12/1967
2. WLYC House and Games Committee Minutes 5/4/1955 to 18/11/1963.
3. WLYC Sailing Committee Minutes 27/7/1956 to 18/9/1962.
4. On loan from John Batten; WLYC 'Season'— referred to in this text and footnotes as club 'Yearbooks'. Most give full lists of members, their boats and a racing calendar. The years available have been 1914, 1919, 1920, 1922, 1923, 1924, 1951 to 1964 inclusive, 1971 and

1975. WLYV Rules and Regulations, May 1947, 1961.

5. On loan from Jim Morgan: WLYC 'Press Cuttings 1954—1969', an excellent record of race reports and social events, mostly taken from the *Southport Visiter* and *Southport Guardian*, all placed in chronological order and dated.
6. On loan from Kirk Wilson: 'Offshore Sailing Negotiations 1961/2; Correspondence with the Corporation and a Copy of Conditions for Off-shore Sailing: 18 May 1962'. 'Notices and Reports—New Club House Phase 1 1964–66/ Phase 2 1973–4, Copy Land Lease—Marine Drive'. 'WLYC 1st Church Service—4th April 1965, St Andrews Church, Southport'. Photograph album, with photographs, press cuttings and miscellanea from c. 1960 to 1971.
7. Project '65. A Report on Progress and Plans for the New Clubhouse by the Development Sub-Committee, 1965.

Royal Mersey Yacht Club (RMYC)

1. Register of Members c. 1872 to 1945.
2. Register of Admiralty Warrants c. 1880 to 1927.
3. Minute Book of the Secretary of the Royal Mersey Yacht Club, 1862 to 1913.
4. Holdings of *Hunt's Yachting Magazine* (HYM), *The Yachtsman* (YM) and *Yachting World* (YW), used as indicated in text.

Southport Reference Library

1. Microfiche holdings of *Southport Visiter* and *Southport Guardian*, used for period c. 1860 to 1970 as indicated in footnotes.
2. Local directories: Slater's Southport Directories, 1880, 1881, 1882–3, 1886, 1887, 1887–8 and Seed's Directory of Southport, 1904, 1906, 1908–9, 1910–11, 1914, 1920–21, 1924–5, 1927–8, 1930–1, 1933–4, 1936–7.
3. Southport Pier Company Minute Books (PCMB). PCMB Nos 1 to 9 are available, covering the period 1860–1929.
4. 'Pier Box'. Includes misc. maps and items relating to the Pier Company and the Ribble Estuary. Includes plans and maps with ref. HLB1, 1885 and HLB2, 1934. There are also Plans A to F of pier and foreshore c. 1943. Other pam-

phlets and tracts realting to the Bog Hole are indicated in text footnotes where used.

5. Southport Council Minutes. A printed series, used from *c.* 1880 onwards as indicated in footnotes.

Lancashire Record Office (LRO)

1. Blackpool Sailing Club 1907–9, DDX 734 1/1, Blackpool and Fleetwood Sailing Club Minutes.
2. Local directories: Barrett's Directory of Blackburn and District, 13th edn 1915; Kelly's Directory of Lancashire, 1913, 'Exclusive of the Cities of Manchester and Liverpool'; Slater's Manchester, Salford and Suburban Directory, 1919.

Merseyside Maritime Museum Record Centre (MMMRC)

1. 'Seabird Box' 1980–442 (to be listed). A miscellaneous collection which includes; WLYC Season 1915, 1936, Yearbooks; a blueprint plan of Southport Pierhead moorings 19 May 1910.
2. Lloyds Register of Yachts; 1878, 1879, 1880, 1881, 1882–95, 1897–1903, 1905–1913.

Liverpool City Library

1. Lloyds Register of Yachts; 1891–3, 1895, 1896, 1898, 1901–1915.

Secondary Sources

General Articles

Jarrad, F. W., *Ribble Navigation. Report on the Silting in the South (Bog Hole) Channel* (London, 1907).

Liddle, John, 'Estate Management and Land Reform Politics: the Hesketh and Scarisbrick Families and the making of Southport, 1842 to 1914', in Cannadine, David (ed.), *Patricians, Power and Politics in Nineteenth-century Town*, pp. 134–174.

Mountfield, A. S. 'Admiral Denham and the Approaches to the Port of Liverpool', *Transactions of the Historical Society of Lancashire and Cheshire*, Vol. 105, 1953, pp. 123–136.

Vernon-Harcourt, L. F. 'Report on the Extension of the Navigable Channel of the Ribble to the Sea, to the Corporation of Southport' (Southport, 1891).

Oliver M. Westall, 'The Retreat to Arcadia: Windermere as a Select Residential Resort in the Late-nineteenth Century', in Oliver M. Westall (ed.), *Windemere in the nineteenth century* (Centre for North West Regional Studies University of Lancaster Occasional Paper No. 20, 1991 Edition) pp. 34–45.

General Books

Aughton, Peter, *North Meols and Southport. A History* (Carnegie Press, Preston, 1988).

Bailey, Francis A., *A History of Southport* (Angus Downe, Southport, 1955).

Bainbridge, Cyril, *Pavilions on the Sea. A History of the Seaside Pleasure Pier* (Robert Hale, London, 1986).

Barron, James, MInstCE, *A History of the Ribble Navigation. From Preston to the Sea* (Corporation of Preston, Preston, 1938).

Dakres, Jack, *The Last Tide. A History of the Port of Preston 1806–1981* (Carnegie Press, Preston, 1986).

Jarrad, F. W. RN, late Admiralty Surveyor, AInstCE, *Ribble Navigation. Report on the Silting in the South (Bog Hole) Channel. The Result of an Investigation Made in the Months of October and November 1906 to Preston Corporation* (London, February 1907).

Lee, Norman, and Stubbs, Peter. C., *The History of Dorman Smith, 1878–1972* (Newman Neame Ltd, London, 1972).

Marwick, Arthur, *The Deluge. British Society and the First World War* (Macmillan, 1965 edition).

Mowat, Charles Loch, *Britain Between the Wars, 1918–1940* (Methuen, 1955).
Taylor, A. J. P., *English History, 1914–1945* (Oxford University Press, 1975, revised edition).
Vernon-Harcourt, L. F. MA., MInstCE, *Report on the Extension of the Navigable Channel of the Ribble to the Sea, to the Corporation of Southport* (Southport, 1891).
Walton, John K., *The English Seaside Resort. A Social History 1750–1914* (Leicester University Press, 1983).
Walton, John K., *Lancashire. A Social History, 1558–1939* (Manchester University Press, 1987).

Articles about Yachting and other sports

Crump, Jeremy, 'Athletics' in T. Mason (ed.), *Sport in Britain. A Social History* (C.U.P., 1989), pp. 44–77.
Dodd, Christopher, 'Rowing' in T. Mason (ed.), *Sport in Britain. A Social History* (C.U.P., 1989), pp. 276–307.
Lowerson, John, 'Angling' in T. Mason (ed.), *Sport in Britain. A Social History* (C.U.P., 1989), pp. 12–43.
Lowerson, John, 'Golf' in T. Mason (ed.), *Sport in Britain. A Social History* (C.U.P., 1989), pp. 187–214.
Walker, Helen, 'Lawn Tennis' in T. Mason (ed.), *Sport in Britain. A Social History* (C.U.P., 1989), pp. 245–275.
Williams, Gareth, 'Rugby Union' in T. Mason (ed.), *Sport in Britain. A Social History* (C.U.P., 1989), pp. 308–43.
Williams, Jack, 'Cricket' in T. Mason (ed.), *Sport in Britain. A Social History* (C.U.P., 1989), pp. 116–45.
Wrigglesworth, Neil, 'A History of Rowing in the North-West of England', *British Journal of Sports History*, vol. 3, no. 2, 1986, pp. 145–157.

Books about Yachting and other recreations

Anon., *British Yachts and Yachtsmen. A Complete History of British Yachting from the Middle of the Sixteenth Century to the Present Day* (The Yachtsman Publishing Company, London, 1907). (RMYC Archive).
Atkins, Jeremy, *A Hundred Years of Sailing at Oxford University. The Centenary History of the Oxford University Yacht Club 1884–1984* (Atkins, Leamington Spa, 1984).
Bailey, Peter, *Leisure and Class in Victorian England. Rational recreation and the contest for control, 1830–1885* (Methuen, London, 1987).
Barnes, Pam, *The Norfolk Broads Yacht Club. A Short History,* (The Norfolk Broads Yacht Club, Norwich, 1982).
Blake, George, *Lloyd's Register of Shipping 1760–1960* (Lloyds Register of Shipping, London, 1960).
Dear, Ian, *The Royal Yacht Squadron, 1815–1985* (Royal Yacht Squadron, London?, 1985).
Dear, Ian, *The Great Days of Yachting, from the Kirk Collection* (Batsford, London, 1988).
Fairley, Gordon, *Minute by Minute. The Story of the Royal Yachting Association 1875–1982* (RYA, Woking, 1983).
Folkard, Henry Coleman, *The Sailing Boat. A Treatise on Sailing Boats and Small Yachts* (London, 6th edn, 1906). (MMMRC. Lib. 330. FOL)
Heckstall-Smith, Brooke (ed.), *Dixon Kemp's Manual of Yacht and Boat Sailing* (10th Edition, Horace Cox [*The Field* Office], London, 1904). (RMYC Archive)
Irving, John, *The King's Britannia. The Story of a Great Ship 1892/3–1936* (Seeley Service & Co., London, ?1937).
Kennedy, John, *Lytham Yacht Club. Centenary 1889–1989,* (Lytham Yacht Club, 1989).
Knox-Johnston, Robin, *History of Yachting* (Phaidon, Oxford, 1990).
Lowerson, John, *Sport and the English Middle Classes* (M.U.P., 1993).
Mason, Tony (ed.), *Sport in Britain. A Social History* (C.U.P. Cambridge, 1989).
Millar, John, *Anything But Sailing. A History of West Kirby Sailing Club* (John Millar (UK) Ltd., Hoylake, Wirral, 1985).
Simper, Robert, *Victorian and Edwardian Yachting from old photographs,* (Batsford, London, 1978).
Viner, Alan, *A History of Rating Rules for Yachts 1854–1931* (Maritime Monographs and Reports No. 41, National Maritime Museum, 1979).

Appendix I

Year	Revenue £				Costs £				Revenue - Costs £
	Members Subs.	Bar Sales	Other	Total	Wages	Rent & Rates	Others	Total	
1926	223	119	21	363	142	80	154	376	-13
1927	346	453	75	874	306	179	360	845	29
1928	330	475	75	880	332	179	337	848	32
1929	350	486	119	955	338	213	329	880	75
1930	n.d	n.d	n.d	n.d	n.d.	n.d.	n.d.	n.d.	n.d
1931	295	405	108	808	339	209	361	909	-101
1932	286	550	128	964	385	224	378	987	-23
1933	242	412	141	795	358	193	291	842	-47
1934	226	345	113	684	360	155	301	816	-132
1935	234	602	107	943	358	161	287	806	137
1936	261	461	81	803	364	146	304	814	-11
1937	231	371	62	664	275	152	240	667	-3
1938	193	321	60	574	291	113	208	612	-38
1939	173	285	58	516	299	114	142	555	-39
1940	151	328	67	546	305	114	151	570	-24
1941	155	443	85	683	330	114	229	673	10
1942	170	445	90	705	329	114	256	699	6
1943	153	525	73	751	332	113	301	746	5
1944	153	606	84	843	330	113	391	834	9
1945	164	614	120	898	361	117	412	890	8
1946	183	457	73	713	361	122	199	682	31
1947	193	481	52	726	463	126	260	849	-123
1948	218	628	88	934	424	130	349	903	31
1949	235	616	54	905	472	133	443	1048	-143
1950	376	704	61	1141	396	133	539	1068	73
1951	369	796	54	1219	392	137	599	1128	91
1952	374	699	35	1108	420	140	560	1120	-12
1953	363	678	41	1082	446	184	501	1131	-49
1954	339	461	41	841	438	189	425	1052	-211
1955	339	483	38	860	429	189	475	1093	-233
1956	351	460	229	1040	453	198	426	1077	-37
1957	560	293	139	992	455	163	268	886	106
1958	587	364	203	1154	526	203	551	1280	-126
1959	596	406	147	1149	561	196	454	1211	-62

Table 1. WLYC Revenue Accounts, 1926 to 1959.
Source: WLYC Annual Accounts.

West Lancashire Yacht Club
Commodores 1894 to 1994

R. Coddington	1894	R. K. Wilson	1964–1965
W. S. Hayward	1895–1904	E. Whiteley	1966–1967
J. E. Latham	1905	G. A. Hayward	1968–1969
W. D. Coddington	1906–1910	R. I. Atkinson	1970–1971
W. L. Hall	1911–1914	A. G. B. Randall	1972–1973
H. Spurrier	1915–1918	D. Warren	1974–1975
A. Bersi	1919–1922	J. W. East	1976
J. Heyes	1923–1931	J. E. Hayward	1977
H. W. Hatch	1932–1934	C. J. H. Pycraft	1978–1979
F. R. Hall	1934–1935	F. H. Thompson	1980–1981
L. G. Garge	1936–1946	E. A. Brown	1982–1983
H. T. Hall	1947–1951	E. Barton	1984
H. Leigh	1951–1956	T. D. Hewitt	1985–1986
A. Robertson	1957	R. M. Willetts	1987–1988
G. C. Pearce	1958–1959	J. A. Houghton	1989–1990
C. S. Oliver	1960–1961	A. C. Halliwell	1991–1992
C. K. Colley	1962–1963	M. O. Parker	1993–1994

West Lancashire Yacht Club
Presidents 1894 to 1994

Sir G. A. Pilkington	1894	J. W. East	1968
H. Spurrier	1920	R. K. Wilson	1970
H. R. Davies	1924	G. A. Hayward	1973
A. Bersi	1926	R. I. Atkinson	1976
W. S. Moore	1936	R. H. B. Whittam	1978
H. T. Hall	1940	D. Warren	1980
W. Paulden	1941	A. G. B. Randall	1983
H. T. Hall	1951	F. H. Thompson	1985
H. Leigh	1957	O. R. Blenkiron	1987
J. Bond	1960	C. J. H. Pycraft	1990
G. C. Pearce	1962	T. D. Hewitt	1992
C. S. Oliver	1964		

Index

List of Patrons

The Centenary celebrations of the West Lancashire Yacht Club were supported by the following patrons at the time of going to press in early October 1993:

Mr and Mrs R. T. G. Abram
Mr and Mrs I. C. Agnew
Mr J. M. Anderson
Mr W. R. Aspin
Mrs E. Atkinson
Mr E. Barton
Mr V. Basil
Mr J. Batten
Mr and Mrs P. Beachell
Mr and Mrs R. A. Blakey
Mr and Mrs O. R. Blenkiron
Mr and Mrs J. M. Bower
Mr D. L. Byron
Mr and Mrs W. G. Callaghan
Mr P. J. Chester
Mr and Mrs C. T. Danecki
Mr J. W. East
Mrs D. E. Edwards
Mr M. H. Edwardson
Mr A. K. Ellis
Mr G. S. Francis
Mr and Mrs R. P. Gambie
Mr and Mrs P. G. Gardiner
Mr and Mrs P. A. Gilbert
Mrs A. Gloyne
Mr and Mrs R. L. Goulden
Mrs H. Hall
Mr and Mrs A. C. Halliwell
Mr and Mrs M. P. Halsall
Mr and Mrs R. S. Harper
Mr and Mrs J. E. Hayward
Mr and Mrs T. D. Hewitt
Mr and Mrs W. J. Hivey

Mr and Mrs A. J. Houghton
Mr and Mrs B. Ibbotson
Mr I. A. McKinlay
Mrs P. L. McKinlay
Mr and Mrs J. R. Mercer
Mr and Mrs J. L. Moore
Mr and Mrs J. A. Moralee
Mr and Mrs A. F. Moran
Mr J. B. Morgan
Mr and Mrs W. M. Mould
Mr and Mrs H. V. Murray
Mr J. Neil
Mr and Mrs K. Owen
Mr and Mrs M. O. Parker
Mrs B. Porter
Mr and Mrs C. Preston
Major and Mrs C. J. H. Pycraft
Mr and Mrs A. G. B. Randall
Mr and Mrs W. T. Read
Mr and Mrs P. Ridgway
Mr and Mrs W. J. Rimmer
Mr and Mrs G. G. Robinson
Dr and Mrs R. J. Ryan
Mr and Mrs R. Sayer
Mr and Mrs F. Small
Mr and Mrs F. H. Thompson
Mr and Mrs J. G. Thorougood
Mrs P. L. Uttley
Mr and Mrs D. Warren
Mr and Mrs D. A. Westley
Mr and Mrs R. M. Willetts
Mr and Mrs R. K. Wilson
Mr C. G. Wingrove